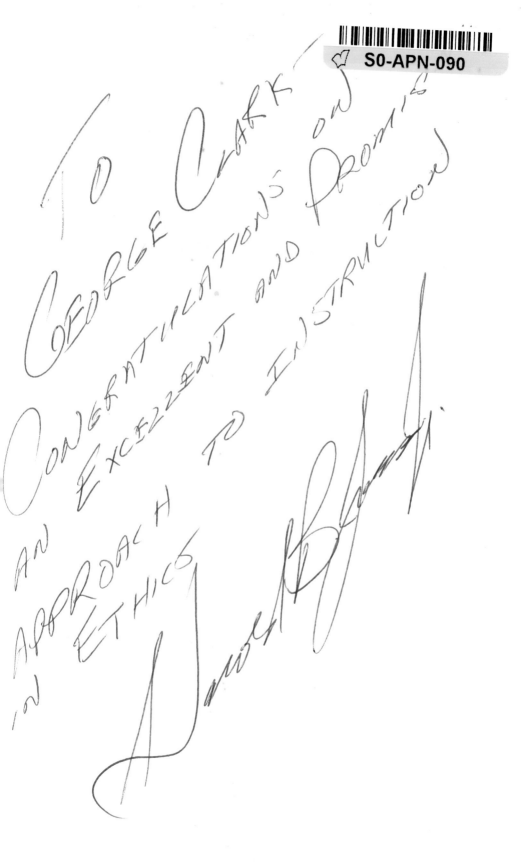

To Clark,

George Clark,

Congratulations on

an Excellent and Promising

approach to Instruction

in Ethics

Personal Character
and
National Destiny

Personal Character

and

National Destiny

Harold B. Jones, Jr.

Paragon House
St. Paul, Minnesota

First Edition, 2002

Published in the United States by
Paragon House
2700 University Avenue West
St. Paul, MN 55114

Manufactured in the United States of America.

Library of Congress Cataloging-in-Publication Data

  Jones, Harold B., 1946-
  Personal character and national destiny / Harold B. Jones, Jr.—lst ed.
      p. cm.
  Includes bibliographical references and index.
  ISBN 1-55778-804-9
  1. Social values. 2. National characteristics. 3. Character. 4. Achievement motiva-
tion. I. Title.

  HM681.J66 2002
  303.3'72—dc21

                                                                    2001051162

10 9 8 7 6 5 4 3 2 1

For current information about all releases from Paragon House,
visit the website at http://www.paragonhouse.com

This book is dedicated to my mother, Elinor Jones. She's looking down on me from Somewhere right now, and she's proud of me for writing it.

I would like to thank my son Paul M. Jones and my colleague Dr. William S. Mounts for their tireless assistance. They have been wise and patient critics, and this book is very much the better for their advice. I could never have written it without their help. I would also like to thank Rosemary Yokoi for her encouragement during the long process by means of which the original manuscript actually became a book. It was a delight to work with her. I am more grateful than I can say to Marlene London for her brilliant proofreading.

.

Contents

Chapter 1

THE ACHIEVING SOCIETY

An old story tells about a Hindu boy who came to his father and asked, "What holds up the earth?" His father told him it rested on the back of a giant turtle. The boy then asked what held up the turtle, and his father said that beneath the turtle was a very large elephant. "But what is under the elephant?" the boy persisted. Realizing that he could keep this up only until he ran out of animals, the father solemnly replied, "My son, it's elephants all the way down."

Now that's the problem with economic analyses. The economist offers a clear and cogent explanation for something and then draws a graph. If a perceptive freshman in the back row asks a question, the professor is ready for him. She nods her head knowingly and draws another graph and if need be a third. Everything can be explained by supply and demand, interest rates, marginal utilities, and marginal costs. If the student persists in his questions "Why?" however, he is sooner or later granted the revelation that it's graphs all the way down.

Economists like to explain things with graphs. They are not much into examining the nonmathematical assumptions that underlie their graphs. That's why they ignored David C. McClelland in 1961, when he wrote, "Japan will move from a status as an 'underachiever' in the economic sphere to that of an 'overachiever,' say by 1970."[1] He didn't have a graph. His prediction was not based on any of the things economists like to use in their graphs: he hadn't assembled data about the Japanese gross national product and drawn trend lines; asked about Japanese fiscal or monetary policy, he would have shaken his head in ignorance. What about Japan's tax rates? No clue. Its balance of trade? Ditto. McClelland was foolish enough to believe he could describe and even predict large events in terms simply of personal values and individual motivation. And so of course he went ignored.

He went ignored, in fact, even after the course of events showed he had been right. In the early 1970s, Japan began its meteoric rise to the role of economic superstar, just as McClelland had said it would. Almost unnoticed by Americans in 1965, by 1985 it had become so powerful that the Reagan administration was forced to negotiate an agreement to protect the American automobile industry from Japanese competition. *The Art of Japanese Management* became a best-seller. Mutual funds with investments in Japan soared to the top of the performance charts, and new funds were quickly formed to follow their lead. The whole world, and the United States in particular, stood in awe of the Japanese economic miracle. And no one, least of all any economists, said, "Looks like McClelland was right. Maybe we should take another look at this stuff."

John Kenneth Galbraith once observed that economists believe it's better to be wrong for the right reasons than it is to be right for the wrong ones.[2] And from the economist's point of view, McClelland's reasons were very certainly the wrong ones. His forecast of Japan's coming day in the sun was based, not on the strength of the yen, but on the strength of Japanese families. He predicted that Japan was going to become an economic powerhouse not because of its economic policies but because of its child-rearing practices. If you want to know about a nation's future, he said, you need to look at the stories it tells, especially the stories it tells its children. Such stories are important because they give us a clue to what people are thinking about, to their values and their purposes, and it is from their thoughts, values, and purposes that all their achievements must ultimately spring.

The key to a nation's prosperity, he showed, lies in the character of its people. The things economists describe with their graphs are symptoms rather than causes. Irving Kristol observed, similarly, that "the economy" may be a deceptive expression because it treats familiar statistics as if they are somehow a reality unto themselves rather than a description of how people are behaving.[3] Economics is the most scientific of the "social sciences," and it can in some circumstances do a wonderful job of explaining how people act. Its explanations, though, are always based on assumptions about personal motivation. Things like national income, interest rates, and unemployment are not eternal verities that irrevocably determine human destiny. They are merely descriptions of the way in which a particular nation is working out its destiny at a particular point in time. The way it does that is the result of the values its people hold and by means of which they direct their lives.

This chapter deals with the nature and the source of the personal values that lead to national prosperity.

The Need for Achievement[4]

McClelland did not begin with economic predictions. He began with a psychological experiment on college students. He wanted to see what an aroused desire for personal excellence would do to the way in which they thought about their world and their lives. But he never told his subjects (victims?) what he was up to. No. What he did instead was tell them that they were about be assigned a series of tasks and that their success with these tasks would be used to measure their intelligence and leadership ability.

Now intelligence and leadership ability are things on which we tend to place an inordinate importance. All of us want to believe, disappointing scores on standardized IQ tests notwithstanding, that we are exceptionally bright. We also want to believe that we have a God-given ability for leading others. (David G. Meyers reported that 70 percent of his subjects rated themselves as being in the top 25 percent of the population when it came to leadership; only 2 percent would admit to being below average.)[5] If there is anything that can arouse college students' desire to excel, it is a representation that their performance will be taken as a measure of their intelligence and capacity for leadership.

McClelland, of course, being a psychologist, was aware of this. He did not really care the first thing about his subjects' intelligence or leadership ability. What he was interested in was the way in which an aroused desire for excellence would affect their thinking. "Ah, yes," he said in effect, "I am very excited about these tests, and as you know, they will have a GREAT IMPACT on your FUTURE."

So the students sat at their desks, waited for the tasks to be assigned, and hoped they could prove themselves by doing a good job. But their wily professor threw them a curveball. "Before we start on the performance tasks," he said, "let's get warmed up. Here's a picture. I want you to write a story about what it means to you." He then gave each of them a picture that would allow for a number of interpretations, a picture of a man with his head bowed, for example, or of a boy sitting at his desk.

It is easy to imagine the discussion that occurred after the stories had been written and handed in. "Thank you very much," McClelland must have said. "What are you waiting for? Why don't you just get up and go home? Performance tasks? What perf...oh, yes, performance tasks! Of course, of course. Performance tasks. We'll do those tomorrow." (Psychologists can be very devious.)

There was also another group of students, who were not told anything about performance tasks or estimates of their intelligence and leadership ability. They were given exactly the same pictures as the members of the first group, and they also were asked to write stories about these pictures. But nothing was done to stimulate their desire for personal excellence. McClelland wanted to see if the stories told by the members of this second group would be different from the stories told by the members of the first.

They were.

Students who believed they were about to be assigned performance tasks that would be used to measure their intelligence and leadership ability wrote stories about people who were trying to accomplish things. Writing under the pressure of an aroused desire for personal excellence, they told stories of self-reliance, persistence, and innovation. The heroes and heroines of these stories often found themselves blocked in their efforts, but they experimented with new methods in the hope of finding a solution. Sometimes their luck was good, and sometimes it was bad, but they kept on trying, no matter what. They made the best possible use of whatever resources they happened to have at their disposal, they worked hard, and they advanced a little bit at a time.

One of the stories about the picture of a boy sitting at his desk, for example, described him as taking an examination. The author of the story said the boy had studied for it, but probably not as well as he could have. He had come up with solutions for most of the questions and was now struggling to think of answers for the rest. Stories about the picture of a man with his head bowed said he was working out a mathematical calculation or trying to come up with the solution to a business problem. In every case, the subjects who believed they were about to receive an important assignment wrote stories about people who were struggling to accomplish something.

But remember there was also another group, the members of which had been told nothing about any performance tasks. The heroes and heroines in their stories were usually more passive. They were not struggling to accomplish anything. They were not so much protagonists as a part of the scenery. The boy sitting at his desk, for example, might be described as daydreaming about life outside the classroom and hoping the instructor would not call upon him. The man with his head bowed was described as taking a nap.

Similar experiments with Navajo Indians and Brazilian students produced similar results.[6] It was found in a number of different cultural situations that those in whom the desire to excel had been aroused wrote stories about people who were struggling to accomplish something in the face of significant obstacles. The common themes of these stories were goals, effort, challenge, persistence, ingenuity, and the careful use of every available resource. The experiments showed the direction in which people's thoughts are likely to move when they feel the pressure of an enhanced desire for personal excellence.

There is admittedly nothing new about stories in which the central figure is struggling to overcome problems of some kind. But here's the thing about psychologists: they like to point to something with which everyone over the age of six is already familiar, put a name on it, and then strut around acting as if they had invented it. A name that jars people's sensibilities is especially good because it can be used as a publicity tool. Sigmund Freud's expression "penis envy" was the greatest terminological coup in the history of psychology. McClelland was less imaginative. The best term he could come up with for the scenes described in the stories that interested him was "achievement imagery." People in whom the desire to excel had been aroused always wrote stories filled with achievement imagery. Those who did not feel the pressure of such a desire usually wrote stories that were devoid of it.

"Very interesting!" McClelland exclaimed. We can almost see him rubbing his hands together. But like everyone else who thinks he's finally figured it all out, McClelland soon discovered a fly in the ointment. There were a few people who, even though nothing had been done to stimulate their desire for excellence, obstinately insisted on writing stories filled with achievement imagery. Even in the absence of suggestions that there were going to be tasks to perform and estimates of intelligence and leadership ability, these people wrote about goals, personal effort, problems, persistence, slow progress, self-reliance, and innovation.

Most people's stories contained achievement imagery only when the experimenter had somehow aroused their desire to excel, but there were a few whose minds seemed always to be filled with images of achievement. They seemed to spend their whole lives thinking about personal accomplishment and overcoming obstacles on the way to it. This latter group, McClelland concluded, might be said to have an inclination, a persistent tendency, a chronic bias, a…a NEED, ah yes, that's it, a need! They had a need for achievement.

The Achievement-Oriented Personality

And thus was born a new psychological expression, "the need for achievement." The idea, to tell the whole truth, was not new with McClelland. It had been suggested by Henry Murray in 1938[7] and probably by somebody else even before that if one had the patience to go back and find out who suggested it to Murray. McClelland attempted to add to its scientific respectability by abbreviating it as *n.ach.*, but he did not invent the term, and he certainly did not invent the type of person whose behavior it describes.

McClelland also examined two other personality tendencies, the need for power and the need for affiliation. The last of these refers to a need for warm relationships, a desire to spend time with others, a need to be liked and accepted. The need for power refers to a desire to dominate, to assert one's claims over other people, and to gain one's ends at their expense. The need for achievement appears as personal effort and industry, the need for affiliation appears as sociability, and the need for power is evident in attempts at control. People with a strong need for achievement are interested in personal accomplishment, those with a need for affiliation are interested in having friends, and those with a need for power are interested in exercising their influence.

These needs are not mutually exclusive. All of us have all three of them, but there is a strong tendency in any given personality for one of them to be stronger than the others. They are like all other human characteristics in that some of us have more of one and others have more of another. Like height, weight, and intelligence, they are, in the buzzwords of psychology, "normally distributed among the population." Some people are dominated by their need for achievement, others by their need for affiliation, and still others by their need for power.

People who are dominated by the need for achievement want above all else to succeed in things that are important to them, and they feel that they must be in control of their own lives in order to do so. The goals they select are a reflection of their abilities and situation. A girl who is bound to a wheelchair might express her need for achievement in ways other than those that would be chosen by an athlete. An achievement-oriented individual might at one stage in his life have his heart set on throwing the winning pass. We might find him years later trying to make a big sale or build a skyscraper. In spite of their differences, these people are all aiming at something specific and at something they have chosen for themselves.

They're all aiming, too, at something they think they can pull off. They want to feel like they're winners, and it is easier to have that feeling if you actually win. Achievement-oriented people pick goals that are difficult enough to give them a sense of victory but not so difficult as to be unreachable. One experiment involved throwing rings at a peg. The participants could choose their own distance. Most tended to throw at random, standing either very close (certain success) or very far away (certain failure). Those who had a high need for achievement were more calculating. They chose a distance that required their best effort, but it was a distance at which success was possible if they made the effort.[8]

Throwing rings at a peg, however, is probably not something you will do perfectly the first time, no matter how carefully you have chosen the distance. It is rather something at which you can improve if you keep trying. People with a high need for achievement want to improve. They do not expect to do something perfectly the first time, but they do expect to become better if they practice.

In another experiment, those who were high in the need for achievement and those who were low in it began at the same skill level. The "lows" completed the task at the same skill level at which they had begun. The "highs" became progressively better as they proceeded. It seemed that they were concerned with doing a good job, and they learned to do it better as they went along. But they did not improve at tasks that were merely repetitive or routine. Things of that kind can be done "faster" but not "better." Only when there was some possibility of gauging improvements in the way one performed the task itself did the achievement-oriented individual become gradually better at it.[9]

People of this kind are not into taking chances. In a pure gambling situation, they will always place the safest bet they can. If they think they can shape the final outcome by means of personal effort and personal improvement, though, they may take what outsiders regard as a long shot. They see failure as temporary and as the result of insufficient effort. The thoughts that run through their minds are along the lines of "If I just work a little harder, if I just try one more thing, if I just keep at it, I'll figure it out. There's a way. There's got to be a way. I know I can find it if I just keep trying."

People who are high in the need for achievement therefore tend to make long-term commitments. They do not expect to do it perfectly on the first try or "have it all right now." They are willing to take whatever time is needed. Their thinking is focused on the future and on the things they intend to accomplish. Ninth graders who were high in the need for achievement remembered more about tasks to be reported on in eight weeks than they did about tasks to be reported on the following day. Adults who were high in the need for achievement anticipated future events well in advance of their occurrence.[10] They seemed always to be thinking about the future, visualizing obstacles and conquering them in their minds before having to face them in reality.

Achievement-oriented individuals think in terms of progress, and so they always want to know how well they are doing. Good feelings are not enough. They seek out objective feedback.[11] They are never satisfied with and may not even care about warm encouragement from their peers. "Hey, bud, you're doing great; we're glad to have you on the team," is not enough; high achievers always have an eye on the scoreboard. They want to measure their progress. A few yards, a few points, a few dollars, a few pages at a time: little by little, steadily, persistently they move toward their goals.

Personality and Progress

So let's take a look at what we've got here. People who are high in the need for achievement take responsibility for their own lives. They choose their own goals. They focus all of their efforts and resources on the accomplishment of specific objectives. They don't like risk, but if they believe they can shape the end result by means of their own effort, they may take what others regard as a long shot; when they place their bets, they bet on themselves. They are time-oriented and think about future successes rather than immediate obstacles or immediate rewards. They are persistent. They like to keep track of how well they are doing, and they are constantly trying to improve.

Achievement-oriented individuals have an entrepreneurial personality. The great economist Joseph Schumpeter described such persons as the universal engine of economic progress. They are the people who start farms and create new businesses. In the process of coming up with improved ways for doing things, they create new products, new services, and new jobs, a "perennial gale of creative destruction" through which outmoded methods and social structures are replaced with better ones.[12] Few of these persons have the wide-ranging genius of Thomas Alva Edison. Few of them ever enjoy the remarkable success of Sam Walton or Bill Gates. But their individual successes, whether great or small, add up, and together they carry their society forward.

This is what happened in Japan. We all know about the great institutions created by men of exceptional genius, Soichiro Honda, for example, or Sony's Akio Morita. And make no mistake about it: the achievements of such men were an essential part of the Japanese success story. But they were not the whole story. Important also were smaller entrepreneurs, who created tiny enterprises to supply the industrial giants with high-quality parts. Important also, as William Abernathy observed at the time, were millions of workers who were excited about their jobs and committed to the production of high-quality cars.[13] (A story from the early eighties tells about a worker who stopped to straighten the wiper blades of every Honda that he passed on his way home from work: he just couldn't stand to see a defect in a Honda.)

A society can advance only if a large proportion of its members work hard, look constantly for better ways to do things, and direct both their efforts and their resources toward long-term objectives. This is the role of persons who are high in the need for achievement. A society with a lot of them will be prosperous, and a prosperous society can afford not merely life's necessities but also such liberal amenities as art, science, and literature. It will very likely be a society that is filled with the materialistic rush and hurry over which modern psychotherapists, social philosophers, and theologians shed their tears. It will also be a society with enough money to give psychotherapists, social philosophers, and theologians the leisure for weeping.

Achievement-oriented individuals, both as the creators of businesses and as employees, are the people upon whom an economy depends. Ayn Rand's *Atlas Shrugged* is a book about the sad fate of a society from which they have begun to disappear. They are people who come up with new ideas, make long-term plans and commitments, and take the initiative. They are not politicians or protesters or poets or philosophers. They are practical people who are trying to build a better life for themselves and their children. They may want to "change the world," but the changes that interest them most are small and incremental changes in things for which they have some personal responsibility. They do not expect to advance by demanding more from "society," but by demanding more from themselves. They set out for specific goals, they plan, they work, they experiment, sometimes they fail and sometimes they succeed, they climb little by little, and on their shoulders they carry their whole society to constantly higher levels of comfort and security.

The Source of Achievement Motivation

If achievement-oriented people are really as important as this seems to imply, we need very much to know where they come from. One could appeal to the modern faith in self-help by arguing that each of us needs to create the achievement motive in himself or herself, perhaps by listening to an inspirational speaker and then repeating a list of positive affirmations first thing every morning. If it could be shown that achievement motivation was the result of work experiences, consultants would be ready to endorse the concept and collect fat fees for facilitating achievement-encounter groups. If this book described achievement motivation as the result of government programs, passages from it would be read aloud from the floor of the Senate, and Hillary Clinton would offer a five-point program for a federal agency to oversee individual motivation, reminding us, no doubt, of an old African saying that it takes a bureaucracy to raise an achiever.

But the fact seems to be that none of these things has anything to do with creating the need for achievement. An inspirational speaker may appeal to it if it already exists. Consultants might be able to help employers create situations to take advantage of it. It is highly probable that government programs can (and do) nip it in the bud. It is absolutely certain that neither motivational speakers nor consultants and least of all politicians have anything to do with creating it.

Achievement motivation is the result of family life. It is the result of the way in which a child is raised. One study involved families from the United States, Germany, Brazil, and Japan. The mothers of eight to ten year olds were asked about the ages at which these children had certain demands and restrictions placed upon them. At what age had the mother expected her child to do things for himself without asking for help, do his homework without assistance, and make decisions for himself? At what age had the child been expected to do well in competition with other children and find his or her own way around the neighborhood? At what ages had these children been required to feed themselves without help in cutting and handling their food, undress and go to bed by themselves, take responsibility for their own possessions, and do household chores?[14]

It was found that children who were high in the need for achievement had been expected to become self-reliant at a comparatively early age. Their mothers had placed relatively few restrictions on them, but the restrictions that were demanded had to be observed at an earlier age. In general, self-reliance training came first; the imposition of restrictions came later. These children were encouraged to master something, and once they had done so, they were not permitted to slide back to earlier levels of dependency.

The mothers of the "lows," by contrast, did not expect their children to be independent at such an early age. These children had more restrictions placed upon them, and they received less encouragement to take responsibility for themselves. They remained dependent upon their parents longer and with regard to a wider area of their lives.

The need for achievement is the result of the way in which a child is raised. The difference between "highs" and "lows" is evident as early as the age of five. Children with a high need for achievement are those who have been required to develop an early self-reliance in many areas of their lives. They have not been neglected, but they have not been coddled, either. Their parents have paid a good deal of attention to the child-rearing process, and an important part of that attention has been a firm insistence that children learn to take a good deal of responsibility for themselves.

Children faced with such a demand and given a little liberty with regard to meeting it soon gain a sense of independence. Left to their own devices, children are compelled to come up with ways to get things done, and they learn about self-trust. Required to make personal decisions and then live with them, children are taught hard lessons about scarce resources and learn to focus on the things that will bring the greatest benefit. They experience the rewards of personal achievement and begin to seek out opportunities for experiencing them again. The earliest rewards come in the form of attention and praise from siblings and parents.

But parents will not raise their children in this way if the society around them does not endorse the values associated with the achievement syndrome. If parents see that enterprise is not rewarded, they will not teach their children to be enterprising. If their society discourages personal initiative and self-discipline, they will not encourage these things in their children. If the prevailing ideology is one of individual helplessness, victimization, and dependence upon large institutions, it pollutes the atmosphere of family life. Children will learn to be dependent upon others rather than self-reliant.

On the other hand, if the social environment endorses the values associated with the achievement syndrome, these are the values that will guide child-rearing practices. As children mature and live according to these values, they will create a prosperous society.

The Values of an Achieving Society

It was popular in the high school textbooks of years ago to say that the United States became wealthy because of its abundant natural resources. It may be true that natural resources do tell a part of the American success story, but they do not tell it all. Russia has some of the best farmland in the world; it also has vast reserves of natural gas, timber, gold, and oil. If natural resources were the secret of national prosperity, Russia would be an economic powerhouse instead of an economic basket case. Japan, on the other hand, with very little in the way of natural resources, enjoyed a quarter century as the economic wonder of the world.

A rich environment is a luxury, not a necessity. It is something that happens by chance, a stroke of luck. Good fortune is wonderful, but national prosperity is the result of what people do with their good fortune rather than the good fortune itself. And what they do with it is the result of the values that guide their lives. It is the result of personal character.

Rose and Milton Friedman have observed that what we do with our lives is the result of two things: chance and choice.[15] We do not get to choose our parents or our childhood circumstances. We do not get to choose which opportunities come our way or which disasters overtake us. Those things happen by chance. But after chance has done its worst, we still have a choice. We can choose either to complain about our situation or do something with it. We can choose to save or spend. We can indulge or discipline ourselves. We can play it safe or experiment. We can work hard or relax. We can choose, in short, what we will do about the things we did not get to choose. The line between success and failure is drawn at the point where we take responsibility for the things that are actually in our power.

This is as true for a nation as it is for individuals. In fact, it is true for a nation precisely because it is true for individuals. If the individuals of whom a nation is composed aspire to high things and struggle to overcome the limitations of circumstance, their society will find the resources and opportunities it needs. If the individuals of whom a nation is composed are always looking for a better way to do things, their society will advance. If they are busily trying to accomplish things, their society will prosper. On the other hand, if they think of themselves as helpless victims and sit waiting for someone else to rescue them, their society will stagnate. A people's fate is decided not by their environment but by what they do with their environment.

We will look at some of history's advancing societies in the next chapter. For right now, it is enough to point out that in every one of them the natural environment was identified as a force to be reckoned with, but not as a force that could always be manipulated or controlled.[16]

The people of achieving societies have recognized that there are some things you just have to accept, and this is the truth they have handed on to their children. One must be prepared for unexpected and perhaps unjust problems and difficulties, they have taught, because these are life's only certainty. When (not if) you run into an obstacle, look for a different way. Accept the uncertainty, make the best decision you can, accept the pain of failure, learn from your mistakes, and move on. There is no telling what you might be able to accomplish.

People who take this approach to their lives insist upon personal liberty. They want the freedom to do the best they can with what they have. They want to use their own talents in pursuing their own goals in their own way. They see themselves, as Walter Lippmann once observed, not as runners who must maintain the same pace and finish together, but as competitors in a fair race that will be won by the best athlete.[17] They understand that things other than effort and ability may play a part in deciding the final result, but they ask that such things be left to chance. No runner should be allowed to elbow his rivals off the track or call upon the judges to declare him the winner when someone else has finished first.

This was the attitude that made America great. People began without asking for guidance or guarantees. They wanted no more than the freedom to make their best effort and an assurance that they would be permitted to enjoy the fruits of whatever victory they might achieve. Few of them found an early or easy success. When Anthony Trollope traveled down the Mississippi in the early 1860s, he described the new settlers as living in caves and sod huts and laboring from dawn to dusk in order simply to survive. And those were the lucky ones. Others (the members of the Donner party, to give a famous example) met with disaster. But the pioneers believed that in time they could bend things to their will, and they kept at it in spite of repeated discouragement and failure.

The story of the American railroads is another tale of disappointment and disaster. It involved the ruin of many fortunes and many lives. But the builders of the railroads followed the example of the first pioneers and continued the struggle. Entrepreneurs like Cyrus

McCormick and John Deere, meanwhile, came up with machinery that made it possible to earn a living on the western prairies. Men like Westinghouse and Vanderbilt gradually improved the safety and efficiency of the railroads. And all of a sudden the railroads that succeeded were carrying the produce of the farmers who succeeded to eastern cities, which were now filled with immigrants who were employed in factories that were the brainchildren of still other entrepreneurs.

No one could have predicted that, or planned it, or legislated it. No less a revolutionary than Thomas Jefferson predicted in 1808 that a transportation system (he was thinking of canals) reaching even as far as upstate New York was at least a century in the future.[18] America's rise to prosperity had little to do with the work of proactive politicians. It was almost entirely the work of individuals, hundreds, thousands, millions of whom, without elaborate or coordinated plans, set out to accomplish things and put their ideas to the test. Many failed, some succeeded, synergies appeared out of nowhere, and the United States became the land of opportunity.

The Situation in Japan

The economists who say Japan's recent woes are the result of its tightly regulated economy can be no more than partially correct. Interference by layer upon layer of government officeholders undoubtedly slows things down, but it does not entirely explain the current situation in Japan. It is well to remember that back in the days when Japan was riding high, there were many who said that government regulation was the cause of it. In 1982, Robert Reich and Ira Magaziner (both of whom would later ride the Clinton administration merry-go-round) published a book entitled *Minding America's Business*, in which they unfavorably compared America's economic performance to that of Germany and Japan. What the United States needed to do, they said, was imitate the Japanese example with an "industrial policy" of alliances between big business and big government.[19] Japanese bureaucracy and regulation, which are now recognized as an obstacle to progress, were then held up as a means to it.

It makes no sense to argue that regulation worked well in the 1970s and '80s but isn't working right now. We can't have it both ways. Something either helps or hinders. It does not do both. It is more logical to say that the Japanese economic miracle occurred in spite of the drag-anchor effect of government involvement in the economy. And if Japan is now in the backwaters, it must be because the forces that once enabled it to overcome the obstacles raised by public policy have lost their strength.

Those forces were personal forces. They were the values and motivation of the Japanese people. And they are not the same today as they were thirty-five years ago. Writing in 1996 and at a low point in the recent economic history of Japan, John Naisbitt came very close to the mark when he said that it has become a nation of risk-averse custodians who fear initiative and cower behind old customs.[20] He described a value set very different from the one McClelland had detected in the stories the Japanese were telling their children during the late forties and early fifties. In those days, Japan was a nation of risk-takers and entrepreneurs, and McClelland predicted that at least for the next generation its economic future would be bright.

But McClelland's success in predicting the Japanese economic miracle is not the only evidence of the relationship between personal character and national destiny. We will look at some additional cases in the next chapter.

Chapter 2 | THE CYCLES OF HISTORY

F. Scott Fitzgerald once said that the test of a great mind is its ability to simultaneously entertain two ideas that are in conflict with one another. By this standard, most academics* qualify as great minds, for nothing is more common among us than our willingness to believe both of two contradictory things. People who insist on either one or the other are accused of being "too simplistic" or perhaps even simpleminded.

There may someday be time to go through the list of mutually contradictory beliefs discipline by discipline, but it will be enough for now to point out two that are cherished by historians. They argue, on the one hand, that each historical event is unique, a thing unto itself, and impossible to duplicate. They warn us, on the other, that those who do not learn from history are destined to repeat it. If historical events are truly unique, however, there can be only one of each, and not even the most systematic and calculated attempt to be ignorant of it will enable us to repeat it, try as we might.

With regard to inconsistency, John Kenneth Galbraith had the vast luxury of being not merely an academic but a socialist, and he seems to

---

* Those of us in the trade prefer to be called "intellectuals."

have believed he could have it both ways at the same time. "It can be said with some assurance," he wrote, "that in economic, social, and political matters, if the controlling circumstances are the same or similar, then so will be at least some of the consequences."[1] In other words, if history repeats itself, it will repeat itself. Maybe.

Galbraith was certainly one of Fitzgerald's "great minds." David C. McClelland, unfortunately, was not. He was an academic, but he was not a great mind because he persisted in a foolish search for simple and comprehensible answers. Asked the question of whether history repeats itself, for example, he set out to discover if there really are some parts of the historical process that can be described as cyclical.

Suppose for a minute that certain things occur in a predictable sequence, he reasoned, and suppose also that we can define these things and measure them. If that is true and if we find that one of these things is happening, we should be able to predict what will happen next. Suppose, for example, that the study of ancient Greece reveals a cycle that runs its course from bottom to top and then back down again. Suppose also that we can see the same beginnings in some modern society. Well then, if the two things really are the same, and if there really is a definite cycle, we should be able to predict the outcome of the current situation. Following this line of reasoning, he predicted (as we have already seen) Japan's economic superstardom a decade in advance of the fact.

In this chapter we will discuss some of the other things he discovered about the historical relationship between personal character and national destiny.

Content Analysis and Historical Categories

The studies described in the previous chapter made use of a technique known as "content analysis." The idea is that we can learn a great deal about people's values and attitudes from the stories they tell us. This applies to all of their stories, not just to those that are developed in the course of a psychological experiment. Without quite intending to do so, writers shape the plot, describe the action, and portray the characters in such a way as to tell us what they, the storytellers, are really thinking about. The tales they tell give us a clue to their ideals and priorities.

This is true also of the stories they enjoy. Readers and listeners prefer stories that convey values to which they subscribe, refer to behaviors they applaud, and describe the victories of people they admire. Stories become popular because they give expression to widely held beliefs. It is therefore possible to learn a great deal about a culture's values by studying the stories it creates, enjoys, and hands on.

This set McClelland's mind running. He had measured his subjects' need for achievement by analyzing the stories they wrote. Now he began to wonder if it might not be possible to measure a society's need for achievement in the same way. If the literature of a particular society was filled with achievement imagery, he reasoned, it was probably because the people who enjoyed this literature liked stories about achievement. If they liked stories about achievement, it was probably because they had a strong need for achievement, and if they had a strong need for achievement, they would probably be busy accomplishing things in the world. They would be inventing, exploring, opening new trade routes, engaging in commerce, and starting businesses. A society filled with such people would be making rapid progress. A literature rich in achievement imagery should therefore be associated with an advancing society.

McClelland began thus to consider the possibility of using literary studies to categorize various historical periods as high, medium, or low on the need for achievement. These same periods could also be categorized as high, medium, or low on their rate of their economic progress. Once those things were done, it would be easy to see if an increase in the achievement motive really did go along with increasing prosperity.

Historians greeted this suggestion with the same good cheer and ready acceptance that rises in the heart of small-town merchants when they learn of Wal-Mart's intention to build a new store in their area. These historians had doubtless insisted somewhat earlier that those who did not learn from history were destined to repeat it, but now they howled in protest at McClelland's absurd suggestion that we could point to concrete similarities between different historical periods. Generalizations are not possible, they argued, because every historical event is unique. Any attempt to define two events as belonging to the same category will force us to overlook the unique qualities of each.

To this McClelland replied, "Of course." Categories are no more than an aid to understanding. They are useful precisely because they leave out the interesting but confusing details. Two animals may have different personalities, be of different sizes and different colors, and still belong to the common category "cow." The categorization is useful in helping us understand them even if each animal does have unique qualities of its own.[2]

Again, consider the category "white male." Some are tall, some are short, some are obese, some are athletic, some are bald, and others have dark, curly hair. In spite of these differences they have certain defining characteristics, and in the absence of things like cross-dressing or hormone treatments they are usually easy to identify. Once the identification has been made, we can predict other, less apparent but more important characteristics. Specific cases may seem temporarily benign, but it is well known that white males are insensitive sexual predators who are responsible for the oppression of women, world hunger, race prejudice, international tensions, pollution, teenage smoking, cancer, tooth decay, and the dreaded gum disease gingivitis. These things are more characteristic of some white males (presumably those with names like Joe and Mike and Bob) and less characteristic of others (who have names like Harold), but no member of the category is entirely free from them.

Historical events are undoubtedly unique, McClelland admitted, just as Joe and Harold are unique. But Joe and Harold (sad to say) are both white males, and some historical periods may have certain things in common with other historical periods. If we can define and measure these things, we can place historical periods into categories. It is possible that periods belonging to one of these categories are consistently followed by periods belonging to another. With regard to the need for achievement, for example, perhaps periods high in it are consistently followed by periods that are lower. It might also be that periods high in the need for achievement are always periods of growth and that periods low in it are always periods of stagnation. It might therefore be true that a declining need for achievement warns of economic and cultural decline. It might not be, but then it might. Why not try to find out?

So McClelland turned to history.

Looking for the Achievement Motive in History

The trouble with history is that it can be used to prove whatever you want it to prove. One historian turns to one set of facts and proves one thing. Another prefers another set of facts or perhaps reads the same set in a different way and proves something else. Some historians treat a man like a hero and others make him out to be a cad. As long as personal preference rules the day in the selection of historical data, all conclusions are suspect and probably misleading.

But what if we quantify things? What if, to put the matter crudely, we just take a count? Instead of selecting our facts according to what we think we will find, we can list all of them and then run totals to see how many of them support our opinion and how many don't. If the count goes against us, we were wrong, too bad, back to the drawing board. But if the count goes strongly in our favor, maybe we were right.

The easiest things to count, when it comes to history, are those related to economic transactions. People tend to keep a record of things that have to do with money, and some of these records have survived. We have, especially in the case of modern societies, elaborate and detailed records with regard to economic transactions of every kind, and these records are an excellent source of information.

But the trouble with records, as anyone who has ever been audited by the IRS will be quick to observe, is that they get lost. You remember thinking that a particular receipt was important and putting it in a place where you knew you could find it. It's just that right now you can't remember where that was. And of course the older a thing is, the more likely it is to have disappeared. When we study societies of the distant past, that's the problem we run into. Most of the records have been misplaced.

Instead of records, we may have to use what are called "artifacts." A good example of an artifact is that big box your microwave came in.

You couldn't find the receipt for that thing to save your life. The microwave itself may be gone. (Perhaps your daughter took it with her to college.) But that box is still sitting in the back of your garage, probably filled with smaller boxes and miscellaneous junk, an eternal and everlasting record that you had enough money to buy a microwave oven, or at least put it on your Discover card, back in 1993. Or was it 1994?

The artifacts in the garages of the ancient world tell us a great deal about various periods' levels of prosperity. Jesus once observed that new wine would break old wineskins and both would be lost. That's why merchants involved in long-distance commerce didn't use wineskins. They used earthen jars. Now the cool thing about pottery is that it remains behind even after the last drop of wine has been emptied from it. It becomes an artifact. It's not what we're interested in, but it tells us a lot about what we are interested in.

When archaeologists find a great deal of the appropriate pottery in a particular place, they conclude that it is a place where there was once a good deal of drinking, as well (one assumes) as eating and being merry. And it's easier to eat, drink, and be merry if you're not broke. Places with a lot of things like the pottery associated with wine and olive oil are therefore thought to have been places where the people were relatively well off.

Both the surviving records and the surviving artifacts tell us something about the level of prosperity characteristic of particular historical periods. The economic course of history is thus comparatively clear. Among historians, in fact, only feminist historians (whose carefully reasoned and tight-knit body of theory on the role of the white male allows them to reach definitive conclusions even before they have examined the data) are more likely than economic historians to agree about the interpretation of their findings.

McClelland and his colleagues could therefore draw on substantial agreement among historians about various periods' levels of prosperity or decline. There remained the problem of determining whether the people who lived in each of these periods were high or low on the need for achievement. This question was answered with a method similar to the one used in gathering economic data. The researchers just took a count. They went though the literature, counted the number of times something was said about achievement, and calculated the average number of achievement images per line.

In the end it came down to two sets of numbers. The first set described the history of a people's economy. The second described the history of their dominant motives. Periods during which a society's literature was filled with achievement imagery were taken to be periods during which the members of the society had a high need for achievement: they liked stories about achievement because they had their hearts set on getting things done. Periods during which the popular literature was less rich in such imagery were taken to be periods when people were less interested in practical accomplishment. Periods during which the popular literature discouraged individual achievement were categorized as periods during which the need for achievement was low.

Two sets of numbers: one told the history of a nation's prosperity; the other told the history of its aspirations. Now the question was, do these two sets of numbers go together?

The Achievement Motive: Historical Examples

The answer was "yes."

Achievement Motivation in Modern Societies

Some of the work[3] involved textbooks intended for the second-, third-, and fourth-grade children of societies in the first half of the twentieth century. Such books are designed not merely to entertain and educate children, but also to guide their values. They are therefore a pretty good indicator of what a society thinks is important. They have the additional advantage (to paraphrase Margaret Mead) of being so simple and direct that even a psychologist can understand them. McClelland wanted to see if there was any relationship between the achievement imagery in these readers and the rate of economic progress in the nations that made use of them.

Among the thirty countries whose children's stories were studied were the United States, Sweden, Australia, Great Britain, France, Germany, the Netherlands, Chile, and (as we have already seen) Japan. It was found in virtually every case that a high need for achievement, as indicated by the values expressed by the stories a nation was telling to its children, was associated with a period of rapid economic progress.

But there was an interesting twist. No one had expected it. And at first it was a little perplexing. After thinking about it, though, McClelland suddenly realized it confirmed his theories because it clarified the cause-and-effect relationship between the achievement motive and economic progress.

Here's what was found: periods of economic progress were always *preceded* by periods during which the stories in children's readers indicated a high and rising need for achievement. An increase in the need for achievement came first. Economic progress followed. This deserves to be emphasized.

- A nation's need for achievement did not rise as economic growth occurred.
- The need for achievement did not rise in the period that came after a period of economic growth.
- A rise in the need for achievement always came before a period of economic growth.

Only nations with a high need for achievement at the beginning of the periods being studied had rates of growth that were higher than could have been predicted on the basis of their previous economic record. Countries whose children's readers indicated a strong need for achievement at the beginning of the period showed a tendency to advance more rapidly than countries whose children's readers indicated a weaker need for achievement. If you would like to study the findings in more detail, please refer to McClelland's Tables 3.4 and 3.5 of *The Achieving Society*.

These findings make it extremely difficult to argue that material progress is the reason for a rise in the need for achievement. If the need for achievement rose only after a period of economic improvement, or if it rose as the economy improved, we might be inclined to say that material progress leads to an increase in achievement motivation. But that isn't the way it works. In virtually every case, the findings showed that the level of achievement motivation rose first and material progress followed. A nation's progress is the result rather than the cause of a generally high need for achievement among its people.

The Need for Achievement in Ancient Greece

Although rich and varied, the history of ancient Greece is easy to summarize.[4] It went through a long period of gradual progress, enjoyed about a century of grandeur, began to decline, and was eclipsed by Rome in the first century BC. The following dates may be used as mile markers:

- 900 BC to 476 BC   The Age of Growth
- 475 BC to 363 BC   The Age of Ascendancy
- 362 BC to 100 BC   The Age of Decline

The Greek economy began with agriculture, but it was overseas trade that made Greece rich. In its day, Athens was the chief port of call for ships from all over the Mediterranean. There was an active business in dried fish, salted meat, iron, lead, wood, and ivory, but at the heart of Greek commerce were wine and olive oil. These the Greeks exchanged for the grain of Sicily, the rugs of Persia, and the perfumes of Arabia.

Greek wine and olive oil were transported in large earthenware jars, many of which have been discovered by archaeologists at places all around the Mediterranean. Such discoveries have been used to map the history of the Athenian trading area. In the sixth century BC it spread over some 1.2 million square miles in a narrow band along the northern shores of the Mediterranean. During the fifth century it expanded to 3.4 million square miles, which included northern Africa, Persia and the area around the Black Sea. During the fourth century, Greek trade with Persia and Italy began to decline, and its trading area shrank back to 1.9 million square miles. These estimates about the extent of Greek commerce correspond with historians' estimates of its economy on the basis of other factors. They also fit with the periods of rise, ascendancy, and decline described at the beginning of this section.

Literary pieces were chosen at random from each of the three periods, and the Greek level of achievement motivation was calculated as the average frequency of achievement imagery per one hundred lines. (The reader who wants to examine the findings in detail is referred to McClelland's Table 4.2 of *The Achieving Society.*) It was found that for every type of literature, achievement imagery was highest in the period of growth, lower in the period of ascendancy, and lowest during the period of decline.

This is exactly what the theory of achievement motivation told us we would find. People with a strong need for achievement will be busy accomplishing things; the society of which they are a part will be making rapid progress and reaching out to the rest of the world. People who have a weaker need for achievement will accomplish less, and their society will be stagnating or declining.

Ancient Greece: Examples from Literature

It is interesting to consider specific examples from Greek literature. The poet Hesiod, who lived during the Greek age of growth, recognized and endorsed the desire to excel. The poor man notes the success of someone who has become rich, he observed, and begins to seek riches for himself. He plows and plants; he fixes up his house and his barn. The potter seeks to make a place for himself in the world by doing a better job than his competitor, and so does the carpenter. This struggle to imitate and improve upon the success of others, Hesiod said, enriches both the competing individuals and their society. In their age of growth, the Greeks admired achievement.

Xenophon wrote during the Greek age of ascendancy and was less optimistic than Hesiod. He reports a conversation between Socrates and Critobulus, in which Socrates observes that the management of an estate is not an easy task. Even if a man does happen to get ahead, Socrates says, he will often waste his profits on foolish pleasures and luxuries. So what's the point of all this work? Socrates adds that although he is himself a poor man and Critobulus is rich, Critobulus has so many responsibilities that in many ways Socrates has the advantage over him.

The Greeks who liked this sort of thing must have been less achievement-oriented than their ancestors were. The piece has some achieve-ment imagery, for Xenophon describes Critobulus as wanting to do a better job of managing his assets, and Socrates observes that it is always possible to learn something from the mistakes of others. Still, there is far less about achievement than in Hesiod, and the primary emphasis is on the difficulty of accomplishing anything of lasting value.

By the time of Aristotle, Greece was sliding into its period of de-cline. In talking about the management of an estate, Aristotle put the emphasis not on getting things done, but on what was proper and suit-able. He said a man should give due attention to overseeing those who work for him and avoid giving them wine, which will make them inso-lent. A free man should never engage in manual labor because it makes the soul unfit for true virtue.[5] Manual labor was for slaves, whose lives were a matter simply of work, punishment, and food. He advised against buying energetic slaves who tried to think for themselves.

Aristotle also said that while a certain amount of wealth was neces-sary for living, there were some people who were too anxious to get more of it. If they could not be trained to moderate their ambitions, they should be legally forced to do so.[6] In this disdain for the upwardly mobile, Aristotle shared the bias of his master Plato. Plato complained about conspicuous consumption among the mercantile bourgeoisie, said that free trade and commerce were no better than war, and suggested that "philosopher kings" should set strict limits on the amount of wealth a person could legally accumulate.[7]

Hesiod praised people who were trying to get ahead, and his writ-ing was popular during ancient Greece's age of growth. As their civiliza-tion began to decline, the Greeks became interested in the ideas of writers like Aristotle and Plato, who wanted to slow things down. A faith in the value of competition among individuals, each of whom should be free to do the best he could with his own life, accompanied the Greeks in their rise to greatness. A belief in hierarchies and an insistence that the government get control of things accompanied them in their descent from it.

The struggle between these two tendencies is apparent as early as the sixth century BC in stories about the brothers Hermes and Apollo.[8]

The former was the patron of upwardly mobile Athenian merchants, and the latter was the patron of the traditional propertied classes. The stories about them reflect the aristocracy's unhappiness over efforts by the nouveaux riches to claim a place in the social structure.

Hermes' entrepreneurial tendencies are clear from the first. He wants to get ahead and takes a positive delight in his schemes for doing so. He makes the best possible use of his time: he sets out on his quest almost at the moment of his birth, he is constantly on the move, and he never wastes a second. He develops new technologies to suit his needs, turning a tortoise shell into a lyre, for example, and inventing wicker sandals to avoid leaving his footprints on the road. He is oriented to things and money. He tells his mother that he intends to follow the career with the most profit in it because he prefers a life of luxury to living in a cave. The story of his stealing his brother's cattle and then convincing Apollo to let him keep them is an allusion to the landed gentry's feelings about the commercial upstarts who were usurping their place in society.

These stories come from the Greek age of growth. Hermes was a mythical role model for people who were high in the need for achievement. The popularity of stories about him suggests that during the sixth century BC, Greek society had many people of this kind. They thought in terms of effort, improvement, material progress, and social mobility. Two centuries later many Greeks were beginning to fear change. They came to resent the person who had his mind set on practical accomplishment, and they nodded in approval when teachers like Plato and Aristotle condemned the man who had become "too successful."

The Death of Achievement Motivation

But the need for achievement among the Greek bourgeoisie was destroyed neither by the resentment of established interests nor the pontifications of philosophers. It was destroyed instead by the success of the very people it had carried to power. By the last quarter of the sixth century BC, most Athenian families were wealthy enough to have slaves. It was common among the "best" families for each child to have two of them—a nurse and a pedagogue to take the child to school. Slaves, who were heavily dependent upon the goodwill of the family, would be the last people in the world to insist that a child become self-reliant at an early age. The very existence of the slaves tended to keep children dependent upon others for a longer period of time than their parents had been, for the grandparents had never been able to afford slaves.

Raising children is one of the most difficult tasks assigned to us. Anyone who has done it will sympathize with Athenian parents' desire to delegate the responsibility just as soon as they had money enough to do so. Some of their slaves, furthermore, were clever and well educated, the product of civilizations more advanced than that of Greece, and parents may have reasoned that the slave could teach children things that the parents themselves could not. And the fact that a family could afford not merely slaves, but the best slaves, was a validation of its importance in the community. It was the ancient equivalent of a new Mercedes in the driveway.

There were some old fogies (including Socrates) who remarked upon the declining moral fiber of the young, but they were obviously out of touch with the realities of a progressive society. Slaves were a great convenience, and besides, everybody was doing it, and what would the neighbors think of those who were so foolish as to insist upon raising their children themselves? So people delegated a large measure of their parental responsibilities, children failed to develop an early self-reliance, and achievement motivation began to die out among the Greeks.

Athens became wealthy because of her vigorous middle class. They gave her freedom and security by demanding a role in the government and by building a powerful navy to protect their trade. They were the source of the wealth that funded art, philosophy, and literature.[9] Athens had some notable political leaders, but everything they did was built on the foundation of a successful economy. As the desire to maintain that foundation died out, so did everything else. By the end of the third century BC, Greek freedom was a thing of the past. By the end of the second century the age of Greek supremacy was passing into memory.

England

As we approach the end of the chapter,[10] there may be some readers who are approaching the end of their patience. All this about economic foundations is well and good, they may be thinking, but is that all there is to it? There are more important things than money.

The discussion of economic matters may perhaps be defended with the observation that people who insist that there are "more important things than money" are usually (a) asking for money, (b) already have a lot of money, or more often (c) both. That issue aside, it does deserve to be asked if there is any relationship between the need for achievement and noneconomic forms of cultural expression. We can take a step toward an answer by looking at the history of England.

In the year 1400, England did not seem to have much of a future.[11] Asked to pick from among the world's nations the one with the best prospects, futurists of the time would have placed their bets on China. Forced to choose from among the nations of Europe, they probably would have chosen Spain. But not England. In 1400, England was small, weak, and backward, an almost primitive agricultural community on the European periphery. Four and a half centuries later, though, it was the most advanced civilization on the planet, the wealthiest, and the most powerful, and both China and Spain were in decline. The thing that made the difference was a rise in the English people's need for achievement.

McClelland and his colleagues examined this in a study of English literature. The years between 1400 and 1830 were broken up into seven approximately equal periods, and the level of achievement motivation during each of these periods was calculated with the same method that had been used in the study of ancient Greece. (The results are summarized in McClelland's Table 4.6 of *The Achieving Society*.) The English people's need for achievement increased until about 1600, leveled off, and then began to decline. It fell over the course of the next century and then began to rise again, reaching its peak in 1830.

The English economy also had some ups and downs. There was no period of decline like that of ancient Greece, but there were periods during which improvement was faster than it was in others. If we consider periods of accelerated progress as periods of advance, and periods of slower progress as periods of (relative) decline, a clear picture emerges. For most of the years between 1400 and 1500, the English economy was stagnant, but it began to improve toward the end of the fifteenth century. Between 1500 and 1635 it grew by leaps and bounds. The rate of progress declined after that, hit a low around 1770 or 1780, and then began to pick up again.

The reader who is interested in a graphic representation of these findings is referred to McClelland's Figure 4.3 of *The Achieving Society*. The upper part of the graph shows the rate of economic progress and the lower part shows the average frequency of achievement imagery in popular literature. The two lines seem to be almost parallel, but that is an optical illusion. The scale of the lower graph is set back fifty years. The year 1550 on the lower graph corresponds to the year 1600 in the upper graph, 1600 to 1650, and so on.

Okay, so what does all this tell us? It tells us that changes in the English people's concern for practical accomplishment, as reflected by the literature they enjoyed, came **before** changes in their rate of economic progress. A rise in the need for achievement was followed by a period when the rate of progress increased, and a decline was followed by a period during which the rate of progress slowed down. A change in values and purposes comes before a change in economic circumstances. First people change, and then, either for the better or for the worse, they change the world they live in.

But a change in the way people think about themselves and their world shows up in more than just their economic behavior. It shows up also in their contributions to the arts and sciences. We have already noted that the literature of the late sixteenth and early seventeenth centuries point to a high need for achievement among the English. In the periods that followed (in other words, in both halves of the seventeenth century), England was remarkable for her production of persons eminent in music, science, and literature.

We saw also that the latter half of the seventeenth century was a period during which the need for achievement was lower. The following period (that is to say, the early eighteenth century) was one of economic and cultural stagnation: English businessmen were less enterprising, and the per capita volume of trade with America fell off. English universities declined, and the Royal Navy (which once had been and would again become a force to be reckoned with) languished. The great outpourings of the English Enlightenment did not begin until the middle of the century.

This is not to say that nothing important happened. During the early eighteenth century, England established itself as a parliamentary democracy. English law was codified, and Blackstone published his famous legal commentaries. Some other research, however, found that periods during which there is a strong interest in politics, in particular periods during which there is a strong interest in codifying legal standards, are usually periods in which the advance of science and business is comparatively slow.

Conclusion

Mark Twain once said that if history does not repeat itself, at least it rhymes. Persons and events are unique. No trend is the perfect image of another. The research described in the present chapter shows that it is possible in spite of this to identify certain dominant tendencies. It shows also that a dominant tendency of one kind is usually followed by a dominant tendency of another. Periods during which there is a high and rising need for achievement are followed by periods of social and economic advance. Periods high in the achievement motive are followed by periods during which it is lower, and these are followed by stagnation or decline.

Karl Marx said that material changes come first: people shape their thinking to fit the technology by means of which they earn their living. The need for achievement research shows that he was mistaken. Changes in ideas, values, and character come first. Other things follow. People develop new technologies to match their new aspirations. History's driving forces are not material but spiritual.

Marx also said that every status quo contains the seeds of its own destruction, and here he may have been right. The stories of both England and ancient Greece indicate that periods of prosperity are periods during which the need for achievement declines. And a declining need for achievement bodes ill for the future.

We cannot say, however, that a period of relative poverty must be followed by a period of progress or that a period of comfort must followed by a period of decline. The force that drives a people's history is not to be found in the level of their material well-being. It is in their thinking. It is in their values. It is in their character. These may change suddenly, unexpectedly, and in ways no one could foresee. The next chapter will deal with a change of just this kind.

Chapter 3

THE APPEARANCE OF CHARACTER

Under one of his journal entries for the year 1778, Rev. John Wesley tells us about a sermon he delivered to a group of disadvantaged children. "I endeavored to warn them," he tells us, "and all that bring them up, against that English sin, ungodliness, that upproach* of our nation, wherein we excel all the inhabitants of the earth."[1]

Anyone who has even the slightest knowledge of child psychology knows that this was absolutely the last thing in the world those children needed to hear. They needed to hear about the positives of both themselves and their nation, not the negatives. They needed encouragement to go out and do what they wanted to do, not warnings about things they should not do. The use of the word "sin," in particular, was a major *faux pas.* You can almost see the spirit of Dr. Spock raising his finger to his lips and waving wildly in a desperate attempt to catch Wesley's attention and hush him up before he did irreparable damage.

Perhaps we can better understand Wesley's inappropriate message if we set it against the background of his own experience as an abused child. His mother had displayed an inordinate faith in the biblical in-

---

* Modern Americans would say "reproach."

junction against spoiling the child by sparing the rod. In raising her children, she said, she was guided by two principles (both of which would raise warning flags in the minds of modern psychologists): to break the unregenerate will of the child; to guide him by a strict discipline in the way he ought to go.[2] The family was a large one and very poor, so Wesley was from an early age deprived of adequate parental attention except in the little-desired form just suggested. It is hardly surprising that he and his brother Charles played leading roles in a widespread countercultural rebellion (called the Evangelical Revival), the many excesses of which shocked decent people in both England and America. It is a wonder that his sermons were no more offending than they were.

He was at least more moderate than the most famous of his colleagues, George Whitefield. On one of the occasions when he listened to Whitefield preach, Benjamin Franklin expressed his amazement at the admiration showered upon him by the members of his audience, "notwithstanding his common abuse of them by assuring them that they were naturally *half beasts and half devils.*"[3]

One might suppose that, having listened to sermons of this kind, people would go out and commit suicide (or at the very least organize a protest against clergy brutality). They went out instead and became rich. Consider for example the testimony of James Lackington, son of a poverty-stricken, drunken shoemaker. At the age of sixteen he became a Methodist. He borrowed some money from the Methodist Lending Society, started a business, and became a wealthy bookseller. "If I had never heard the Methodists preach," he said in his later years, "I should have been at this time a poor, ragged, dirty cobbler."[4]

But it wasn't just the Methodists. The Baptists, too, and the Quakers, and the Pietists, and a hundred other small sects, and before any of them, the Puritans, all displayed the same curious connection between strictness in their religion and success in their material endeavors. Wesley could see what was happening. "For religion must necessarily produce both industry and frugality," he wrote, "and these cannot but produce riches."[5] In cases without number, the members of England's wretched masses listened to the words of preachers who were interested only in preparing them for the next world and suddenly found themselves doing very well in this one.

Walter Lippmann once observed that religious experience gives people a new confidence in their power and potential as human beings. The feeling that one stands in the immediate presence of God is associated with inner assurance, inner discipline, inner strength. The distinctions of this world lose their importance, the pretensions of rulers are rejected, and a person begins for the first time to feel the full significance of individuality.[6] A new self-confidence and self-trust show themselves in every area, including the economic, and the empowered individual begins to do great things with his life.

The dawn of the eighteenth century, as we observed in the last chapter, found England at a low tide in both the need for achievement and its rate of economic progress. A futurist of the time might well have concluded that it was about to retrace the path of ancient Greece to decline and oblivion. It set out instead to become, over the course of the next 150 years, the most advanced, the most prosperous, and the most powerful civilization on the planet. Something happened to change people's values, priorities, and aspirations—and therefore their destiny. That something, according to McClelland, was the Evangelical Revival.

In this chapter we will examine the historical relationship between religion, character, and social progress.

The Rule of St. Benedict

There are many places at which we might begin, and AD 500 is as good as any. At this point in history, the once-mighty Roman Empire was a shambles. Violence was so common that no one remarked upon it. Trade had come to a halt; intellectual life was at a standstill; it was impossible to be sure about who was in charge.

In the midst of this chaos, some of the devout felt themselves called to rise above the demands of the flesh and serve God in the seclusion of a monastery. Now there was nothing new about rising above the demands of the flesh or lives of seclusion or monasticism. They were all tried, true, and even trendy. Simeon Stylites, whose name was as familiar then as Elvis's is today, lived on a pillar east of Antioch for 36 years and is said to have put his feet to his forehead 1,244 times in a row. Other monks lived in cells so tiny that they could neither stand at full height nor lie at full length. Still others went for long periods of time without sleep or for days without food.[7] Like many another religious movement and most political speeches, this was all quite entertaining but not very useful. The most extreme monks were called "the athletes of God," and crowds came to look at them, but they didn't get much done.

At around the beginning of the sixth century, though, a man who is known to history as Benedict of Nursia had a better idea. He invented a new and improved brand of monasticism. First of all, he said, there would be no more going it alone. The monks would live as a community. Second, instead of relying on alms and charity, they would work to support themselves. Third, there would be a definite standard, a standard that came to be called the Rule of St. Benedict.

This Rule was simple enough, but there was no doubt about what it meant: "Poverty, chastity, obedience."[8] The monks were required to live in poverty. No matter how successful their work might be, the monks were not allowed to spend any more than was necessary to keep body and soul together. They were not allowed to have any contact with women. And they were expected to do whatever their superior told them to do. There were no bonuses for high productivity, no retreats for the sake of team-building, no vacations, no consciousness-raising seminars, no weekends in the big city, no time off for good behavior (which was required), no escape from those eternal and unexciting demands. Day after day after day it was the same dull round of poverty, chastity, obedience, poverty, chastity, obedience, poverty, chastity, obedience, poverty, chastity, obedience.

As a means to the surrender of life's physical and material pleasures, this was a standard that could hardly be improved upon. As an incentive plan it had some obvious defects. In spite of the many shortcomings in the management system under which he labored, the monastery plan participant was expected to work hard and make good use of his time. Writing late in the fourteenth century to those who were seeking to attain perfection in the monastic life, Thomas à Kempis said, "Never leave your time quite unoccupied; always be either reading, or writing, or praying or doing something for the good of the community."[9]

Any suggestion to the effect that one had a right to find fulfillment in his work would have fallen on deaf ears. A desire for personal fulfillment would have been the last thing to come up in a polite discussion among a group of monks, many of whom had in any case taken a vow of silence and did not get involved in polite discussions. Some days the work might go well and some days it might not, but that was irrelevant. Work was regarded as a means, not to fulfillment, but to subduing the desires of the flesh. It was a means to self-control.

To sociologist Maurice Line's question, "Why isn't work fun?"[10] a man like Thomas à Kempis could only have stared in dumb amazement. He had never entertained the slightest notion that it ought to be fun or rewarding or fulfilling. One put his back into his labors precisely because there were more important things than enjoyment.

Nobody ever told the monks that their work ought to be fun. The strong implication, upon the contrary, was that they were doing it precisely because it wasn't fun. It was a discipline. The ascetics who once sat on top of pillars or tortured themselves in cages had at least been able to draw admirers, but the monks who worked under the Rule of St. Benedict were denied even that. Copying manuscripts, cleaning stables, and plowing fields do not work well as crowd-pleasers. There was nothing in these things but the work itself, work that was done not for the love of it or because anyone would notice or even because a man could expect to enjoy the fruit of his labors, but simply because it had been assigned.

A study done in 1984 described four concerns that were widespread among students entering the workforce at that time. The first of these was employment under supervisors they did not respect and could not follow with commitment. The second was not being able to earn enough to live as well as they wanted, and the third was being forced to work in an organization they did not like just for the sake of an income. Finally, they were afraid their abilities might never be recognized.[11]

One suspects that their experience in the years since then has shown them that these concerns were, if anything, overly optimistic. Bosses we do not like, financial strains, and a less than perfect place of employment are not strange things or unusual. Unrecognized genius is a proverb. Heavy burdens they may well be, but they are burdens that are laid at one time or another upon the backs of us all. Whoever designed the world and human life did so without giving adequate consideration to our desire for frequent and positive reinforcement. The person who cannot be at peace with this fact cannot be at peace. And so the monks worked, expecting nothing from their labors but the inner assurance that they had done their duty and would in God's good time be rewarded as faithful servants.

Their reward, as it happened, usually came much sooner than they had expected but in a somewhat different form. We have no hard data with regard to their fate in Eternity, but it is a matter of historical record that the monks' patient efforts often led to earthly success. The grounds of the medieval monastery were characteristically clean and well kept, its farms almost invariably became the most prosperous in the area, and its coffers were usually brimming. It is true that this was on some occasions due in part to the bequest of a wealthy merchant, but it is also true that the monasteries did very well for themselves even in the absence of such bequests. Diligence, industry, and frugality produced wealth.

Feudal magnificence was built on an unsound economic foundation. In the midst of it, the monks led quiet, sober, inconspicuous lives, applied themselves to the tasks at hand, never wasted a second, spent very little of what they earned, and grew rich. It was not intended that the monastery's wealth should be used for the benefit of individual monks, who were expected to adhere steadfastly to their vow of poverty. Even in the cases where this principle was faithfully followed, though, the obvious prosperity of the monastery always occasioned a pious commentary. Here these men were, the critics intoned, supposedly serving God, and yet growing rich in the things of the world. One could not serve God and Mammon. If these institutions were growing rich, it was said, it could only be because they had somehow gone very badly astray.

Local princes, whose profligate style of living kept them poor, did what they could to keep the monasteries on the path to perfection by robbing them with some considerable frequency. Monastic funds were also drained off for the service of Christ and the aid of the poor through the construction of great cathedrals and bishops' residences. In spite of such assistance in remaining true to the faith, monasteries continually fell from grace by growing rich. New monastic orders arose to protest the material comforts and declining rigor of their predecessors, imposed even sterner disciplines, and in due course also became prosperous.

The Protestant Reformation

Martin Luther was a monk. He was also a spiritual hypochondriac. Poor, chaste, and obedient in perfect conformity with the Rule of St. Benedict, he still felt the need to go over his soul with a fine-tooth comb, relentlessly searching for every hint, suggestion, or implication of anything similar to, bordering on, or tending toward sin. He would confess whatever he found to the vicar of his monastic order and then perform the assigned penance.

The said vicar, one John von Staupitz, eventually grew weary of this. To get Luther's mind off his sins, he assigned him the task of lecturing on the biblical books of Psalms and Romans, a task Luther undertook late in the summer of 1513. As it turned out, more than just keeping Luther busy, the job changed his religious perspective. In 1512 the central theme of his thinking was dark concern over his sins. By 1517 it was his excitement over the passage that said, "The just shall live by faith."[12]

Whether this insight came gradually to Luther in his study or (as a famous story has it) suddenly as he climbed stone steps on bleeding knees and in obedience to a penance that had been assigned him, it was a turning point in the history of Western civilization. The dominant conception up to this time had been of the Church as the only means of grace. The Church was conceived of as a vast repository, into which were deposited all the merits of the saints, and from which small increments of salvation could be dispensed at the discretion of ecclesiastical officials. And salvation usually came at a price: in the words of the ditty over which Luther was to fight the first of his battles, "As soon as the coin in the coffer rings, the soul from Purgatory springs."

It was believed that apart from the grace distributed by the Church, a person was doomed to an eternity in the fires of hell or at the very least to the extended discomfort of purgatory. *Nulla salus extra ecclesiam*: "There is no salvation outside the church." No, Luther replied, *sola fide*: "Faith alone." Grace comes by faith. One's relationship with God is direct, personal, and complete. It is the result of individual faith. It is neither mediated by an institution nor granted in small increments.

The particular institution that claimed it could grant little bits of grace and charge for them was as enthusiastic about this insight as modern oil companies would be about a solar-powered minivan capable of carrying six people, three sacks of groceries, and a large dog at ninety miles an hour. John Hus had been burned at the stake in 1415 for saying almost exactly the same things Luther had begun to say by 1517. We have not here the space to go into the congeries of political and ecclesiastical rivalries that protected Luther. Suffice it to say that he lived and that his idea became a movement.

The Appearance of Individualism

During the Middle Ages it was believed that those who became members of a monastic community did so because God had called them. Kings, princes, cardinals, and bishops were also regarded as having been placed in their positions by an act of God. There was nothing special, though, about the life of the average Joe or the average Jane. Such persons existed only to provide money (and of course subjects) so that kings and princes could rule and cardinals and bishops could administer the incremental disposition of grace.

Luther's experience with Thomas Munzer and the Peasants' Rebellion led him to believe that it was entirely possible to be in too big a hurry about disabusing people of these notions. As soon as he saw people acting on the practical implications of his insights, he began to draw back from them. A person should not rebel against his or her place in the world, he declared, because that place is the direct result of God's decision with regard to that particular person. Everyone has a divine calling, and that calling is to stay right where they already are. The evidence of one's calling was to be found in the obligations imposed by the realities of daily life.[13]

These arguments were as effective as a decision to close the barn's door after all the cattle had gone. Luther's idea of a "calling" was an attempt to preserve the social status quo, but once people have begun to think of themselves as standing in the immediate presence of God, any status quo based on belief in hierarchies and divinely chosen rulers is doomed. If one's place in the world is a God-given responsibility and if each is directly accountable to God, each will personally decide the way in which his life should go.

Luther wanted to preserve the past, but later generations of Protestants used his ideas to point to the significance of the present. A century after Luther, we hear the Puritan divine John Angier urging the members of his flock to "spiritualize their calling and earthly business." The theologian William Perkins added that worldly callings thus spiritualized became "the matter of good works."[14]

They were saying that one's work was important for more than just securing the means of existence. It had an eternal significance, and the way in which one did it gave expression to the nature of one's relationship with the Divine. For most people, economic activities were not merely the best, but probably the only way in which one could serve God.[15] Religious services and worship had their place, and a definite time was to be set aside for them. In other times and places, though, the individual was called to faithfulness in the things of daily life.

This new emphasis on the importance of everyday living led to new attitudes. People had once admired the person whose great spirituality had led him to withdraw from the world and serve God in a monastery. They now admired the man who served God through faithfulness in his daily responsibilities. They had once stood in awe of kings and princes. They now began to focus on the importance of their own individual lives.

The full effect of this reorientation would not be felt until after the middle of the eighteenth century, but the tendency was already clear at the beginning of the seventeenth. Scotland's James VI (later James I of England) could not see how Puritan divines could be so vocal about the depth of their own sins and their unworthiness before God and yet so willing to defy the royal decree. In his mind, their awareness of their low standing before the Almighty should have increased their willingness to obey one such as himself, the divinely appointed ruler. He did not understand that the person who believes himself to be in personal contact with God, and who therefore accepts his own conscience as a sufficient measure of divine approval or displeasure, feels no need for the commands of a king.

Beginning very cautiously with Luther and becoming more audacious with the appearance of each new sect, Protestantism gradually changed the locus of responsibility. At the beginning of the sixteenth century, people looked to the institutions of church and state for their definitions of good and bad, right and wrong, strong and weak. By the end of the eighteenth, many of them were looking into their own hearts. The great issues, they had come to believe, were not the issues occupying the time of the political and religious hierarchy. The great issues were those pertaining to the way in which they led their own lives.

The Protestant Ethic

The *New York Times* best-seller in late-sixteenth and early-seventeenth-century Protestant bookstores was Foxe's *Book of Martyrs.* If there had been a video, it would have been rated "R," and parents would have been cautioned against showing it to their children because it contained extreme violence, in particular scenes of explicit torture. The surgeon general would have attached a warning against its being viewed by persons with pacemakers, heart trouble, or weak stomachs.

Wherever it had the support of a king or queen, the Roman Catholic Church expressed its warm acceptance for conflicting faiths chiefly through the cruel murder of their adherents. Elizabeth's predecessor, for example, is known to history as "Bloody Mary" because she threw the weight of the English throne into the execution (no pun intended) of just such a policy. Protestants were not necessarily opposed to the use of force in encouraging conversion or the painful extermination of heretics, but they had such force at their disposal in only a comparatively small number of cases. In the religious struggles of the sixteenth and seventeenth centuries, they were more often the persecuted than the persecutors.

All of this made for some very bad feelings. None of the early Protestant sects could see much that was good about Roman Catholicism, and they would not have appreciated any suggestion to the effect that they were endorsing the continuation of practices begun by the medieval church. Yet in more ways than one, this is precisely what they were doing. The so-called "Protestant work ethic," for example, was essentially an adaptation of monastic standards to the new emphasis on the importance of individuals.

This is a significant point. The early Protestants saw nothing admirable about monasticism and never would have consciously set out to imitate it. Yet once people begin to take life seriously and as something with more than a merely transient value, they are very likely to fall back on the principles to which the Rule of St. Benedict had given expression.

"Poverty, chastity, obedience." Add "pain" and "sickness" and we have the list of life's five least desirable conditions. The person who accepts such privations, said sociologist Emile Durkheim, does so to gain control over irrational instincts or, in the language of religion, "the demands of the flesh."[16] In gaining this control, the medieval monk found the freedom of indifference toward the chaos of secular life, and with that freedom the power to rise above it. Although more enmeshed in the world than the monk had been, the devout Protestant sought a similar freedom and a similar power.

Work and the Quest for Perfection

"Poverty, chastity, obedience." These are most easily discussed if their order is reversed. For the medieval monk, "obedience" meant the faithful execution of whatever had been assigned by his superior. Such assignments were often given without any regard for a man's talents, limitations, or preferences. Peace was to be found, not in the work itself, but in the self-control that stifled the angry emotions it provoked. The person who could bring himself to a wholehearted and perhaps even an enthusiastic commitment to a disagreeable task found his way eventually to both competence and enjoyment.

Fate is more arbitrary than any human superior. You can devote your energies either to railing against life's injustices or to doing what you can in the midst of them. The members of the early Protestant sects settled upon the latter course. "Obedience" became a willing surrender to the inevitable and a determination to make the most of it.

Everything that happened, they believed, happened because it was the will of God. But the purposes of God were inscrutable. Not merely the outcome of one's earthly endeavors, but even one's status in eternity remained always in doubt. The Puritans held to a doctrine of strict predestination, according to which God had from before the foundations of the earth assigned some to be damned and others to be saved. There was no way either to know one's destiny or to change it. The Methodists, more lenient, believed the evidence of salvation could be found in the testimony of one's heart. On the other hand, they believed a person could easily fall from grace and warned the faithful against the dangers of unconscious sins and "backsliding."

They expressed it differently and argued endlessly, sometimes even uncharitably, over whose formulation was the best. In the end, however, the Protestant sects agreed upon a fundamental and inescapable uncertainty, in the face of which their members were encouraged simply to persist and never to lose heart. The Methodist was urged to be vigilant about remaining on "the more excellent way."[17] The Calvinist who came to his pastor with concerns over his eternal fate was told that all he could do was be faithful to his calling.[18]

In either case, it was to their daily tasks that they returned for assurance, and it was in the effectiveness of their daily labors that they found comfort. They sought evidence for their spiritual progress in the gradually increasing perfection with which they carried on their economic activities. Obstacles to efficiency could not be tolerated. They believed God would bless those who persisted in their efforts to find a better way.

The immediate precursors of the Industrial Revolution were the seventeenth-century inventions of the English textile industry. All of these, as Walter Lippmann once observed, were the work of operatives who were faced with practical problems.[19] But those difficulties had been there for so long that most people had learned to take them for granted. It was only with the appearance of the new faith that steps were taken toward dealing with them. If necessity is the mother of invention, the other parent is a belief that one can somehow find the power to meet its strict demands.

The Greeks' disdain for manual labor had meant that the best minds never came into contact with the problems of production.[20] The attitude of a man like Aristotle was "let the slaves worry about it." But the slaves had no incentive for making improvements. No one, not even the slaves themselves, saw any significance in what they did. And anyway, if they found a better way to do something, their masters would just find more things for them to do. It was not until people began to see a higher value in their labors that they learned to identify problems and work with them until they were solved.

The Fleeting Moment

The early Protestants also reaffirmed the monastic disciplines in their attitude toward time. Remember that late in the Middle Ages, Thomas à Kempis had advised his monastic readers to make use of every moment. Seventeenth-century New England Puritans mirrored this attitude: a Massachusetts colony statute of 1633 said that "No person, hawseholder or other, shall spend his time idely or unproffably, under pain of such punishment as the court shall thinke meet to inflicte."[21] The General Conference of 1766 gave this command to the Methodists: "We must never forget the first rule, 'Be diligent. Never be unemployed for a moment. Never be triflingly employed. Never while away time; neither spend any more time in any place than is strictly necessary."[22]

Set against the vastness of Eternity, the span of a human life was so brief as not to be worth mentioning. There was barely enough time to make sure of one's salvation, so it was necessary to make the fullest possible use of every single moment. Unnecessary socializing, idle conversation, and too much sleep were all condemned. Not even times of quiet openness to the Divine Power should be allowed to come at the expense of one's employment. Sunday has been provided as the day of worship, said one Puritan minister, and it was usually those who neglected their callings during the week who had no time for God on Sunday.[23]

Fidelity, Honesty, and the Family

The Rule's second injunction had been to "chastity," which for the medieval monk meant celibacy. The great German sociologist Max Weber said that the sexual instinct is so little subject to rational control that the person who could discipline it was regarded as having a "gift of grace" (this is the correct translation of the word *charisma*).[24] In committing themselves to marriage with complete faithfulness to a single spouse, the early Protestants sought to demonstrate such a gift, and not without some justification. It is as difficult to be faithful to a single spouse as it is to remain celibate. The person who seeks the satisfactions of marriage is easily led to believe that life's remaining dissatisfactions (of which there will always be many) are the result of a flaw in his or her mate. The search for inner peace, and with it the habit of consistent behavior toward other people, is at least as difficult in marriage as it is in a monastic community.

This discipline has important implications for economic behavior. Honesty to the marriage vow is the fundamental honesty. Franklin Roosevelt covered up his affairs with Lucy Mercer and Missy Le Hand. In 1932 he ran on a ticket that promised to reduce the size of the American government—and then launched the New Deal. It was said of him that his first instinct was always to lie. He would on occasion begin a statement and then change it because he realized that for the present purpose the truth would work as well as a falsehood.[25] Lyndon Johnson was a far-ranging philanderer and such an open liar that the expression "credibility gap" was invented to characterize the statements of his administration.[26] Marital infidelity opens the door to other infidelities, to one's employer, to one's customers, to the public.

The reliability evident in their marriages was evident also in the economic transactions to which the members of the Protestant sects were a party. Quakers and Baptists certified their religious merit by maintaining fixed prices and a reputation for reliability.[27] People were drawn into the shop of a devout artisan because they knew they could trust him. Employers sought out the Methodists (and in Germany the Mennonites) because of their willingness to learn the new methods demanded by emerging technologies and because they were known for their honesty.[28] Piety opened the door to material success: we all prefer to do business with people we can trust. It was said of the Quakers that they came to America seeking to do good and found themselves doing well.

The commitment to marital fidelity was also a commitment to one's family. A couple's devotion to each other was reinforced by their devotion to their children. Little ones were brought up in the "fear and admonition of the Lord," had tasks for which they were responsible, and were often employed in the family business. They were also likely to be involved in an intensive home schooling program. John Wesley's mother taught her children the Lord's Prayer as soon as they could speak, began their education in reading when they reached the age of five, and had the older children assist her in the training of their younger siblings.[29] The honor that in the Middle Ages had gone to solitary ascetics or to members of a monastic community went now to the parents of honest, courteous, and hardworking children.

Attitudes Toward Money

With material success and a family came the temptation to indulge oneself in a luxurious display of one's wealth. In the hands of the Protestant sects, the Benedictine injunction to "poverty" became the rule that one should always live well within one's means. We are stewards of the things that have been entrusted to us by the grace of God, they believed, and will be held accountable for the way in which we have used them. Money spent for personal enjoyment or ostentation is money lost for the sake of some higher purpose. The successful individual made modest provision for himself and his family, gave something for the work of God and the assistance of the deserving poor, and then saved the rest, or more probably, invested it back into his business, which then grew even more rapidly than it had before.

Personal Character and Economic Progress

This, then, was the Protestant Ethic. Work hard. Look for a better way. Persist. Make good use of your time. Be honest. Save. Weber saw the appearance of this standard as a unique event in the history of the world and as the first step in the creation of a competitive economy. McClelland took a less sweeping view. It was, he said, no more than a large-scale outbreak of the same thing he had studied in primitive societies, in the rise of ancient Greece, in medieval England, and in the modern world. It was a codification, perhaps even the institutionalization, of the need for achievement.

It was that, to be sure, but it was more than just that. It was also the first appearance of what would come to be known as "character." Honesty and fidelity are not directly derivable from the need for achievement. They are in fact conspicuously absent from the personality traits the Greeks attributed to Hermes, their mythological embodiment of achievement motivation. More interested in ends than in means, the ancient Greeks admired craftiness and low cunning. The Protestant reformers and the leaders of the Evangelical Revival did not. What they endorsed was not prosperity itself, but the strict, disciplined, and self-sacrificial style of living that often led to it. And this, said William James, is precisely what we mean by "character": a purpose and a structure that the demands of the inner life have imposed upon the outer life.[30]

In developing his thesis on the relationship between the Protestant Ethic and the rise of the modern economy, Weber said that the significance of the great religious movements was primarily in their educative influence. This influence, he added, generally made itself felt only after "the peak of the purely religious enthusiasm was past."[31] In other words, there was a lag effect. The religious movement came first. The economic impact came later.

This is exactly what we have already observed about the need for achievement. McClelland's research showed that an increase in the literary use of achievement imagery preceded periods of economic progress in ancient Greece, in late medieval and early modern England, and in the modern world. The educative influence came first. Individuals went out to change their world only after they had experienced a change in their ethical standards and aspirations.

In the seventeenth and eighteenth centuries, this change came at first because of the new converts' participation in the worshiping community and their frequent exposure to sermons in which the new values were upheld. These new values soon appeared in child-raising practices that encouraged independence and mastery training. The rearing of children was treated with the same seriousness as the rest of life, and the same disciplines that parents imposed upon themselves were visited also upon the heads of their little ones, as in the case of Rev. John Wesley, with which this chapter began.

People were encouraged, indeed required, to read the Bible for themselves, and this was urged upon children as well as adults. Children were thus directed not merely to take care of themselves but to think for themselves. The inevitable consequence was a generation that had an extraordinarily high need for achievement. It happened in the early seventeenth century because of the Puritans and again in the eighteenth because of the Evangelical Revival. Exposed twice to the influence of persons who were high in the need for achievement, England became first the greatest commercial and then the greatest industrial society the world had ever seen.

The role of the radical Protestant sects in the second of these transformations is especially clear. Accounting for an average of only about 6 percent of the British population in the years between 1725 and 1850, they produced more than a third and perhaps as many as half of its industrial innovators.[32] They also provided a supply of workers and managers who were willing to master and employ the new methods of production with which these innovators supplied them. Members of the lower classes raised themselves to prosperity, and it was not long before ordinary employees found themselves blessed with a level of comfort that not even kings had enjoyed two centuries before.

Personal Character and Political Freedom

Among the many of McClelland's studies not discussed in the previous chapter was one that examined the folktales of preliterate tribes throughout the world. Tribes who told stories low in achievement imagery were found to believe that one could come into contact with the Divine only through the mediation of a priest or the representative of a religious institution. Tribes high in the need for achievement were likely to believe in the possibility of individual contact with God (or the gods). They were also likely to be filled with small entrepreneurs and to feel that they had the freedom to try new things.[33]

This research spanned a wide variety of social structures, climates, means of subsistence, and levels of technology. Across all of them, tribes with a high need for achievement were readier both to recognize the rights and power of the individual over the central issues of his or her own life and to adopt more efficient means of earning a living. The sense of a personal responsibility for one's own religious life, it might be suggested, creates the necessity of individual thought, and individual thought is the prerequisite of economic creativity.

That is the central theme in the evolution of the ethic we have just described. Thrown increasingly back on themselves and upon their own convictions and experiences in their relationship with Eternity, people came also to trust their own ideas in dealing with the things of this earth. And instead of expressing their faith only by means of participation in a religious institution, they learned to testify to it in the way they did their work.

The first freedom they demanded was not economic but religious freedom. Their first demand for freedom of assembly was for the sake of religious meetings. Scorning the services and the ministry of the established church, Puritans assembled in small "conventicles" to interpret Scripture for each other and to decide upon its implications for the events of their times. To the state, attendance at such meetings was both heresy and treason. The common people were permitted neither to have thoughts of their own nor to share them with one another, and their assemblies were frequently disturbed. Their leaders were taken to the Tower. In time, some of the devout began to look overseas, where they hoped they could meet in quietness and peace.[34]

The combination of the printing press and a strong emphasis on the Bible as a source of authority made for the appearance of a widespread intellectualism among the laity. The ordinary individual was for the first time in history recognized, at least in his own mind and by peers, as having meaningful opinions on the central issues of life. It was possible to have ideas other than those endorsed by the Crown and its organ of propaganda, the established Church. There remained of course a large element of the population that was willing to believe what we would today describe as "spin" about the unimportance of immorality in high places in view of the government's obviously benevolent purposes. But now there was also a substantial minority that dared to believe something else.

The first Puritans were highly educated clergymen who because of their convictions and social background were unable to obtain positions in the established Church. They were extremely critical both of the uneducated priesthood and of bishops who held high positions because of their connections at court. The Puritans believed that the ministry should be the work of those with the gifts and graces to perform it.[35] They were saying, in effect, that church careers should be open to talent. Success should come as the result of ability and effort, not the good favor of one's superiors. Those who lacked the necessary skills should give way to those who had them.

What they accepted as true for careers in the Church came to be accepted among the Protestant sects as true for careers in general. Success should go to those with the ability to achieve it. High positions should be earned in a free competition. The will of God would be revealed as the most talented and the hardest workers rose to the top. The only government with which the early Protestants were familiar was closed to careers of this kind. Their religious convictions, moreover, which they wore pinned to their shirtsleeves, excluded them from careers in the government. For most of them the only path open to a career based on talent was a career in business. That is where they turned and, by applying the disciplines ingrained by their religious training, that is where they prospered.

From these attitudes sprang demands for limitations on government. If each stood as an individual in the eyes of God, then no one had the right to rule over another. If each could read and interpret the Bible as an individual, then no one could speak as the final authority on ultimate truth. Only the individual could decide upon the divine purpose for his life or hers. The greater the power of a government, the more likely it was that its power would be used to somehow hinder the efforts of the individual who was attempting to do the will of God.

The radical Protestants believed that regardless of one's place on the social scale, human beings were equal in the sight of God and had an equal right to make what they could of their lives. Experience taught that a person might begin at a very low place and rise to a high one. Differences in talent and effort meant that if opportunity was equal, the final results could not be. All that could be asked was the elimination of artificial barriers; no one should be favored at the expense of another. It was not for the government, at best a very unworthy servant, to make general decisions about relative merits. If individuals were left free to pursue the will of God for their own lives, God could be relied upon to reveal His decision in the actual turn of events.

These were the political and economic implications of the faith the passengers of the *Mayflower* and their successors carried with them to America. On the basis of this faith, they laid the foundations of the greatest achieving society the world has ever seen. We turn now to tell that story.

Chapter 4

THE LITERATURE OF HOPE

While feminist historians are agreed upon the malign influence of the white male, they disagree as to when this influence was the worst. The General Evil Theory regards it as a historical constant, equally bad at every point in time, and beginning to abate only in the last decade of the twentieth century, when Mr. Gore paid a prominent feminist fifteen thousand dollars a month to advise him on how to become an alpha-male. The Bad-Worse-Worst Theory of history, on the other hand, identifies some periods as more viciously masculine than others.

Among those who subscribe to the latter theory, the late nineteenth century, in particular late-nineteenth-century England and America, always rate at least a "worse," and in the opinion of the most exacting scholars, a "worst." On a scale from 1 to 10, with 1 being "not too bad" and 10 being "just terrible," this period of time and these nations get a 13. This was the age, and England and America were the places, in which white males exercised the greatest freedom in oppressing not merely women but the entire world. They even went so far as to make comparisons between their own culture and the cultures of other civilizations and to openly regard their own as superior.

In our calmer and more rational time, and with our liberated modern attitudes, we can look back and see how foolish they were. We now know not only that women are the same as men (except for being better), but that all cultures are equally good, each in its own way. Some cultures prefer freedom. Others prefer bondage. Who are we to say that one is better than the other? Some cultures favor a high and rising standard of living. Others favor tradition and stagnation. To avoid the chaos and uncertainty associated with progress and increasing abundance, some nations bravely choose poverty, filth, outmoded technologies, immutable status differences, and an elite class that uses law, custom, and (in Russia and Iraq) war to protect its own comfortable position. Who are we to say they're wrong? Who are we to suggest that our values are better?

In their insensitivity and ignorance, the white males (and sad to say, also the white females) of nineteenth-century England and America could not grasp the insights of cultural relativism. They held blindly, even obstinately, to the belief that there was something unique and important about their own particular values. Alfred Marshall, for example, completely failing to stick to his tasks as an economist, openly took pride in the fact that Anglo-Saxon civilization was the richest on the earth and offered its people the widest range of freedom, opportunity, and comforts the world had ever seen. All of this, he said, was the result of the values upon which it placed a premium: energy, initiative, enterprise, freedom, rationality, innovation, industry, reliability. Less advanced peoples, by contrast, were not held back by a cosmic injustice for which the citizens of prosperous nations were somehow to blame, but by their own idleness, indifference, obedience to custom, ostentation, dishonesty, and waste.[1]

Marshall, it should be added, is guilty of more than just politically incorrect opinions with regard to the relative quality of his own culture. He is also to blame for fiendishly discovering the role of supply and demand in the determination of prices and thus for inflicting the pain of rigorous thinking on countless generations of students in Economics 101. In his defense, it can be said only that he was an equal opportunity oppressor, for the discomfort of understanding economists' graphs has been evenly distributed over both male and female students.

Now the interesting thing about Marshall is this: although he was one of history's greatest economists, he was hesitant (as many of his successors have not been hesitant) about attempting to explain everything in terms of economics. He would of course have been the first to recognize that economics can explain a great deal, including a great deal that politicians would prefer to explain away. But he understood that it couldn't explain everything. Supply and demand, for all their importance, do not explain themselves but must be explained as the result of something else. And that something else, Marshall said, is character.[2] The graphs of economics are an accurate description of reality only if economists have made accurate assumptions about the character of the people whose behavior they are seeking to explain.

One of economists' assumptions, for example, is that we can increase a person's desire to work by increasing wages. But as Marshall recognized and as his great German contemporary Max Weber emphasized, people do not by nature seek to earn more and more money. The tendency is rather to earn only as much as is necessary to support a familiar standard of living. Early attempts to industrialize West Africa were hindered by workers' habit of working for a few weeks, collecting their pay, and returning to their villages. The first European manufacturers found that workers responded to an increase in piece rates by maintaining their previous income with the production of fewer pieces.[3]

Adam Smith argued that the effect of high wages was to increase employees' diligence, but this was in the last quarter of the eighteenth century and in England, where the Evangelical Revival (Smith specifically mentioned the "methodists")[4] had already begun to exert its powerful influence. People work harder than is absolutely necessary and then make it a point to set some of their earnings aside only if they are working for something other than a paycheck. The medieval monk turned his eyes toward Eternity, lived by its strict demands, and saw the monastery become a center of prosperity. The Puritan, the Baptist, and the Methodist treated their work as an outward and visible sign of an inward and spiritual grace, disciplined their appetites, and grew wealthy. Nineteenth-century entrepreneurs, as we shall see in the next chapter, thought in terms of making America great and made both themselves and their country rich. In every case great material accomplishment grew out of something other than a desire simply for material accomplishment. It grew out of the feeling that one's endeavors were serving somehow to give expression to higher principles and a greater truth.

This is not to say that achieving societies have in any way downplayed the importance of material accomplishment. Their strong tendency, however, has been to regard success as important primarily because it testifies to the truth of the values they endorse. Seventeenth-century Puritans despised the greedy but admired the person who grew rich by means of obedience to the standards of the Protestant Ethic. In the eighteenth century, Methodists and Baptists condemned avarice but regarded the success of a fellow sectarian as evidence of God's blessing. And up until nearly the end of the nineteenth century, most Americans believed that achievement in the world of facts and material things was important less as an end itself than as evidence of the truth in the values to which they subscribed.

This chapter and the next tell the story of the achievement ethic in America.

From Rags to Riches in Colonial America

Benjamin Franklin was raised in Boston, an old Puritan stronghold. He could trace his lineage back to the sixteenth century and to Protestant ancestors who had defied the decree of Bloody Mary with a clever device for hiding their Bible as soon they heard the police knock at the door.[5] His older brother James used his newspaper to continue the family tradition of challenging authority and got himself thrown into jail, leaving teenage Benjamin in charge of the enterprise. The two brothers began to quarrel shortly after James' release from prison, and Benjamin set out for Philadelphia.[6]

He now encountered a series of surprises and used them to build his fortune. He traveled by sea, survived a shipwreck, and was on the verge of destitution by the time he arrived in Philadelphia. He was lucky enough to find a job and unlucky enough to be sent to London by a prominent man who never made good on his promises to help young

Franklin set up his own business. He found a job in London and did well but spent too much, made some unwise loans, and had to delay his return to America. Back in Philadelphia, he returned to his old job, worked hard, and was soon running the place. The father of a fellow worker said that if Franklin would provide the brains, he would provide the capital to get the two young men started in a printing shop of their own. The partnership didn't work, and Franklin was hard-pressed to come up with the funds for buying out the other man. He finally managed to do it through the kindness of some friends. He did a good job with the business and accumulated enough money to retire by the time he had reached his middle forties.

This was the model later generations of authors would use in designing their stories for young people. It is a story of both good luck and bad, a story that is constantly taking turns for the worse and then for the better. Even as Franklin finishes his *Autobiography*, there is some doubt about how it will end. The only certainty it illustrates is the truth that good character can use life's vicissitudes for the achievement of worthwhile ends.

But what kind of character was it? We happen to have a little information on the subject because Franklin records that early in his life he drew up a self-improvement plan based upon a list of habits he wanted to cultivate.[7] He identified thirteen cardinal virtues, but six of them stand out: Silence, Order, Frugality, Industry, Chastity, and Justice. The first ("Avoid trifling Conversation") and second ("Let each part of your business have its time") are traceable to the religious emphasis on the importance of time. The third ("Waste Nothing") speaks to the careful use of material resources. Industry ("Be always employ'd in something useful") is about hard work, and again, about time. Chastity, pointing to the necessity of controlling the sexual urge, and Justice are injunctions to honesty in every area of one's life. These are the first-generation descendants of the Protestant Ethic, and they bear unmistakably the family traits of first cousins to the Rule of St. Benedict. They are eighteenth-century adaptations of the sixth-century standard: "Poverty, Chastity, Obedience."

Coming from a Presbyterian background, Franklin could never have acknowledged his debt to the standards of monasticism, but he never forgot his debt to Christianity. Early in his *Autobiography* he describes himself as a "doubter," but the second paragraph of the book reads like a prayer of gratitude. He attributes all his success and happiness to God, "Whose kind Providence…led me to the means I used & gave them Success."[8] Franklin was like most Deists, and for that matter many of the French *philosophes*, in that he wanted to avoid narrow doctrinal disputes but had not the slightest interest in giving up religion. He never had any doubt about the immortality of the soul or the reward of the just and the punishment of the unjust. The closest Franklin ever got to leaving the faith of his fathers came when he developed a list of the precepts for what he regarded as a "purely rational" (as opposed to a religious) morality:

- Do not do to another what you would not have done to yourself.
- Give everyone his due.
- Honor your parents.
- Adore God.[9]

In the first of these, he repeats Jesus and anticipates Kant. The second comes from the Old Testament prophets' insistence that employers should not hold back or delay the payment of a worker's wages. The third and the fourth are affirmed at several places in both the New Testament and the Old. Franklin could not have conceived of character without religion, and it was his conviction that a nation composed of persons without religious convictions was doomed.

No man is an island, though, and least of all Benjamin Franklin. Writing in 1774, Horace Walpole said, "A single man sometimes gives a new color to an age. This proved to be the case with Dr. Franklin."[10] But he was overstating it. Franklin did not so much give color to his age as describe the hues that were coming into vogue. He demonstrated a unique capacity for the attainment of practical virtues, but he was not unique in seeking them. We know the values he held were widely approved because of the success enjoyed by the most famous of his publications.

Poor Richard's Almanac began in 1732 as a calendar of important events in the agricultural year, into which Franklin inserted, as he put it, "the wisdom of many ages and nations."[11] It soon ran to over ten thousand copies a year, and Franklin continued to publish it for 25 years.[12] The advice it contained came straight from his Puritan upbringing. Idleness, folly, and pride, he said, are far more costly than even the most burdensome taxes. If you love your life, don't waste your time, because time is all you have. Keep your conscience clear and you have nothing to worry about. There is no gain without some pain. Pay attention to your business, whatever it is, and be careful with your money: "What maintains one vice would bring up ten children."[13]

In 1757 the advice was assembled in a single volume entitled *The Way to Wealth*. But the title should not be taken too literally. Franklin's intention was not to describe wealth as an end itself but "industry and frugality as the means of procuring wealth."[14] It would never have crossed his mind to suggest that people should devote their lives to the accumulation of a fortune. Writing from England to a friend back in America, he said, "London citizens, they say, are ambitious of what they call *dying worth* a great sum. The very notion seems to me absurd."[15]

It was not that he had anything against making money. Writing about an opportunity that came to him late in his first trip to England, he said it would have created a means by which "I might get a good deal of money" and added that if it had come earlier he would have delayed his return to America.[16] There was nothing wrong with making a fortune, but it was the way of living that led to it rather than the fortune itself that occupied his mind and writing. "Wealth and content," he said, "are not always bedfellows," and again, "Avarice and happiness never saw each other." His primary emphasis was always on the improvement of personal character. "Be at war with your vices," said Poor Richard, "at peace with your neighbors, and let every New Year find you a better man." "Search others for their virtues, thyself for thy vices."[17]

The way to self-improvement, Franklin taught, led through self-control. "'Tis easier to suppress the first desire than to satisfy all that follow it" and "To lengthen thy life, lessen thy meals." The way to prosperity led through hard work, honesty, and the careful use of both time and money. "Be always ashamed to catch thyself idle." "He that riseth late must trot all day and shall scarce overtake his business at night," and "Beware of little expenses, a small leak will sink a great ship." "The art of getting riches," said Poor Richard, "consists very much in *thrift*. All men are not equally qualified for getting money, but it is in the power of everyone alike to practice this virtue."[18]

Franklin also placed a premium on innovation, which he advocated as a way of serving God through the service of humanity. He was himself a highly successful inventor. He became famous for his work with electricity, and he invented the damper, a number of smokeless chimneys, two new stoves, and a new hearth called the Pennsylvania Fireplace. The latest medical innovation of his time was inoculation for smallpox. When Franklin's famous contemporary Ethan Allen submitted to such an inoculation, the doctor who administered it was jailed for trying to interfere with the ways of God. Franklin, who lost a small son to the disease, was more open-minded. In 1737 the following opinion appeared in *Poor Richard's Almanac*:

> God offered to the Jews salvation,
> And 't was refused by half the nation;
> Thus (thou 't is life's preservation)
> Many oppose inoculation.[19]

Also worthy of mention is Franklin's emphasis on families. He was close to his own parents, and in the *Autobiography* he goes on at some length about the assistance his father gave him in choosing a line of work. Attributing much of his own success to his spouse, he quoted an old English proverb: "He that would thrive must ask his wife."[20] His greatest pride in setting young men up in business by forming partnerships with them was that these enterprises provided the means "by which several families were raised."[21] Poor Richard also had some opinions on the subject. "Let thy child's first lesson be obedience," he said, echoing the sentiments of John Wesley's mother, "and the second will be what thou wilt." With regard to marital happiness, "Good wives and good plantations are made by good husbands" and "Keep your eyes wide open before marriage, half shut afterwards."[22]

It has been observed that Benjamin Franklin did not always adhere to the virtues he espoused. His failures, though, were mostly during the latter part of his life, after his virtues had made him rich and famous. There is not the slightest doubt that he sincerely aspired to them when he was young. Nor is there any doubt that his success in attaining them, admittedly imperfect, had a good deal to do with what he made of his life.

More important, the popularity of *Poor Richard's Almanac* shows that many Americans held values similar to Franklin's. In terms of the McClelland thesis, his success as a writer is important because it is indicative of the values to which his readers subscribed. These are the values by which they attempted to live and the values they handed on to their children. They are the values that laid the foundations of American prosperity and political institutions. They are also the values that shaped American thinking for most of the nineteenth century.

McGuffey's Reader

The authors of modern textbooks know that all value systems and even nonvalue systems are equally good. The classroom is no place to insist that one is better than another. The student should learn to be objective, disinterestedly weighing the pros and cons of various approaches and never taking a personal position on anything. The people who put together the first American textbooks were less enlightened and made a serious attempt to inculcate a definite morality. The authors of such works as the *New England Primer* and *Webster's Elementary Speller* thought of moral behavior as an end in itself and as more important than any of its by-products.[23]

None of these authors would have been much impressed by arguments to the effect that character was unimportant as long as a person knew how to do the job. It would never have entered their minds to think that job performance could be separated from the rest of one's life. Without character, they believed, it would be impossible to remain steadfast in the disciplines necessary for reliable behavior in real-world situations. Beneath the surface or behind the scenes, the person without character would be involved in things that would prove to be damaging to the interests of those he claimed to serve. Character was the only real guarantee of job performance.

The *New England Primer* was first published in 1690. It was America's most popular textbook for over a century, but by the early 1800s its day had passed. In 1833 a Presbyterian minister/college professor named William H. McGuffey accepted the task of putting together something to replace it.[24] Over the course of the next twenty years, he and his brother Alexander created what may well have been the most successful educational tool in the history of the planet. The six volumes of *McGuffey's Reader* provided an education in everything from elementary reading to Shakespeare and from penmanship to science.

And yes, the *Reader* taught values. Its authors regarded the propagation of morality as a primary purpose of the educational process. The *Reader* was less doctrinal than the *New England Primer* ("In Adam's fall we sinnéd all") but no less concerned with the building of character. The titles of the stories it contained are suggestive: "Mr. Toil and Hugh Idle," "Try, Try, Try Again," "The Honest Boy and the Thief," "Harry and the Guidepost."[25]

The *Reader* described for the student exactly the world that the age of Benjamin Franklin had sought to create, a world where opportunity was open to anyone who would soberly and steadily pursue it. There was no suggestion that anything either was or ought to be guaranteed. In spite of one's best intentions and best efforts, trouble was certain and could be overcome only by going back and back again to the same old difficult and disagreeable tasks. A few of the McGuffeys' heroes and heroines did pretty well for themselves, but most of the stories were along the lines of a poor boy helping his widowed mother feed the family by clearing snow from the paths around neighbors' homes.

If what was preached was, as some have said, a gospel of success, the good news was simply that one could by means of persistence, honesty, and effort find a place in the world. There were no stories about visionaries, rebels, dissenters, or skeptics. All of life's great benefits were traced back, not to the visions of social reformers, but to the efforts of Mr. (or Ms.) Toil.[26]

Good fortune, when it came, always came as the answering response to an expression of personal character. George Ellet in the *Second Reader* inadvertently broke a store window. He ran away but upon reflection went back to confess the crime and to pay for it with the dollar he had just received as a New Year's gift. There was no Clintonesque wrangling over the precise meaning of the words "throw" or "snowball." He admitted to the crime and accepted responsibility for it. Virtue was its own reward (he felt good about himself because of his honesty), but it turned out to have other rewards as well. The storekeeper, who had been looking for a reliable employee, returned the dollar, added another to it, and hired George. In time there was a partnership and George became a wealthy man.[27]

At no place in the six volumes of *McGuffey's Reader* was there any suggestion that one should spend long hours splitting fine hairs with regard to whether personal success was "socially responsible." It was assumed that real achievement was always of benefit to others. Ernestine, in the *Fifth Reader*, was rewarded for her ability to read a letter to the king.[28] She would doubtless have been criticized by modern educators for failing to share the reward with those whose efforts had played a part in enabling her to read the message and by modern psychologists for wounding the self-esteem of the two page boys who had been unable to read it.

The McGuffey story, by contrast, showed that what she did was of value in itself. Because of the effectiveness with which she read, a draftee was restored to his widowed mother and later received an opportunity to paint the king's portrait. Her father became the royal gardener. The page boys were inspired to improve their education and eventually rose to positions of prominence. Like ripples spreading outward from the splash of a pebble, her achievement expanded to touch and bless the lives of everyone within her circle.

In the year 2000, a school board's decision to purchase texts of this kind would have been attacked by the Reno Justice Department on the grounds that the use of material written by a Presbyterian minister was a prima facie case of violating the separation between church and state. (Given her boss's record, Ms. Reno might have been especially offended by the suggestion that there was something to be said for telling the truth.) Special interest groups would have united in a class action law-suit, arguing that the McGuffey series demeaned them by suggesting one should advance through one's own effort rather than through the agitation of the special interest group that claimed to represent him or her. The local teachers' union would have marched in protest against (a) the books' failure to recognize the importance of "diversity" and (b) the necessity of actually having to teach something.

A series of textbooks attempting to propagate values would not, in short, enjoy much popularity in modern America. Things seem to have been different 150 years ago, because the *McGuffey's Reader* was popular from the first. It was not that there was any shortage of competition: fifteen sets of American school readers were published between 1820 and 1841. The *Reader*, however, took an early lead and didn't begin to lose it until almost 1900. The first volume came out in 1836, and by 1843 sales had reached a million copies a year. By 1860 annual sales were over 2 million. The original publisher was unable to fill all the orders, and others were licensed to share the bounty. After the Civil War, an edition for the South was produced by the Methodist Book Concern in Nashville. The series sold 60 million copies between 1870 and 1890. It was adopted as the standard schoolbook in no less than 37 states, and rich with portents for the future, there was a Tokyo edition with alternate pages in English and Japanese.[29]

The *McGuffey's Reader* was popular for almost sixty years because the values it espoused were the values to which students' parents and in time the students themselves subscribed. The *Reader* appealed to Yankees, Irish, Scotch, and German settlers, and later even to the people of what had been the slave states. The watchwords of Industry, Creativity, Persistence, Frugality, Honesty, and Independence were simply another rendition of the value set endorsed by the Protestant Ethic and reaffirmed in the writing of Benjamin Franklin, the values that are fundamental to the need for achievement. This set of values would also find affirmation in the teaching of nineteenth-century America's best-known philosopher.

The Philosophy of Achievement

Like Benjamin Franklin, Ralph Waldo Emerson was born in Boston. The son of a minister, he tried at first to follow in his father's footsteps. After a few years he threw off the cloth and went out on the lecture circuit, where he soon became a star attraction. When he came to Pittsburgh in 1851, businesses closed early so that young clerks could go listen to him. Many were expecting to find themselves bewildered: it had been said of his philosophical works that his appeal arose from the fact, not that people understood him, but that they believed minds such as his should be encouraged. Nor were the titles of the lectures ("The Identity of Thought with Nature," for example, or "Instinct and Inspiration") at all encouraging. But when he began, the confusion cleared, and those who attended the lectures reported that what he said was just common sense.[30]

Emerson lived in the great age of the *McGuffey Reader*. His first book was published in 1836; his last lecture was delivered in 1871. The philosophy he preached was a philosophy to which those familiar with the McGuffey stories could readily subscribe. Brook Farm Transcendentalism, the movement with which his name is often associated, is long forgotten, but his appeal for individual effort, personal responsibility, innovation, persistence, and achievement remains vital.

He was in fact one of the first to recognize that socialistic experiments of the kind conducted at Brook Farm had little chance of success. "The scheme offers," he said, "by the economies of associated labor and expense, to make every member rich, on the same amount of property that, in separate families, would leave every member poor."[31] He observed that although capable persons might be drawn into such communities with the first rush of enthusiasm, they would soon leave and go out to see what they could accomplish on their own. Nathaniel Hawthorne, for example, put some money in the deal, worked at Brook Farm for six months, and then departed. "A man's soul may be buried and perish under a dungheap or in a furrow of the field," Hawthorne said, "just as well as under a pile of money."[32]

Those with leftist inclinations might decry such a remark as self-seeking, "the perennial Western malady," as Auguste Comte described it, "the revolt of the individual against the species."[33] Emerson, wiser, saw that without individual achievement, social progress was impossible. Driven by the desire for personal prosperity, we learn to use the secrets of nature in the service of our neighbors. The pulpit and the press condemn widespread aspirations to wealth, he said, but "if men should take these moralists at their word and leave off aiming to be rich, the moralists would rush to rekindle at all hazards this love of power in the people, lest civilization should be undone."[34]

We are meant to be rich, Emerson said, and we begin to grow rich just as soon as we apply our own unique talents to our own specific tasks. Each of us is incomparably superior to others in some area, and exceptional accomplishment is always the result of keeping yourself to those tasks for which your superiority is the greatest.[35] Apply your talents to the task at hand, work steadily and persistently even if no one notices or pays you for it, and success is inevitable. It comes sooner or later to those who remain at their tasks in spite of discouragement and disappointment: "No matter how often defeated, you are born to victory."[36]

But don't look for applause, he warned. A new undertaking is an almost certain target for criticism, especially if it does not meet with an early success (which it probably will not). Rely on your own instincts and stay with the project until you understand what is needed to make it succeed. If your experiment appeals to a truth, the universe will respond, your critics will become your admirers, and the world will beat a path to your door. "Adhere to your own act and congratulate yourself if you have done something strange and extravagant and broken the monotony of a decorous age."[37]

But self-confidence and persistence are not enough. It is necessary also to pay attention to the way in which you use your resources. A wise farmer is careful with his money, Emerson said, because he understands how hard it is to earn. "He knows that in the dollar he gives you is so much discretion and patience, so much hoeing and threshing."[38] The same discipline that kept him faithful to his tasks aids him in preserving the wealth that his faithfulness has produced. The secret of prosperity lies not in the size of one's income but in the relation of income to expense. Unearned income seldom leads to lasting wealth because its recipients have not learned this truth. They have an effect without a cause. They do not know how to discipline their appetites, and the treasure is soon spent.[39]

Our wants are unlimited. Our resources are not. We will make no progress until we bring the former into subjection to the latter. Without self-control, self-reliance is impossible. "Let a man keep the law— any law—and his way will be strewn with satisfactions."[40] The exceptionally gifted may describe their vices as trivial in comparison to the size of their contribution, but self-indulgence reduces both a person's contribution and the ability to contribute. The same disciplines that make for a real contribution make also for admirable character, and the value of a man's work "is less for every deduction from his holiness, and less for every defect of common sense."[41]

Faithfulness to your calling, innovation, work, persistence, the careful use of resources, self-control: these are the secrets of happiness and success. Emerson admitted that vice may sometimes seem to triumph and virtue often meets with disasters that have nothing to do with personal character. In the end, however, justice will prevail, just as a stone that has been thrown upward soon begins to fall.[42] The ways of Providence are always just but seldom obvious and never easy: "It is of no use to try to whitewash its huge, mixed instrumentalities, or to dress up the terrific benefactor in a clean shirt and white neckcloth of a divinity student."[43]

Campaigns for sweeping reforms collide with the fact that it is impossible to fully understand the ways of Providence or to change its laws. A man who works hard and applies himself to "that plot of ground which is given to him to till"[44] can know his own business, do it well, and make a real contribution. As soon as he begins to talk about "society," though, he is out of his element. Two people who are equally sure of their own good intentions are certain to argue if they disagree on a matter of policy.[45] Let each be faithful to his own duties, and they will accomplish more for the general welfare than they ever could with debates over things that neither of them fully understands.

The expression "social justice" is an absurdity. It is not society, but individuals who are just or unjust, fair or unfair, ethical or unethical. The vices we attribute to "society" are our own vices writ large because now they are multiplied by the number of people who display them. When two boys were frightened by their own shadows in a dark hallway, their grandfather said, "My children, you will never see anything worse than yourselves."[46] The ratio of good to evil that we see in the world around us is the same as the ratio of good to evil in our own souls.

Social reform begins with the reformation of individuals. The person who preaches about the failure of institutions but never deals with his own failures becomes "tediously good in some particular but negligent or narrow in the rest."[47] In the years between 1992 and 2000, for example, smoking was forbidden in the White House; Mr. Clinton's other and more famous diversions were described as simply "letting off steam." It was said that the man would be concerned about sex between teenagers only if it led to a cigarette afterward. Every crusade that insists on reforming others without beginning with the reform of oneself ends in hypocrisy and vanity.

There is no record of collusion between Ralph Waldo Emerson and the McGuffey brothers. If they ever got together to devise a plan for misrepresenting and distorting the mind of their time, the conspiracy is one which historians have yet to disclose. Perhaps their names will someday be as tightly linked as those of Marx and Engels. Until their plot is uncovered, though, we may be excused for believing that what they said was popular because it offered support for the values that tied Americans together. People believed in the importance of personal character and in individual achievement as one of the ways in which it expressed itself. They enjoyed stories and essays about hard work, honesty, and self-control. As the century wore on, the highbrows of academia and their parrots in the press began to talk in terms of vague and sinister forces that were not responsive to virtue and effort, but most people continued to believe that if there was a will there was a way. Their faith was affirmed in the stories of nineteenth-century America's best-selling novelist.

The Last Hurrah

As a boy, Horatio Alger Jr. was subjected to the cruelest imaginable form of child abuse: Horatio Sr. was a minister, and he forced his son to listen as he practiced his sermons. The not very surprising result was that Horatio Jr. was the worst little hellion in the schoolyard.[48] After a halfhearted attempt at the ministry, he began to write books for children. Between the Civil War and the end of the century he published over one hundred of them. These included biographies of Lincoln and Garfield, but the great majority had titles like *Bound to Rise, Luck and Pluck, Sink or Swim, Strive and Succeed.* At a time when the American population was around 75 million, sales of Alger books ran to over 16 million copies and maybe to as many as 20 million.[49] (Danielle Steel, eat your heart out.) Most were sold in the years immediately after his death as a part of the paperback revolution and as dime novels, but even before that and at $1.25 a copy (a lordly sum in 1880 or 1890), Alger was a best-selling author.

He was popular because he spoke to the mind of his time. A. K. Loring, Alger's first publisher, said, "He is outstanding today because he is the first to record lives with which we are all familiar. In centuries to come he will be outstanding because he was the first to record, in the fiction form, the narratives of everyday life." Frank A. Munsey predicted that Alger would go down in history as "the greatest literary figure of his time."[50] As the nineteenth century drew to a close, "intellectuals" had their noses in the novels of Henry James and discussed the works of William Dean Howells, but the country was reading Alger. Scarcely a family in America was unfamiliar with him, and he was as popular with adults as he was with children.

Most of his books were the result of his experiences at the Newsboys' Lodging House, which was created to serve as a haven for the hundreds of twelve to sixteen year olds who had been mustered out of the Union Army after their brief service as drummer boys. The institution's founder, one Charles L. Brace, believed that charity in the form of handouts led to long-term dependency, so he organized the lodging house around the principle of self-help. The boys were required to work. Most of them earned an income as cooks, bootblacks, delivery boys, or news carriers, the very trades Alger celebrated in his novels. They had to pay for their beds and their meals, and they were required to go to classes (and bathe once a week).[51]

Alger wrote his novels with the intention of inspiring young men of this kind. The stories he told were less about success than about the role of character in achieving it. He never said much about the hero's (or in one book, the heroine's) latter days on the high plateau of prosperity and comfort; his plots are almost entirely about the agonies and victories of the climb.

Consider, for example, *Joe's Luck*, a fine little piece from late in his career. Alger's protagonists were often firstborn sons who had come to the city in the hope of getting a job and saving the family farm, but Joe Mason is an orphan. After some initial hardship he discovers that his aunt passed away and left him $56.75. This is less than a fortune, but the year is 1851, and Joe hopes it will be enough to buy passage to California, where he can dig for gold. A clever swindler cheats him out of the money and Joe is left waiting on the dock. He is lucky enough to run into someone who has a ticket and has just discovered he can't make the trip. Joe gets the ticket in exchange for a promise to repay the man as soon as he can.

Immediately upon his arrival in California, he goes to work. The wages are high, he discovers, but so is his cost of living, and he has to pinch every penny. He is robbed and left with nothing. He helps a man named George Morgan defend himself from thieves, and Morgan loans him enough money to buy a restaurant. Joe works hard, befriends others, saves his money, pays back the loan (not to mention the price of his ticket to California), and soon has a thriving business. He eventually leaves his business in the hands of a partner and heads for the goldfields.

Joe works even harder at digging gold than he had at running the restaurant, and little bit by little bit his fortune accumulates. One of the others who is out there with him (the very man who had cheated him earlier in the story, as it happens) spends little time working and a great deal of time complaining about his bad luck. Alger reminds us, though, that "it wasn't luck but industry he lacked."[52] At last Joe makes a substantial strike. He returns to San Francisco, discovers that his business has prospered marvelously, and decides that he can now go back east and marry Annie Raymond, his childhood sweetheart. At the story's end we are told that he has a wonderful family and that "his domestic happiness is by no means the smallest part of Joe's luck."[53]

All of this takes us back to the first chapter of this book and to the stories McClelland's subjects told when they felt the stimulus of a desire to excel. Hard work, the careful use of every resource, challenges, and persistence—these are the condensed essence of what McClelland called "achievement imagery." They are the kinds of ideas that circulate in the mind of the person who is intent on getting things done. Writers like Alger, Emerson, the McGuffeys, and Franklin added the Protestant Ethic emphasis on personal morality to this imagery and turned achievement motivation into character. This, they said, is the real secret of success: not your opportunities or your family background, not your resources, nor even your intelligence, but your character. With that, all things are possible, and without it, nothing.

And character, they all agreed, was something that appeared in families. They did not engage in such sophisticated analyses or come to such detailed conclusions as those described in chapter 1, but they understood families as both the foundation and the purpose of individual accomplishment. In one of his periodic lectures to the residents of the Newsboys' Lodging House, Alger urged them to keep thinking ahead to the day when they would have homes of their own and reminded them that happy homes were impossible without the right kind of wife. Giving voice to a sentiment that would almost be forgotten a hundred years later, he advised them to become worthy of a good wife: "Yes, you must make yourselves worthy and deserving."[54] He was pointing the boys not just to prosperity but to the creation of families in which character could grow. If they had been asked for their opinion, Franklin, the McGuffeys, and Emerson would have certainly agreed with this as a proper point of emphasis.

These authors talked almost entirely about human effort, but a guiding Providence was implicit (and on occasion explicit) in every line. When Emerson referred to God, he was admittedly thinking of something more like Hegel's Universal Mind than the Puritans' Jehovah, but not even Emerson could have conceived of personal character apart from personal faith. It is certain that when those attending his lectures heard him talk about God, they thought he was talking about the God of the Bible, the same God that was in the minds of Franklin, the McGuffeys, and Alger. And Alfred Marshall, too, the great economist with whose opinions this chapter began, insisted upon religious faith as the source of the values to which he attributed the remarkable success of Anglo-Saxon civilization.[55]

Character, families, faith: building on this foundation, the United States began as a primitive agricultural community and became the most advanced civilization on the planet. The next chapter will illustrate the process by reviewing the lives of two men who played a key part in it.

Chapter 5

THE AGE OF ACHIEVEMENT

A lady on one of the morning talk shows told about her husband's efforts to clear the walks of leaves in front of their Connecticut home. She made it a point to mention that because his leaf-blower was electric rather than gasoline-driven, it could not harm "the environment." She no doubt believed that the power generation system at the other end of the extension cord consisted of ten thousand windmills raised entirely by hand to take advantage of the wind that comes sweeping down the wide Connecticut plain. Or perhaps she had read somewhere of the ten billion guinea pigs New England Power had purchased to generate electricity by running on tiny treadmills.

The story illustrates the basic problem with many of those who want to march under the banner of "the environment." They cannot see the conflict between the lifestyle they enjoy and the values they think they espouse. They drive their SUVs to a meeting at which they sign a petition for lower gasoline prices and a treaty to reduce emissions. They live by one set of values, proclaim another, and demand that those who provide them with the means to live by the first set measure up to the second.

In so doing, they are being faithful to the most hallowed traditions of their faith. The man who turned "the environment" (his buzzword was "conservation") into a political cause was Theodore Roosevelt, who demonstrated his desire to leave our children a living planet by going to hunt big game in Africa just as soon as William Howard Taft replaced him in the White House. (Congressmen raised a toast: "To the lions!")[1] He killed 296 lions, elephants, and other wild animals and posed for a publicity shot with his large rifle resting on the corpse of a water buffalo.[2]

Theodore Roosevelt was the first major politician who sought to advance his career by demonizing great business leaders. He said he found it difficult to like men who were preoccupied with making money, but he was gracious enough to set this conviction aside and ask a group of prominent businessmen to pay for his hunting expedition. He was so open-minded that he was even willing to wire home for more money when his funds began to run low.[3] Technically a Republican, he was in fact the first of the modern liberals. He was critical of great economic accomplishment but only too happy to enjoy the bounty it conferred upon him. Like the dear lady who was so proud of her husband's electrically powered leaf-blower, he was unable (or unwilling) to trace his comforts back to their source.

That is exactly the story of character and prosperity in nineteenth-century America. It occurred in two overlapping phases. In the first phase, persons who were motivated by the values described in chapter 4 turned a vast wilderness into farms and cities, created new industries, and made their country the most desirable place on the planet. In the second phase, those who played the leading roles in this process were portrayed as malefactors by the very persons who had benefited the most from their accomplishments. This chapter will talk about two of the greatest achievers. The next will describe their critics.

Andrew Carnegie

The first of Horatio Alger's best-sellers was published in 1867, when Andrew Carnegie was still in the very early stages of his climb to wealth and fame. If it had been published thirty years later, Alger might have been accused of modeling his tales on Carnegie's biography. The dimensions of the Carnegie story, however, far exceeded those of even the most incredible fictional hero. He began lower, worked harder, had more lucky breaks, and rose higher than anyone ever conjured up by the imagination of a writer. As a novel, his biography would never have made it into print. It is believable only because it actually happened.

The Industrial Revolution created infinitely more jobs than it destroyed, but it was hard on those whose livelihoods were tied to outmoded technologies. The textile industry was the first to be transformed. Small entrepreneurs could not compete with giant factories, and in order to put food on the table many weavers had to sell the hand looms that had once been the source of their security. Carnegie never forgot the day when his father came home to tell him, "Andra, I can get nae mair work."[4]

The family scraped together some money by borrowing from friends and left for the United States. They found to their dismay that the situation there was far from promising. The big mills in America were as ruinous to the prospects of a hand weaver as the big mills in Scotland. Carnegie's father got a job, but he found factory life intolerable and soon was unemployed.

And so it was that thirteen-year-old Andrew Carnegie became his family's chief means of support. He worked from six in the morning to six at night in the local cotton mill, earning $1.20 a week as a bobbin boy. He later moved to a different mill, where he worked in a cold, dark basement and earned $3.00 a week by tending a steam engine and dipping spools of cotton in a vat of oil. His new employer gave him the opportunity to learn bookkeeping, at which he excelled. The financial records were kept in single entry, though, and Carnegie hoped that he could raise himself in the company by selling his boss on the merits of the double-entry system. During the winter of 1848–49, he went into Pittsburgh two or three nights a week to study accounting.[5]

It was at this point in his career that Carnegie had the first of his lucky breaks, and he made the most of it. The communications revolution of the mid-nineteenth century was the telegraph. The first line, which ran from Washington to Baltimore, was completed in 1844, and by the end of 1861 it was possible to send a message all the way to

California. Carnegie's uncle happened to mention in the spring of 1849 that an old friend of his had become the manager of a telegraph office and was looking for message carriers. Carnegie went over the next day and got a job. He memorized names and locations and was soon recognized as the most efficient of the delivery boys. Within six months he was managing the delivery service. He watched the telegraphers, studied Morse code at night, and zoomed through his early-morning cleaning duties to give himself time to practice on the telegraph. He was the first person in Pittsburgh (and the third in the country) who could take a message by ear instead of having to read it off the tape, and crowds of onlookers gathered to watch his amazing dexterity.

Among those impressed by these feats of skill was the Pennsylvania Railroad's Thomas A. Scott, who hired Carnegie to be his personal telegrapher. Once again Carnegie made the most of his lucky break. One morning when Scott was late in coming to the office, an accident delayed passenger traffic and brought freight traffic to a standstill. Carnegie sent out the orders to correct the problem and signed Scott's name. He realized that he would be unemployed and maybe even imprisoned if the orders were mistaken, but he was pretty sure he could get things straightened out, and so he went ahead. Everything worked perfectly. Scott made it a point for some time after that never to come in late, but he realized that young Carnegie was someone who could be trusted and soon charged him with responsibilities far exceeding those of a mere telegrapher.

Scott heard about someone who wanted to sell his shares in Adams Express, and he loaned Carnegie the money to buy them. Within a few years Carnegie was receiving annual dividends of fourteen hundred dollars. Not long afterward, a chance meeting with an inventor led Carnegie to invest in a company that made sleeping cars. This in turn and by means of yet another chance encounter led to a part ownership in the Pullman Palace Car Company. There were other investments, too, including an oil field, Western Express, an iron foundry, and the Keystone Bridge Company, and most of them were "lucky." As long as the Civil War continued, Carnegie felt obliged to remain at his position with the Pennsylvania Railroad, but when it was over he resigned and devoted himself full-time to his investments.

Character and the Creation of an Industry

By 1872, Carnegie was, although not yet famous, one of the richest men in the world. He had reached his goals. If all he cared about was money, he could easily have hung up his hat. Observing that he did not, but went on instead to accumulate an unimaginable fortune, one unfriendly biographer described Carnegie as "the greediest little gentleman ever created."[6]

To use the word "greed," however, is entirely to miss the point. Men like Carnegie, said Allan Nevins, are not motivated primarily by the desire for more money. They are driven rather by the desire to beat their competitors, to express themselves, to impose their will upon the world around them.[7] They are driven, in short, by the need for achievement. Years later, complaining about the "joys of retirement," Carnegie put it this way: "It is the *pursuit* of wealth that enlivens life. The dead game, the fish caught, can become offensive in an hour."[8] For such a person, money is not the real goal. It is simply a form of feedback, a convenient measure of achievement.

At precisely the point at which he could afford to lean back and take it easy, Carnegie set out for his greatest achievement. He was, as he told the story, visiting a British steel mill when he first saw the full potential of the new Bessemer process. "The day of iron has passed,"[9] he exclaimed, and he caught the next ship for the United States, where he proceeded to play a (more precisely, the) major role in the creation of the American steel industry.

Carnegie had been interested in steel for some time. He learned about the limitations of iron early in his experience with the Keystone Bridge Company and set out to find something better. He began experimenting with the Bessemer process in 1861 but found that it had serious flaws. His decision to go full-time into steel was probably more the result of discoveries that remedied those flaws than of anything he saw in England. Once he had committed himself to steel, he worked relentlessly to improve the speed and efficiency of its manufacture. In the middle of the 1870s, his Edgar Thomson plant became the first

American steelworks with an open-hearth furnace, which was an advanced and as yet unproven technology. Later in life he would say that "Pioneering don't pay,"[10] but he was always a pioneer.

Most people would have described the moment of Carnegie's decision to go into steel as the wrong one. In September 1873 the great Philadelphia banking house Jay Cooke and Company failed, and it pulled a large number of businesses down with it. Companies that had grown along with the railroad construction following the Civil War suddenly found that they had neither markets nor credit and were forced to close their doors. Carnegie, though, had avoided speculation, had set some money aside, and was in a position to plunge ahead. Steel mills all over the country were idle, and manufacturers were willing offer him substantial discounts on the equipment he needed. He raised the Edgar Thomson Steel Works in the midst of a depression for about three-fourths of what it would have taken to construct the same plant three years earlier or three years later.[11]

Carnegie's motto was "Thine own reproach alone do fear."[12] He adhered to the highest possible standards of both personal and business morality. He insisted that rails delivered by Carnegie Steel be always of the best quality, and he flew into a rage whenever he got a complaint. He had done the same thing years earlier in the Keystone office when he heard about the faulty construction of a bridge. Toward the end of his career he was accused of delivering defective armor plate to the navy, and the newspapers made the most of it. The judges were told what to find, and like Judge Penfield Jackson in the Microsoft case a century later, they came down on the side of the accusers. Robert Heilbroner, similar to other leftists in his desire to find flaws in the character of the great achievers, used a 1960 *American Heritage* article to hand this finding on as if it were the gospel. The fact is that the armor plate had no difficulty in passing the most rigid ballistics test the navy was capable of imposing, and Carnegie Steel remained among the navy's primary suppliers.[13]

The not very surprising result of Carnegie's emphasis on efficiency, innovation, and honesty was an incredibly successful business. When he began, Great Britain was far and away the world's leading producer of steel. When he retired, the annual output of Carnegie Steel alone was 695,000 tons more than the combined output of all the steel mills in the British Isles. When Carnegie began, iron rails were the standard and steel rails were a luxury at over $100 a ton. When he retired, steel rails were a necessity and cost $12 a ton.[14] He allowed himself to be bought out for a little under a half a billion dollars by a syndicate organized by J. P. Morgan. Carnegie's share of the proceeds was around $300 million.

The Mind of the Millionaire

Carnegie is the archetype of a self-made man, but before he made himself, he had been shaped by his mother. As a wee laddie, Carnegie adored his father and dreamed of following in his footsteps, but it was his mother who sowed the seeds of greatness. Margaret Carnegie was the one who taught her son to work hard and mind his pennies. She was the one whose approval he always sought. She was the one who demanded that he live up to high standards, and she was the one who protected him from the influence of men who did not. She mortgaged her home to help him pay back the loan he had taken to make his first investment. While visiting in Europe, Carnegie left the management of his business to his younger brother Tom. Tom complained about difficulties, and Carnegie advised him to talk to their mother: "I always found her ideas pretty near the right thing."[15]

Carnegie's success was in large measure the result of his emphasis on the most efficient possible use of every resource. He never asked about the profits, one of his partners would recall years later, but "He always wanted to know the costs."[16] That, too, was something he had learned at his mother's knee. On his first day in school, the teacher called upon each of the children to stand and quote a passage from the Bible. Young Andrew stood up proudly and gave a line from the only catechism he had ever memorized: "Take care of your pence; the pounds will take care of themselves."[17] The schoolmaster, a student of the Scriptures, could not recall having seen that one in his own Bible. For Carnegie, though, it was a central tenet. Everything he did to consolidate the steel industry, his interest in innovation, and all his efforts at both vertical and horizontal integration can be explained in terms of it.

This emphasis could lead him into difficulties, for some of the resources he used were human, and he had a tendency to push men beyond their limits. He once told one of his managers about the pleasure of a recent trip to Europe. "You cannot imagine the abounding sense of freedom and relief I experience as soon as I get on board a steamer and sail past Sandy Hook," he said. "My God!" the manager replied. "Think of the relief to us!"[18]

Late in his life Carnegie gained some notoriety as an atheist. This notoriety aside, he never got very far from Scotch Calvinism. He disclaimed the God who from before the foundations of the earth had predestined the innocent to hell but never doubted the reality of a Providence that rewarded the just and punished the unjust. He believed in a Power that was with him to aid him in his earthly endeavors even if he never called upon It by Name. The words of his dour Calvinist schoolmaster were never far from his mind: "Ye hae na been put into this world to enjoy yoursel', but to do yair duty."[19] He remained to the end a very pious atheist and even devout, insisting always on the highest both in himself and in others. Describing a debate that went on for weeks among the friends of his youth, he wrote, "We young men were getting to be pretty wild boys about theology, although more truly reverent about religion."[20]

He was describing his attitudes during the years when he worked for Thomas Scott. It was during this period of time that Col. James Anderson of Allegheny opened his personal library to any young workingman who wanted to take out a book for the following week. Carnegie, always a voracious reader, was one of the leading borrowers. Among his favorites was Bancroft's *History of the United States*, the introduction to which concludes with these words: "A favoring Providence, calling all our institutions into being, has conducted the country to its present happiness and glory."[21] Bancroft was a best-selling author until almost the end of the nineteenth century because his words gave beautiful expression to Americans' feelings about their country. They looked at the events of their times, rejoiced in their freedom, and thanked God for the place in which they lived.

For such feelings Carnegie felt a hearty sympathy. He was irritated by narrow theological disputes, disliked pious humbug, and regarded bishops and ecclesiastical hierarchies with contempt. He had not the slightest doubt, however, about a benevolent and guiding Power that was carrying his country to great things. He called it "Progress," but it was exactly the same thing Benjamin Franklin was talking about when he spoke of "Providence." It was the Power that enabled an individual to make his own way in the world and to make the world better as he did so.

Carnegie the Philanthropist

The way in which Carnegie disposed of his fortune shows that like Benjamin Franklin he believed the best service of God was the doing of good for human beings. While he was still in the process of accumulating his fortune, he published an essay in which he argued that a millionaire was under a moral obligation to distribute his wealth during his own lifetime. A wealthy man, he said, is "but a trustee for the poor; entrusted for a season with a great part of the increased wealth of the community, but administrating it for the community far better than it could or would have done for itself."[22] A part of this administration, he said, lay in putting together the ideas and resources that created industries and jobs and prosperity for the thousands and the millions. The other part lay in sharing the wealth one gained in the process.

The redistribution of a fortune, he believed, was not a task that could be safely entrusted to someone whose only qualification for the job was an expressed desire to benefit humanity. (For one thing, as we shall observe in the next chapter and again in the tenth, it is always possible that the part of humanity such a person is most interested in benefiting is himself.) Even in those exceptional cases where the desire might be completely sincere and disinterested, generalized feelings of goodwill do not in themselves provide any insight with regard to how money may be effectively used in giving expression to it. Money is a powerful agency, and in the wrong hands it will do more harm than good.

Carnegie had learned from his own experience that the cure for poverty was not money. It was enterprise. The only proper goal of charity was that of providing those who wanted to improve their lives with the opportunity for doing so. And only those who had served their own apprenticeship to wealth would understand how it could be used to open doors for the person who was willing to similarly begin at the bottom. It was their duty to do exactly that.

And so Carnegie gave away his millions. The most famous of his benefactions, Carnegie Hall, the Hague Peace Palace, the Carnegie Endowment for International Peace, and the Carnegie Corporation, are the least interesting. More interesting is the fact that he built three thousand libraries; he believed that in libraries, ambitious persons could gain the knowledge by which to raise themselves. Free libraries were almost unheard of in the 1880s. A generation after Carnegie began building them, they were serving 35 million persons a day. Toward the end of his life he would boast that the sun never set on Carnegie Free Public Libraries.[23]

The libraries' popularity became the basis of an accusation that Carnegie was using them to win public favor. No such accusation could have been made with regard to some of his other philanthropies. He created private pensions for a large number of people, including Booker T. Washington. In 1890 the great liberal (today we would say "conservative") scholar Lord Acton announced that he would have to sell his magnificent private library in order to meet the demands of his creditors. He hated to see the eighty thousand volumes sold piecemeal and requested that Prime Minister Gladstone search for an institutional library to purchase the entire collection. Gladstone asked Carnegie to buy the library and donate it to a university. Carnegie agreed to purchase it for ten thousand pounds on the condition that Lord Acton would be allowed to keep it for the rest of his life and that no one, not even Carnegie's wife, would ever know about it.[24]

At Carnegie's death, public speculation put the size of his estate at a half billion dollars. It was in fact something under twenty-three million. "How much did you say I had given away, Poyton?" he would ask his private secretary; "$324,657,399," Poyton would reply. "Good Heaven!" the withered old man would mutter. "Where did I ever get all that money?"[25]

John D. Rockefeller

Horatio Alger told stories about success that was the result of "pluck and luck." Carnegie, although a hard worker, benefited from a great deal of "luck." The story of John D. Rockefeller is almost entirely about "pluck."

In comparison with Carnegie's childhood, Rockefeller's was comfortable, though by no means luxurious. He was raised in Ohio, the home state of *McGuffey's Reader*, and on a farm. After a year at Folsom's Commercial College, where he easily mastered the rudiments of bookkeeping, he made a list of businesses he thought would be suitable employers and went to Cleveland to knock on doors. He visited every establishment on the list but got no offers. So he went the rounds again, again without success. The third time around, when he called on the offices of Hewitt & Tuttle, he was asked to show a sample of his handwriting. "We'll give you a chance," they told him. He climbed onto the tall bookkeeper's stool and went to work for $3.50 a week. He was sixteen years old.[26]

He met a young Englishman named Maurice Clark in 1858, and in 1859 the new produce-shipping firm of Clark & Rockefeller opened its doors. Half of Rockefeller's investment in the new company came from his savings; the source of the other half was a one-thousand-dollar loan (at 10 percent) from his father. The practice of borrowing money to make money was one he learned early and well. The new business was successful at least in part because it offered "liberal" advances against the value of every consignment, which meant that it had to borrow during its busy seasons in the spring and fall. Rockefeller's new partner described him as "the greatest borrower I ever saw."[27] By 1865 the firm (with a new investor now and operating as Andrews, Clark & Company) owed over $100,000, and Clark began to grow nervous. After a brief argument he took his money and left.

A great deal of the borrowing had been occasioned by Rockefeller's involvement in the emerging petroleum industry. Lamps had been lit for centuries with whale oil, but in the 1850s the price of whale oil became prohibitive. It was possible to extract kerosene from coal, but this, too, was extremely expensive. Colonel Edwin Drake's discovery of oil in western Pennsylvania was widely regarded a fluke of nature that would give out as quickly as the West's gold and silver mines, but many saw it as offering an opportunity too good to miss. Rockefeller was incapable of generating within himself the boom-or-bust mentality that flourished in the oil fields, but the more staid business of refining had a certain appeal for him, and he turned to that.

Refining was not without risks of its own, however, and these were especially large in Cleveland. Pittsburgh was closer to the oil fields, to the coal that was used to fire the refineries, and to the export market in New York. Most of Cleveland's refiners complained about these disadvantages but accepted them as facts of life. Rockefeller did not. After a careful study of the problems, he assembled a four-prong attack on costs. He directed his attention first to increasing the efficiency of the refining process, which meant that he had to borrow to increase the capacity of his plants. Costs could also be lowered if one stocked up at times when the wildly fluctuating price of crude oil was low. That, too, meant borrowing. And a refiner could lower the cost of its export business (which in 1866 accounted for 70 percent of his company's output) by handling it in-house rather than entrusting it to jobbers.[28]

The remaining cost was transportation. Competition among the railroads was such that shippers who could promise a large and steady flow of traffic were in a position to set their own rates. As long as the oil industry was made up of a large number of small and highly competitive firms, no one of them could enjoy a luxury of this kind. Rockefeller therefore set about to join Cleveland's refiners in a cartel, the productive capacity and therefore the bargaining power of which would be infinitely greater than that of any single member. Opened later also to Pittsburgh refiners, the scheme gained notoriety as the South Improvement Company.[29]

Such a cartel, the oil producers realized, could use its buying power as effectively in demanding concessions from them as from the railroads, and in a well-publicized meeting they agreed to shut down their wells until the South Improvement Company had been disbanded. A few papers gave Rockefeller's scheme a sympathetic hearing, but most attacked it as an assault on free enterprise. For the first time in his life, Rockefeller found himself being condemned by the press. Having already become unhappy with the railroads' efforts to gain control of his plan, Rockefeller gave up on it.

All of this happened at a low point both in the history of the oil industry and of Rockefeller's own life. The price of refined oil was dropping, but the cost of crude remained steady, and many refiners were going out of business. Rockefeller began to sell off shares of stock in his own company, which by now was known as Standard Oil. "All the fortune I have made," he said years later, "has not served to compensate for the anxiety of that period."[30]

He was desperate. He felt that if he did not get control of things, and quickly, he was finished. But his fears do not seem to have been primarily financial. He wrote his wife to tell her that no matter what happened in the oil industry, their other investments were more than adequate. The thing he was frightened about was the possibility of failing at something. There are many things the high achiever can take in stride. Failure is not one of them.

Rockefeller decided to bring order to the oil industry by taking control of it. His plan was the essence of upright propriety. Competitors who agreed to look into his offer would have the value of their plants appraised by impartial judges, and the owners could take their payment either as cash or as shares in Standard Oil. Many of those who agreed to sell were left as the managers of the plants they had once owned. Times were hard for everyone in the oil industry, and many were only too willing to accept Rockefeller's offer. Years later, when times were better, those who had taken their payment as shares in Standard Oil found to their delight that Rockefeller had made them rich, rich beyond their wildest dreams, richer by far than they could ever have made themselves. There would then be accusations and complaints from those who had sold for cash, including widely publicized accounts of events that never occurred, but no one complained at the time. Many realized that they had received far more than their companies were worth.

Rockefeller's interest in gaining control of the oil industry was the result of a desire to impose order on chaos, not for monopoly profits.

The true monopolist seeks to raise prices in complete disregard of market forces, but as Rockefeller's control of the oil industry increased, the price of kerosene declined. He never had a complete monopoly, and it is unlikely he could have gained one. The expenses involved in gaining such control as he could raised his cost of doing business and forced him to charge higher prices than might otherwise have been necessary. High prices always attract competition, especially when the costs of entering a business are as low as they were in the oil industry of the 1870s and 1880s. Standard Oil, furthermore, "the Colossus of Cleveland," became less efficient as it grew larger. Smaller, tighter organizations could always beat it in niche markets. When one competitor was eliminated, two more sprang up to take its place, and these new competitors moved much more quickly than Standard in the adoption of such new technologies as shipment by means of long-distance pipelines.

For one brief, shining moment in 1879, Standard controlled 90 percent of the oil industry (which was a very small one in the decades before the appearance of the automobile), but its grip was already beginning to loosen. Within four years its share had declined to 80 percent, and things went downhill from there. An enterprise can gain a lasting monopoly only with the support of the government, and this is something Standard Oil never had or sought.

A Study in Character

Rockefeller was always close to his parents. Years later the press would accuse his father of cheating on his mother, but if this was true, Rockefeller himself seems never to have known about it. He thought his father had been an ideal parent, a man who did not drink, a man who spent time with his sons, who taught them to swim and shoot and trained them in the ways of business.[31]

But it was his mother who made Rockefeller great. It was his mother who taught him to work and who put him to work in the garden when he was still very young. It was also his mother who taught him about rules, one of which was that ice-skating at night was strictly forbidden. The effect of this rule, needless to say, was to make ice-skating at night the most enjoyable of all possible activities. On one of the occasions when they engaged in it, Rockefeller and his brother saved a neighbor boy from drowning. When their mother heard of the deed, she praised them for their courage and then gave them a whipping for their disobedience.

She never had much doubt about the value of corporal punishment. One time, suffering for a crime of which he was not guilty, young Rockefeller managed to present a convincing case for his innocence. "Never mind," his mother replied, "we have started this whipping and it will do for the next time."[32]

A good Baptist, young Rockefeller never imitated Carnegie's mistake with memory verses, but not every passage he memorized came straight from the Bible. Always there hung in his mind the lines repeated so often by his mother: "Willful waste makes woeful want" and "Save when you can and not when you have to."[33]

That was an emphasis he took to heart. At the height of his business career he was watching finished cans of oil being soldered shut and suddenly had an idea. "How many drops of solder do you use on each can?" he asked. The foreman told him that the number was forty. Rockefeller suggested that they try doing a few with only thirty-eight. Some of these cans leaked, but with thirty-nine they could all be sealed tight. The savings amounted to several thousand dollars a year.[34] When he was old and wealthy beyond belief, he defended his practice of keeping chickens on the estate to supply fresh meat and eggs as more than merely a luxury. They could get forty cents a pound for the birds, he said, "and we can sell the surplus at a fair profit and save enough to eat next spring and to breed a new supply."[35]

With such an orientation to financial detail goes the keeping of careful records. Both Rockefeller and Carnegie kept ledgers. They always knew what to do because they always knew how they were doing. Asked late in life about the secret behind the success of Standard Oil, Rockefeller attributed it to the fact that "We never deceived ourselves."[36] He kept records of his own income and expenses, and he frequently reviewed the records accountants kept for his company.

Rockefeller's religious faith was cast in a more conventional mold than Carnegie's. He was baptized by immersion in 1854, and the church was always an important part of his life. As a young man in Cleveland, he attended the Erie Street Baptist Church, the congregation of which consisted of ordinary workingmen and their families. He went to the morning service, the evening service, and the Friday night prayer meeting. He seldom missed a church social. Most businessmen of the time migrated to more prestigious churches as their fortunes advanced, but Rockefeller did not. The Baptist church always suited him, and after he had become rich the most frequent visitors in his home were ministers and temperance workers.

Rockefeller had begun as a young man with high aspirations. Even as he looked for his first job, he would say years later, "I was after something big."[37] But the "something big" was more than money. Money was no more than a measure. He was hoping to achieve personal greatness through the creation of a business that would conspicuously bless the lives of humanity. "I saw a marvelous future for our country," he said, "and I wanted to participate in the work of making our country great. I had an ambition to build."[38] Toward the end of his life, when he was widely known as "the world's richest man," he regarded the epithet as distasteful. "Wealth isn't a distinction," he said. "If I have no other achievement to my credit than the accumulation of wealth, then I have made a poor success of my life."[39]

Innovator and Philanthropist

One of Rockefeller's last great battles was the one he fought over the Lima, Indiana, oil fields. He made an investment in them in spite of the fact that existing refineries could do nothing with the bad-smelling oil they produced. He believed his chemists were on the edge of discovering a means for making this oil useful, and he held on for long years, facing criticism from within the company and without. Herman Thrash hit at last upon a way to cleanse the Lima crude of its sulfur, and Standard was for a short time the world's largest oil producer.[40] With the discovery of oil in Texas, though, and with the appearance of competitors like Gulf and Texaco, that distinction would pass to other companies.

Rockefeller invented no new products or technologies, but he did bring the inventions of others into the market. He did not discover petroleum jelly, but it was his company that made Vaseline a household term. He often did lead the way in marketing methods, as for example in the elimination of middlemen through the use of tank wagons to carry kerosene directly from the producer to the consumer. That particular maneuver, he noted, made him plenty of enemies "but we made oil far lower in price than it had been before."[41]

He was by this time in his life interested in other things than Standard Oil. He had always given systematically to worthy causes, primarily the church of which he was a member. By 1889 his wealth was beginning to accumulate so rapidly, and requests for donations were becoming so numerous, as to make his older habits of charity inadequate. He hired a Baptist minister named Frederick T. Gates to aid him in his benefactions. These began with $600,000 for a struggling little college on the shore of Lake Michigan; before he was done, Rockefeller would give this institution (the University of Chicago) $80 million. In 1901 he gave away well over $2 million, over $5 million in 1902, over $13 million in 1905, over $39 million in 1907, and over $71 million in 1909. In 1919 he gave away over $138 million. His giving supported the General Education Board, which pioneered educational, medical, and social development in the South; the Rockefeller Institute for Medical Research, which soon became known for its campaign against yellow fever; and the Rockefeller Foundation, which has supported a wide range of research. All told, he gave away over a half billion dollars.[42]

Personal Character and National Prosperity

In concluding the stories of Carnegie and Rockefeller with a record of their benefactions, we run the risk of falling back into the superstition that there is something wrong with exceptional accomplishment. During the Middle Ages, a wealthy merchant would often donate large sums to the Church as a way to atone for the sin of having become financially successful. The cathedrals that his money raised, however, did much less for the general welfare than did the "sin" of creating a successful business. It was the late medieval and early modern revival of commerce (not beautiful places of worship) that provided the foundation for personal freedom and widespread prosperity.

Men like Carnegie and Rockefeller did more good for America in accumulating a fortune than they did in giving it away. Carnegie made his managers millionaires by giving them tiny fractional interests in Carnegie Steel, provided countless workers with the jobs that enabled them to raise their families, and played a major role in making America's standard of living the highest in the world. Inexpensive steel provided the framework for transportation systems (the New York Elevated, for example), bridges, and buildings that improved the lives of millions. Rockefeller created fewer millionaires and fewer jobs, but the industry he led revolutionized the American standard of living. Before Rockefeller, illuminants were so expensive that the average workingman had to go to bed at sundown. By 1890 the life of every American family extended late into the evening.

And Carnegie and Rockefeller are only the tip of the iceberg. John Deere and Cyrus McCormick produced machinery that made America's farms the most productive in the world. The Armour brothers found ways to get the beef and pork of western farms onto eastern tables. The Pillsburys of Minneapolis-St. Paul got western grain into eastern ovens. Frederick Weyerhaeuser provided farmers with milled lumber to raise beautiful homes. George Eastman's Kodak camera provided people with an inexpensive and convenient means for recalling important moments in their lives. It would take many pages to give the whole list. Thousands of small and large entrepreneurs, motivated by their need for achievement, turned America into a pantry that could feed the world.

But no one thanked them for it. No one, for example, wrote long paragraphs in the newspapers praising Carnegie for the innovations he had sponsored, the conveniences he had made possible, or the jobs he had created. On the contrary, he was blamed for the fact that in spite of all he had done, the world remained a hard place in which to live. Describing the community around the steel mill, novelist Hamlin Garland wrote, "The streets were horrible; the buildings poor; the sidewalks sunken and full of holes...Everywhere the yellow mud of the streets lay kneaded into sticky masses through which groups of pale, lean men slouched in faded garments."[43]

This was hardly fair. Long before there were any steel mills, and even before the Carnegies migrated from Scotland, Pittsburgh was already familiar to European travelers as the filthiest and ugliest city in America.[44] In 1840, though, it was filthy and jobs were hard to find. In 1890 it was still filthy, but there were jobs in abundance. Those jobs had been created through the genius of men like Andrew Carnegie.

Hamlin Garland, moreover, is a less-than-credible witness. He doesn't seem to have liked anything. He was as insistent about the miseries of life in the areas untouched by industry as he was about the misfortune of the steel towns. Describing his feelings as he traveled west from Chicago, he said, "The ugliness, the endless drudgery, and the loneliness of the farmer's lot smote me with stern insistence." And again, as he arrived at the old homestead, "My dark mood was deepened into bitterness by my father's farm, where I found my mother imprisoned in a small cabin on the enormous, sunburned, treeless plain, with no expectation of living anywhere else."[45] Perhaps he could have suggested that she move to Pittsburgh, where at least there would be someone to blame. But who (or Who) do you blame for South Dakota?

Garland was in his own words a "militant reformer." He was one of that first generation of professional complainers who, having done nothing to create the prosperity surrounding them, were very anxious to find fault with it. We will consider them more carefully in the next two chapters.

Chapter 6 | DIRECTOR'S LAW

Rockefeller was now an old man. He had been troubled for years by alopecia, the results of which are similar to the side effects of chemotherapy. Once a handsome man who took pride in his appearance, he was now disfigured. His hair and even his eyebrows and eyelashes had fallen out. He bore the affliction bravely, and he was sitting there in the Euclid Avenue Baptist Church in the same pew that he occupied every Sunday morning.

In another pew not far away was a young journalist. She had never been there before. She would never come again. She just wanted to see Rockefeller up close. In the article she wrote about him, she said he looked like "a living mummy," "the oldest man in the world," more like a "dead jellyfish" than a human being. She described his "lipless" mouth and blank eyes. His flesh was "diseased and unclean." In his face she saw "concentration, cruelty, and craftiness." All things considered, she said, he was "indescribably repulsive." She went on to share the rumor that his father had once been forced to move because he been indicted for rape, as if somehow to imply that Rockefeller himself should bear the guilt for his father's sin.[1]

The young woman's father had been a producer in the oil regions.

Just as the earliest experiences of Carnegie and Rockefeller had included a catechism of thrift and responsibility, so her earliest experience had included a catechism on the evils of Standard Oil. Time and again she had heard about the pernicious South Improvement Company, that great threat to the American way, that vast conspiracy against all that was right and just and fair. Her father had known precisely who to blame for his own misfortune, and as she grew to adulthood she knew who to blame for the many things wrong with the world of her own day. Her name was Ida M. Tarbell. Her *History of the Standard Oil Company*, first as a serial in *McClure's* and then as a book, made Rockefeller the most hated man in America.[2]

Something of this kind happened to the reputation of virtually all America's great business leaders in the last decades of the nineteenth century and the first decade of the twentieth. A new generation, unfamiliar with the struggles of their ancestors, college educated, raised in the new prosperity of industrial society, living in the midst of new comforts, and enjoying a new level of security, looked out on the world around them, saw its faults, and found someone to blame. Then they ever so humbly suggested themselves as the ones to set things right.

This chapter is about that new generation and its vision for America.

The New Aspirations

The Declaration of Independence was not the only political document to be published in 1776, maybe not even the most important. The first edition of Adam Smith's *The Wealth of Nations* came out the same year. Smith argued that the liberty of the individual citizen could be protected only by severely limiting the power of the government. There are three things, he said, with which a government should provide its people. First, it should protect the nation from armed aggression by other nations. Second, it should establish a system for the administration of justice and thereby restrict the freedom of individuals at the point where their action might endanger the freedom of others. Third, it should erect and maintain social assets like bridges and roads.[3] As soon as any government begins to stretch itself beyond these three things, he said, it begins to interfere with personal freedom.

Smith was drawing upon the same intellectual tradition Thomas Jefferson drew upon when he wrote the Declaration of Independence. The rights Smith was seeking to defend were precisely those of the individual citizen to "life, liberty, and pursuit of happiness." All of these are what political philosophers refer to as "negative rights." They add up to the right to be left alone.

It is well to remember that the first step toward the American Revolution was taken in 1761, when a plump little lawyer named James Otis stood before the Supreme Court of Massachusetts and argued against the British government's writs of assistance. These were generalized warrants granting customs officers the right to search for smuggled goods wherever they chose: in warehouses, in stores, and even in homes. They were, Otis said, a violation of the rights of Englishmen. "A man's house is his castle, and whilst he is quiet, he is as well guarded as a prince in his castle."[4]

The unoffending citizen, in other words, had a right to be left alone. His life, his liberty, and his property were not to be invaded or infringed upon. No one could grant him happiness, and no one should be required to provide him with it. As long as he respected the rights and the freedoms of others, though, he should be left alone to pursue his own happiness as best he could.

John Adams was in the court as Otis spoke. Looking back on the case years later and seeing it with the clear perspective of hindsight, he wrote, "Then and there the child Independence was born."[5] The American Revolution was less about freedom from England than about freedom from an intrusive government. This was the freedom that the men who framed the Constitution sought to preserve for themselves and their posterity. Let the government limit itself to the things it can actually do, they said, and let it leave the citizens free to do what they could do. In his inaugural address of 1801, Thomas Jefferson set forth the ideal of a "wise and frugal government, which shall restrain men from injuring one another, which shall leave them otherwise free to regulate their own pursuits of industry and improvement."[6]

In restricting the power of the rulers, the authors of the Constitution were assuming a large measure of virtue and wisdom on the part of the average citizen. They assumed that if the government limited itself, citizens could be relied upon to take care of the rest. They assumed people would for the most part be able to identify their own best interest and seek it in a way that would leave others free to engage in pursuits of their own. The Founding Fathers specifically did not believe it was the duty of the government to define the goals to which people should commit themselves or tell them how they should act. They assumed free individuals could be relied upon to set and pursue worthwhile long-term objectives. They assumed that with comparatively few exceptions people knew how they ought to behave and would behave appropriately most of the time. They assumed, this is to say, the widespread existence of character.

Adam Smith, it should be added, began with a similar assumption. He does not seem to have been aware of it, but then we are seldom aware of what we take for granted. The most famous passage in *The Wealth of Nations* is probably the one in which Smith says our neighbors' self-interest is the primary source of the benefits with which society provides us. The butcher is not in business to secure our health and happiness, but his own. If the meat with which tonight's pot roast began was fresh and reasonably priced, it is not so much because the butcher wanted us to enjoy a delicious stew as because a good reputation and competitive prices help keep him in business. The butcher provides us with the things we want because he knows it is in his own best interest to do so.[7]

If that is true, however, it is true because the butcher's wisdom goes far beyond the skills of his trade. It could not be true if he believed he could enrich himself only by impoverishing us. It could not be true if he had not somewhere learned to take a long-term view, thinking not of making the most he could on this particular sale, but of creating a continuing series of transactions. (There are places in the world even today where the merchant thinks of profit only in terms of each individual exchange.)

Smith's thesis could not be true, most of all, if the man who now works as a butcher did not feel he had an obligation to make his own way in the world. "No one but a beggar chuses to depend chiefly upon the benevolence of his fellow citizens,"[8] Smith said, using the term "beggar" as if it were a badge of shame. But it hadn't been a badge of shame four hundred years earlier. In the Middle Ages, beggars were regarded as a fourth estate, the purpose of which was to provide the wealthy with an opportunity to gain religious merit through acts of charity. Francis of Assisi was a beggar before he was a saint, and the haste with which he was canonized was the result as much of his dependent poverty as of his good works. Not until the radical Protestant sects stigmatized begging as an infringement on Christian love (demonstrating a lack of love for the one from whom the beggar sought his sustenance) did the people of the West begin to see any shame in depending upon the benevolence of one's neighbor.[9]

The authors of the Constitution made a long bet on personal character. Raised as they had been in a culture that stressed and encouraged character, they did not realize they were making a bet, but they were making one nonetheless. And it paid off handsomely. The spirit of competitive achievement was as intense in nineteenth-century America as it had been in the Greece described by Hesiod. Every man was stimulated by the evidence of his neighbor's prosperity to seek his own, looking for opportunity in new places and with new methods. Even the South Dakota landscape that so depressed Hamlin Garland was a place people chose because it gave them the chance to have lives of their own. The inevitable consequence of such behavior was the most widespread prosperity in history. By 1900 the average American workingman enjoyed a level of material comfort, security, and personal freedom that would have been unimaginable a hundred years before or at any other place in the world.

But those who had been raised in the midst of this prosperity could not see it for what it was. They compared it not to the hopes and dreams with which it had begun but to the aspirations it had encouraged. By every historical standard the rate of progress had been breathtaking, but to those who had never known anything else it did not seem fast enough. They looked out on the world around them, saw many desirable things that were not being done, and blamed the economic system under which they labored. They did not see that the constraints imposed on their high-flown ideals were the constraints of reality, not of capitalism. They lived in the midst of such abundance that they could not grasp the fact of limited resources. They were incapable of understanding that the doing of one thing might for the present hinder the doing of another. They felt it all should be done immediately.

The New Villains

There was undoubtedly much to be done. The growth of the American economy in the last decades of the nineteenth century encouraged millions to crowd onto ships headed for the United States. In America there were jobs. In America there was freedom. In America there was opportunity. In America, as Carnegie would brag in *Triumphant Democracy* (which went through several printings, including one in paperback, and was translated into both French and German), the person who was willing to work could climb as high as he wanted to go.

The only problem with Carnegie's book was its failure to recognize that progress brought problems. "It's all sunshine, sunshine, sunshine, sunshine," complained one of his critics. "Where are the shadows?"[10] The shadows were in slums that had been hastily constructed for one generation of immigrants and then left standing to house the next generation and the next and the next one after that, until at last they were swept by fire. The shadows were in terrible working conditions, in twelve-hour days, in men and even boys left maimed by the huge machines, in the empty stare of orphans and widows.

Poverty, filth, and hopelessness were not, of course, invented specifically for the discomfort of late-nineteenth-century America. Monsters from hell they may well be, but they have stalked the earth ever since the gate to Eden closed behind Adam and Eve. In 1697, shortly before the dawn of the industrial era, John Locke wrote a board of trade report on the problems of poor relief. A laboring man and wife, he said, could support no more than two children. He said children who were three years of age and older should be sent to schools where they could be taken care of and trained in the skills of spinning and knitting.[11] The occupants of the miserable hovels housing Marx's beloved cottage industry had a very drab existence even in the best of times, and were as much subject to economic fluctuation as the American workers laid off in the calamitous depressions of 1873–77 and 1893–97. Set beside conditions in India (which Carnegie visited) and even Europe (which he visited many times), things in America, even at their worst, were comparatively cozy.

But they were not perfect. The imperfections were clear when seen in the light of Herbert Spencer's optimism about the future and in photographs of life in the factory towns. They were especially obvious to those who had been raised amid better things, a generation, as Harvard professor William James said in 1902, "When we of the so-called better classes are scared as men were never scared in history at material ugliness and hardship."[12] He would have known. The people he was describing were his students, his friends, himself, people, he said, who would "quake at the thought of a child without a bank account and doomed to manual labor." They had been born to comfort, and the thought of discomfort terrified them.

They were terrified also by the chaos of constant change. They wanted the world to settle down, or at least they wanted to somehow control the pace of things. If there were no new factories, there would be no titans of industry living in mansions and no ragged labor force living in slums. There were many points at which they would disagree with Karl Marx, but they shared his romantic view of the Middle Ages, when there were no industries, when change was slow and every man had his proper place. They read Henry Adams' *Mont St. Michel and Chartre* and found in the world of the twelfth and thirteenth centuries the order and harmony for which they longed. They gave no thought to medieval society's terrible poverty, underemployment, injustice, infant mortality, cruelty, and superstition. They saw castles and cathedrals; they turned a blind eye to the thatched huts of hopeless, illiterate, ill-clad peasants, who froze and starved when the winter came.

The Middle Ages provided reformers not only with the picture of a perfect world, but also with an epithet for those whom they chose to blame for the imperfections of the real world. In the fourteenth and fifteenth centuries, some nobles had taken to the robbery of passing merchants. The appearance of towns, the gradual liberation of the peasantry, inflation, and their own insistence upon living up to their place in society (rather than within their means) had left many members of the upper classes in dire straits. Professional warriors who were now faced with a declining demand for rapine and indiscriminant slaughter, they used their military skills either to support the collection of high tolls from those passing along nearby rivers and roads or else in outright plunder. They also did their best, as we noted in chapter 3, to help prosperous monasteries return to the "poverty" part of "poverty, chastity, obedience." These men were known as "robber barons."

American reformers borrowed the term and applied it to their own time. Its application to upper-class bandits was forgotten. Popular writers applied it instead to the industrialists who created and consolidated industries, provided jobs, lowered the average person's cost of living, and made the United States the richest nation on the planet. Among the more notorious of these villains were Duke, Brown, Colgate, Stanford, Johns Hopkins, Cornell, and Vanderbilt. The leading malefactors were Andrew Carnegie and John D. Rockefeller, who in 1915 were denounced by the Congressional Committee on Industrial Relations as "menaces to society."[13]

The popular media are not in the business of discovering and propagating the truth. They are in the business of selling advertising, and advertising is hard to sell when accompanied by a cool and unbiased description of the facts. Members of the press offer simple answers that appeal to popular prejudice, and the prejudice against the person who has achieved remarkable success in a commercial endeavor has an ancient pedigree. It is at least as old (as we have seen) as the works of Plato and Aristotle, and it flourished in medieval superstitions with regard to the prosperity of the monasteries. It views the economic process as a zero-sum game and assumes that one person's gain is someone else's loss. The obvious source of society's many ills, from such a vantage point, were those who created great businesses and made fortunes in doing so. The few who had made it to the top were to blame for the plight of the many still struggling on the slopes.

The robber baron stereotype, said John Tipple, was the result of a popular desire to explain the uncomfortably rapid transformation of American society in the closing decades of the nineteenth century.[14] Those who are looking for simple answers to complex phenomena slip easily into what he called the "devil view" of history, and quickly trace every misfortune to the wickedness of identifiable villains. Leading proponents of the "social gospel," men like Washington Gladden and Walter Rauschenbusch, who had long ago ceased to believe in Satan, clung nonetheless to the belief in a personal evil. They now preached, not against the prince of darkness, but against the captain of industry. Thinking themselves wise, they had become fools.

Now and again those with a mind for reform took a more balanced position. Consider the words of Henry Gantt:

> If the amount of wealth in the world were fixed, the struggle for the possession of that wealth would necessarily cause antagonism; but [since]…the amount of wealth is not fixed, but constantly increasing, the fact that one man has become wealthy does not necessarily mean that someone else has become poorer, but may mean quite the reverse, especially if the first is a producer of wealth.[15]

Not even Gantt was always that objective. And he was not, in any case, preaching a sermon or writing for a popular periodical. Those who did offered simple solutions and had no difficulty in identifying specific evildoers.

The New Model

They had no difficulty, either, in identifying the society they thought theirs should imitate. They enjoyed Henry Adams' romantic portrait of the medieval world, and they believed America should follow the example of a nation that had emerged only recently from its medieval form. It was, of all the industrialized nations, the one that still bore most clearly the marks of the Middle Ages.

The word "Germany" was for long centuries descriptive of a geographical area and a cultural heritage but not a national unity. Allowing for a variety of dialects, Germans spoke the same language but did not have the same ruler. Their system of organization went back to the eighth and ninth centuries, to Charlemagne, and to what had once been known as the Holy Roman Empire. As the result of the Thirty Years' War, Germany had been artificially stabilized at a medieval level of political organization. It was not a nation-state, but a collection of petty principalities, each with its own currency, its own laws, its own system of government, and its own tariff barriers. Germans dreamed about the possibility of national unity along the lines of the American and English models, but the wonderful visions always ended when the dreamers rolled over and bumped into the question of sovereignty. The question of sovereignty is fundamentally a question about the legitimate use of force, and in the case of Germany it went unanswered until it was taken up by a man who was willing to use force in dealing with it.

The "Iron Chancellor," Otto von Bismarck, was a member of the old Junker aristocracy, whose remarkable military prowess played a decisive part in his campaign to unify his nation. Germany came together as a nation-state under the leadership of Prussia, whose semifeudal autocracy, civil service, and officer corps now became the model for the entire country. Its industrialization was achieved within a social structure ruled by an established and traditional elite, the members of which delegated the management of society to an obedient, efficient, and impersonal bureaucracy.

It was Bismarck's goal to bring all of Germany into subjection to the will of the Kaiser. He had no use for parliaments or popular assemblies. The purpose of the government, he believed, was to command the people and control them, not to set them free for the pursuit of purposes they had chosen for themselves. He destroyed political parties whose agenda was opposed to his own. He gave Germans the right to vote, but he ruled with an iron hand, and individual citizens were for all practical purposes completely without the ability to influence national policy. Bismarck created a democracy that became the means to despotism because it failed to set limits on the power of the government.

He quieted complaints by instituting the most elaborate social welfare policy the world had ever seen. Between 1883 and 1889 and in alliance with the labor unions, he assembled a comprehensive scheme to insure every worker against the hazards of accident, sickness, and retirement. "Whoever has a pension for his old age," he observed, "is far more content and far easier to handle than one who has no such prospect"; he "will put up with more because he has a pension to look forward to."[16]

The most important effect of extensive government control, observed the Nobel Prize–winning economist F. A. Hayek, is its impact on personal character.[17] People learn to trust less in themselves and more in the powers that rule them. They become more compliant, less willing to challenge the existing scheme of things, and less willing to seize the initiative. In a society organized from the top, people cease to regard themselves as free moral agents and accept instead the role of appointed functionaries. Their income and their social status are not what they create for themselves but what the government allows them. Attitudes do not change all at once, but they do change. The German sociologist Max Weber watched the change as it occurred. Bismarck left behind him, Weber said, a nation that was less free and politically less mature than the one he had found.[18]

Lacking Weber's perspective and perhaps lacking as well much faith in the notion of free individuals shaping their own destiny, the members of what James described as America's "so-called better classes" began to look admiringly toward Germany. For about two hundred years, observed F. A. Hayek, Anglo-Saxon ideals of personal liberty and limited government had been spreading eastward. The rule of freedom and law that had been achieved in America and England seemed destined to spread all over the world. But now the tide shifted and the wave of the future became the tide of government control. In Germany, American reformers found the model for which they had been searching. It was a social welfare state in which the average citizen was cared for from the "cradle to the grave," and in which business leaders had only a limited power to act without government permission. It was a country in which political leaders could tell the people what to do and how do it.

The so-called "progressive" movement was in large measure the expression of a desire to create this situation in America. What the crusaders did not notice was that no one was migrating from the United States to Germany. Migration ran very heavily the other way. If things were really so awful in America and so wonderful in Germany, how was one to explain this strange phenomenon?

The question was never raised. In Germany, at least, things were under control, and the reformers wanted to get them under control in the United States. The obvious mechanism was the same one that had worked so well in Germany, a powerful national state. Theodore Roosevelt was popular with the Progressives in part because he was one of them: old money, well educated, and ignorant of economics. He was popular also because of his personal charm and his reputation as a hero, although it seems improbable that the animals he killed in Africa found him either charming or heroic. Roosevelt's greatest appeal, however, was his belief in a powerful government and in the malice of private enterprise. "The absolutely vital question," he said on assuming the presidency, "was whether the government had the power to control the trusts,"[19] "trusts" being a convenient catchall for the work of men like Carnegie and Rockefeller. His feelings about the role of the government were captured in Wilson's response to his platform in the campaign of 1912. "I do not care how benevolent the master is going to be," Wilson said. "I will not live under a master."[20]

But Wilson's criticism of Roosevelt's platform was disingenuous. His own political program of a "New Freedom" was as much a step back toward the old despotism as anything of Roosevelt's. As far as substantive issues were concerned, the three-way contest of 1912 offered a choice between Larry, Curly, and Moe. Taft, Roosevelt, and Wilson were distinct only as personalities. The difference in the policies they represented was not great. All three were carried in the political tide that came crashing down on American shores in the form of a larger and more intrusive government.

The New Regulation

In his *Rerum Novarum* of 1891, Pope Leo XIII said that it was "shameful and inhuman to treat men like chattels to make money by, or to look upon them merely as so much muscle or physical power." Coming as it did from the representative of an institution that had only recently given up the practice of castrating choirboys in order to extend their high voices into adult- (not man-) hood, a statement of this kind seems more than a little hypocritical. (There was a castrato in the Vatican choir as late 1903.) Hypocritical or not, the words spoke to an emerging sentiment. As the nineteenth century drew to a close, large business institutions were likely to be regarded as somehow a threat to both their customers and their employees.

Guilt by Association

It began with the dispute over railroad rates. In 1875, Albert Fink of the Louisville & Nashville suggested that the roads could protect themselves from cutthroat competition by dividing up their markets and agreeing to rates that would guarantee a profit.[21] Such an agreement could be effective only if all competitors were faithful to its terms, which few of them ever were. One of the methods they employed in being unfaithful was that of posting the agreed-upon rate and then granting rebates to favored shippers. Of course the word on that always got out quickly, and none of the railroad pools remained healthy for long. In markets where there were a number of competitors, rates were always— well, competitive. There was never any complaint about the charges for long hauls between heavily populated cities.

When it came to short hauls, though, and to areas served by only one line, the story was a different one. In places where a railroad enjoyed a monopoly, it tended to act like a monopolist and charged all the market would bear. Policies of this kind were possible only because of federal land grants, which had created the monopolies in the first place, and collusion between railways and statehouses. The wounded public, though, seldom looked behind scenes to identify the real source of their woes. All they saw was the private greed that displayed itself as higher rates for short than for long hauls. The Populist movement, a rural version of Progressivism, began as a campaign for the regulation of the railroads.

More than one emerging business would find itself in the public spotlight because of its dealings with the railroads. John D. Rockefeller, for example, was an unknown when he first appeared before the Hepburn Committee in 1879. Merchants who believed the roads had discriminated against them had pressed for an investigation, and the name of Standard Oil soon appeared as an example of a company that had received rebates. There was never any suggestion that Rockefeller had done anything to harm consumers. The efficiency of Standard Oil had been rather hard on some of Rockefeller's competitors, though, and the unsuccessful competitors demanded their day in court.[22]

It turned out that Standard was only one of the many companies that had received rebates. More than half of the long-haul traffic traveled under special contracts, and in spite of rebates the oil traffic was the railways' most profitable business. When a rail executive pointed out that Standard was no longer getting any rebates, one of the Hepburn Committee's lawyers dismissed the testimony. Standard had become a monopoly, he said, and no longer needed the rebates.

Politicians love words that turn on the emotions and turn off the thinking processes, and in America "monopoly" is a word of that kind. Compared to a railroad, Standard Oil was small fry, and any near-monopoly it might have almost enjoyed was terminally ill at the moment of birth. It did not take much money to build a refinery, and if Standard charged too much or delivered low quality kerosene to some area, an independent producer soon took over that market. Refineries, Rockefeller complained, were in the air. And the independents were every bit as successful as Standard had been in getting favorable rates from the railroads.[23] The entire oil industry, furthermore, in the day before the automobile, accounted for a minuscule percentage of GNP. It was about one-third the size of the shoe industry.[24]

But never mind the facts; it was enough to make the accusation. When the Democratic Party published its cartoon "Alphabet of Joyous Trusts"[25] (from the Apple Trust to the Zephyr Trust), Standard Oil was one of only two mentioned by name. (The other company thus singled out was Kodak, whose domination of the market for inexpensive cameras made it an obvious threat to the public welfare.)

Labor Relations

In addition to the unfavorable publicity they received because of the railroads, businesses had public relations problems because of their disputes with organized labor. Unions' descriptions of the great industrialists were not in themselves persuasive because the unions obviously had something to gain in the contest of wills. "The capitalist class had its origins in force and fraud," said the American Federation of Labor's Samuel Gompers. "This class of parasites devours incomes derived from many sources, from the stunted babies employed in the mills, mines and factories to the leases of gambling halls and the profits of fashionable brothels."[26] But this same selfless servant of humanity, when asked about the objectives of the union, said, "More, more, and then more,"[27] which, given his assumptions, meant less, less, and still less for everyone else. No objective analysis of the facts could portray the union member as somehow more honorable than the successful entrepreneur.

The owners of large businesses, though, often dealt with their labor problems in such a way as to put themselves in a bad light. Carnegie's handling of the strike at the Homestead Works is a case in point. He had inherited a long history of strained labor relations when he bought the plant from Andrew Kloman and its other shareholders in 1883. Elsewhere in the Carnegie system, labor relations were, if not perfectly peaceful, at least harmonious. The first eight-hour day in the industry had been instituted at Carnegie's Edgar Thomson plant in 1877, but it was abandoned ten years later when none of the other steel manufacturers followed suit. Even this disagreeable policy change had been managed in such a way as to maintain the peace and had occasioned little comment from the press.[28]

Carnegie's undoing in the Homestead strike was the manager, one H. C. Frick, whose goal was to break the union. Carnegie told him to close the plant and let the thing blow over, but Frick was aching for a fight and called the Pinkertons in to investigate. The strikers attacked them, the battle made the headlines, and Carnegie was vilified. A few years earlier the unions had referred to him as "Little Andy"; the Brotherhood of Locomotive Engineers had named a division after him and made him an honorary member.[29] He had been a hero to organized labor because he kept his men employed in good times and in bad, even during a depression.[30] All that was forgotten now. Along with men like Vanderbilt, Duke, and of course Rockefeller, Carnegie now became the human embodiment of everything wrong with America. The newspapers raged and the politicians responded.

Aristotle, it will be recalled, living at the time when ancient Greece slid into decline, said that those who could not be trained to moderate their ambitions should be legally forced to do so. Perhaps this is an instinctive response to any success that cannot be attributed to obvious talents or physical advantages. It was in any case the first response of American lawmakers to the achievements of the great industrialists. The systematic organization and consolidation of a large business enterprise was declared illegal. The Sherman Antitrust Act, said its sponsor, would protect "the rights of individuals as against associated and corporate wealth and power."[31] This it purported to do by declaring such "corporate wealth and power" to be against the law.

Its real purpose, though, was not preventive. Its real purpose was an expansion of government power along the lines of what the Progressives saw in Germany. A law that is intended to prevent something specifies both the prohibited act and the penalty for it. The free individual is thus informed with regard to the acceptable line of behavior and to the consequences of nonacceptable behavior. The older of my sons always drives too fast, but the law tells him what he's doing and what will happen to him if he's caught. In the same way, a law with regard to economic activity allows businesspeople to choose between alternative courses based upon their understanding of what the law permits and the consequences of a violation.

The antitrust laws and their more recent regulatory offspring did not and do not provide guidelines of this kind. They have been what Ayn Rand described as ex post facto legislation.[32] They do not provide a clear and understandable guideline for behavior. One cannot know until after the fact and the expenses of a long court battle whether they have been violated. The antitrust laws are so vague as to give government lawyers a wide discretion in deciding whether to pursue a particular case. Justice Department attorneys make their choice not on the basis of the facts, which the law fails to clearly define, but on the basis of either public sentiment or complaints from competitors.

With the first antitrust legislation, the Jeffersonian ideal of a "wise and frugal government" that left individuals "free to regulate their own pursuits of industry and improvement" passed into memory. The Sherman Act lay largely unused for a dozen years, but the door for federal involvement in the economy had been opened.

The first to walk through it, grinning toothily, was Theodore Roosevelt. He was more interested in the symbolic than in the practical significance of his victories. After the Northern Securities case of 1902–04, for example, J. P. Morgan and James J. Hill remained in control of the Burlington Railroad, and they had no difficulty in carrying out their original purposes. But the business community had been put on notice that never again could it safely act without permission from the government. By the end of 1903, Roosevelt had obtained the passage of a bill that created a cabinet-level Department of Commerce and Labor and a Bureau of Corporations to oversee business practices.[33]

The underlying assumptions of the new regulatory environment were threefold. First, the people who operated businesses were somehow in conspiracy against the public weal. Second, the public was helpless in the face of this attack. Third, salvation lay in the creation of a large and powerful government. The Founding Fathers had attributed to the citizenry a large measure of virtue, wisdom, and self-sufficiency, but that attribution was now on its way to being out of style. The new attributions were those of dishonesty on the part of business owners, helpless passivity on the part of the average citizen, and wise virtue on the part of public functionaries.

The New Class

The Bureau of Corporations is an early example of an active and powerful regulatory agency. Under a series of "gentlemen's agreements," businesses (primarily J. P. Morgan and associates) provided the government with information, and the government stamped its Good Housekeeping Seal of Approval on such activities as it deemed to be "in the public interest."[34] The critical question then became that of assigning responsibility for making the decision with regard to what was and what was not in the public interest.

It was understood that the task could not be entrusted to businesspeople. Even those who might have been supposed to have a favorable attitude toward free enterprise agreed that the character of a corporate leader would be not up to the challenge. The leading management consultant of the time, F. W. Taylor, expressed his contempt for those who cared about nothing but "making money quickly" and had "absolutely no pride of manufacture."[35] And as we shall see in the next chapter, Taylor's opinion of business leaders was, by the standards of the time, the condensed essence of charitable moderation.

It was obvious, too, that the ordinary citizen could not be expected to look after his own best interest. He was regarded as neither bright nor decisive enough to take care of himself. There was a need for some third party to become actively involved in protecting workers, consumers, and most of all competitors from the malicious designs of commercial enterprise. Beginning very tentatively with the creation of the Interstate Commerce Commission in 1887 and becoming gradually more deliberate with the creation of new agencies as the twentieth century began, the job was entrusted to federal bureaucracies. The Civil Service Reform Act of 1883 had set forth the ideal of a disinterested and politically neutral professional as the best choice for managing the day-to-day responsibilities of the government. Now that ideal would be applied also to the oversight of private transactions.

The same class of people who had been most vocal in their criticism of businesses and business leaders were not long in suggesting themselves as the best possible choice for the tasks of oversight. They were educated, idealistic, and untainted by close ties with the business community. In college they had learned about what was wrong with the world, and they wanted very much to set things right. It never dawned upon them to think that their view of reality, although of course very different from that of a man like John D. Rockefeller, might be just as much limited by their experience as his view was limited by his experience.

The greatest possible danger to personal liberty, as the Founding

Fathers had seen in the sad experience of seventeenth and eighteenth-century France, is a large bureaucracy backed by the power of the state. Its members may have a good education and the best intentions, but they remain for all that limited and fallible human beings. Sooner or later their tasks force them to make choices that will bring their personal inclinations into play. The fact that they are well informed with regard to the subject at hand serves only to increase the self-righteous confidence with which they hand down their dicta. "I should be underestimating myself as a true bureaucrat," said Max Weber in a parody of the attitude, "if I did not claim to know, much better than these blockheads, what was good for them."[36] His point was that in spite of their ignorance and bias, the blockheads might still prefer to do things their own way. And there is always the possibility that a blockhead, who is familiar with the details of the situation immediately at hand, might know a thing or two that the bureaucrat does not.

This was a possibility that the members of the rising generation never bothered to consider. They could see what was wrong with the world, they had a mind for "reform," and they could think of no one who would be better qualified than themselves for carrying it out. Henry Gantt, for example, was convinced that industrial leaders had risen to positions of power on the basis of things other than their personal merit. In 1916 he organized the "New Machine" with an eye to putting political and economic power in the hands of men such as himself, engineers and consultants. In a letter to Woodrow Wilson, the members of the New Machine called upon the president to put the control of industry "into the hands of those who understand its operation,"[37] i.e., themselves. Employment bureaus should be set up for the better placement of employees, and public service banks should extend credit on the basis of ability and personality rather than a record of practical success.

In suggesting that things be put into the hands of engineers, Gantt was doing no more than giving voice to an opinion that was already widespread. Thorstein Veblen's *The Theory of the Leisure Class* became popular because its idea of social engineering was one for which many believed the time had come. The business community, declared the members of the New Machine, must accept its "social responsibility" (a word rich with portents for the future) and allow itself to be remade for its own best interest. Engineers, who were persons of "few opinions and many facts and many deeds,"[38] should be accorded their rightful place at the head of the economic system. Above all else, things should be done according to a long-range plan. Such opinions were taken very seriously in America, but they were taken even more seriously in the emerging Soviet Union, where Stalin used Gantt's famous Gantt charts for the administration of his Five-Year Plans.

The new overseers were quite selfless but not so selfless as to expect no compensation for their trouble. With the disappearance of a government that was willing to limit itself came also the disappearance of a government that could afford to be (to use Jefferson's words) "wise and frugal." Old notions about the value of federal parsimony were forgotten. The tariff duties that had supported the government since its inception were now to be supplemented by an income tax. Such a tax would be perfectly fair, said the Democratic platform of 1908; there was no danger that it would overburden anyone. It was, moreover, absolutely necessary, given the Republican extravagances of recent years. There was no danger that Congress would ever abuse its power to tax or expand the federal budget in an effort to build up interested constituencies. The income tax, moreover, was a progressive tax, a great equalizer that would at least in some measure relieve the wealthy of their obviously ill-gotten gains.

With the election of 1912, the members of the new generation began to get what they wanted: an academic in the White House, a government with high-minded ideas for overseeing the economy, an automatic penalty for exceptional economic achievement, and well-paid positions of power for themselves. All of this would save American society by making it "more" (not completely) just. It would also guarantee the comfort and security of those who led the way to salvation and justice, the members of the groups who were most vocal in their demands for reform, who now had good jobs as regulators and bureaucrats.

This is what always happens, said economist Aaron Director: those with a plan for saving the world through the power of government find a way to turn the plan to their own advantage.[39] Intellectuals and bureaucrats set themselves up as a new class, whose great plans justify their maintenance at the expense of the taxpayer.

None of this happened, though, without an agreeing nod from the public the new class proposed to save and to tax, not necessarily in that order. The most popular literature of the time gave expression to a widespread conviction that personal character was not something upon which one could safely rely. The type of character that led to economic success was regarded as a particular threat to the general welfare and as something to be reigned in. This new bias is the subject of the next chapter.

Chapter 7

THE LITERATURE OF DESPAIR

At 1:40 the captain told the helmsman to make a turn to starboard, inadvertently giving an order that would bring his ship into the path of a waiting submarine. Aboard the *U-20*, Lieutenant Schweiger struggled for half an hour to get into an attack position off his victim's bow and then gave the command to fire.

The orchestra was still playing for the second sitting of lunch when the torpedo struck. Elbert and Alice Hubbard came out on deck to see what had happened. "Well, Jack," Hubbard called to a friend, "they got us. They were a damned sight worse than I ever thought they were."

"What are you going to do?" Jack asked.

"There does not seem to be anything to do," Alice replied. She took her husband's arm and they returned to their cabin to go down with the ship.[1]

It was the end of an age. America's entry into the First World War marked an end to its independence from the struggles of Europe. With the war came also an end to the relatively small and nonintrusive government that had guided America through the nineteenth century. And with Hubbard's death on the *Lusitania* came an end to the train of writers who had pointed to the importance of personal values and personal character. Their successors would describe the world as a place in which values were irrelevant and character nonexistent.

Between 1900 and 1940 there was a great sea change in American thinking and therefore in American destiny. This chapter and the next deal with those changes.

Elbert Hubbard

He was born in 1856 and in Illinois, the son of a country doctor. His autobiographical remarks include no mention of *McGuffey's Reader*, but given the time and place of his upbringing, that would have been so common as not to merit comment. He was thoroughly familiar with Emerson and the *Autobiography* of Benjamin Franklin, and there may have been a time in his life when he enjoyed the stories of Horatio Alger.

A country doctor in mid-nineteenth-century America was nothing like his modern descendant, who is sure of his fee because most of it is paid by someone other than the patient. There are stories without number of small-town physicians who died in poverty because they made it a practice to forgive the debts of those who could not afford to pay. With a large family and never wealthy, Dr. Hubbard raised no objection when his fifteen-year-old son decided to drop out of school and make his own way in the world.

In the years that followed, Elbert Hubbard found employment as a farmhand, as a cowboy, as a dockworker, as a salesman, as a teacher, as a reporter, and as a printer. He read voraciously. He made what was for the time a small fortune ($75,000) as a partner in a soap factory and used the money to go to Harvard, but he never earned a degree. He journeyed through Europe and settled at last into the creation of well-bound books by founding the Roycoft Press in East Aurora, New York. Tufts College awarded him a master's degree in 1899, but he said, "Since I did not earn the degree, it does not count."[2]

His literary career began as a rearguard action. He grew weary of highbrow periodicals' assault on the values with which he had been raised. He said he had grown tired, in particular, with the newly popular myth of "the downtrodden, honest man looking for work and not being able to find it."[3] His own experience taught him that the man who wanted to work would have no difficulty in finding something to do, although admittedly not always at the wage he might prefer.

He went to G. P. Putnam's Sons with an idea for a periodical called *The Philistine*. He had chosen this title as a way of drawing a clear line between what he had to say and the ideas that were then becoming popular among America's educated classes. "I think I'll start a campaign for the reformation of the reformers," he said, and suggested that instead of trying to fix the world, "each man and each woman set a guard over his own spirit and try to be greater than he who taketh a city."[4] The publishers were doubtful about the market for such ideas, so he had to print it himself. The first issue came out in June 1895. It was successful from the first.

In March 1899, *The Philistine* published Hubbard's essay, "A Message to Garcia." It drew on newspaper reports about how, at a critical point early in the Spanish-American War, a man named Rowan had carried a message from the president of the United States to the Cuban insurgent, General Garcia. Rowan asked no questions about his assignment. He simply began to carry it out. When he ran into difficulties and uncertainties, he did not waste time with inquiries for additional directions. He took the initiative and figured things out for himself. And he got the message through.

This was exactly the kind of man businesses needed, Hubbard said, a self-starter, self-directed, a man who would take the initiative and complete a task without constant questions, whining, and complaints. "Men are needed—honest, loyal men who will do their work."[5]

That month *The Philistine* went out as usual, but there were soon orders for additional copies. When the American News Company ordered a thousand copies, Hubbard asked one of his assistants what was going on. "It's that Garcia stuff," the assistant said.[6] Demand soon outstripped the capacity of the Roycroft Press, and other publishers took over. By the time of Hubbard's death, 22 million copies had been published.[7] The "Message" remained in print for another ten years, and it was translated into 40 different languages.

Circulation of *The Philistine*, meanwhile, had more than doubled and Hubbard had become a celebrity. He went on the lecture circuit, made about 80 presentations a year, and never failed to draw a crowd. An early engagement was at the Waldorf-Astoria. Nine hundred people paid a dollar a seat, 300 were turned away at the door, and the promoter lamented, "Oh! Oh! Oh! Why didn't we charge them two dollars apiece!"[8] A little while later he spoke to a crowd of 2,200 at Carnegie Hall. He was just beginning to reach out for the rest of the world when the *U-20*'s torpedo hit the *Lusitania*.

Upton Sinclair

Among the articles Hubbard published were 180 "Little Journeys into the Homes of the Great," vignettes that described and praised the virtues of persons whose achievements had shaped history. After his death, these essays were collected and bound as fourteen volumes, one of which was about great businessmen. Among Hubbard's heroes were Philip Armour, John Jacob Astor, Andrew Carnegie, and the same James J. Hill whose work Theodore Roosevelt tried to hinder in the Northern Securities Case of 1902-04. These were the men who made America great, Hubbard said, men of vision, men who set practical goals and found ways to reach them. They seized the initiative, found better ways to do things, worked hard, husbanded their resources, persisted in the face of defeat, and eventually found their way to success.

The popularity of such ideas is shown both by the success of *The Philistine* and by Hubbard's success as a lecturer. At the beginning of the twentieth century, Americans still had a strong interest in the values associated with self-reliance and personal achievement. But the balance of power in the battle of ideas was beginning to shift. The new generation of authors looked out on the world around them, discovered that beside its increasingly widespread abundance there remained a great deal of poverty, and decided that those who had created the abundance must be responsible also for the poverty. In the process of trying to assign blame for their world's obvious problems, they denied the importance of the personal qualities that offered the only real solutions.

The danger was described as inherent in the very attempt to achieve things in the world of commercial activity. In the middle of the nineteenth century, Harriet Beecher Stowe had suggested that the explanation for the evils of slavery lay not in the free choices of individuals but in "the system."[9] By the beginning of the twentieth century it had become fashionable to offer a similar explanation for virtually all of humanity's problems. The economic process, in particular, was seen as corrupt and as poisoning everything it touched.

This new trend in literature was called "realism." It described the world as a place where the wicked preyed upon the simple and the clever robbed the virtuous. It was a place where things always turned out badly for the average man. *McGuffey's Reader*, Ralph Waldo Emerson, and Horatio Alger had faced up honestly to the fact that life is hard but put the emphasis on a person's ability to accomplish things in spite of the difficulties involved. The realists described the world as murderously competitive and the ordinary individual as helpless before the onslaught of overambitious achievers.

Probably the most famous of these writers, and the only one whose name is likely to be recognized by modern students, was Upton Sinclair. His novel *The Jungle*, which came out in 1905, outsold every other book in America for a full year.[10] It tells the story of Jurgis Rudkus, who arrives in this country fresh from Lithuania, pure, idealistic, and untouched, the latest rendition of Rousseau's noble savage. He works hard, speeds up his work when asked to do so, defers the gratification of marriage until he can afford a home, and goes to night school. Unlike Andrew Carnegie or Benjamin Franklin, though, whose luck was often good, his luck is always bad. He goes not from rags to riches but from rags to despair. In the end he finds happiness and peace of mind by reading the socialist magazine *Appeal to Reason* and doing his bit for the World Revolution.

Franklin's *Autobiography*, the life of Andrew Carnegie, and the novels of Horatio Alger are stories about the victories of personal character. *The Jungle* is a story about the defeat of personal character. "Realism" in this context apparently refers to something other than a description of reality: it refers not to how things actually happen but to how, given certain gloomy assumptions about human nature and human possibilities, the novelist thinks they "should" happen. Benjamin Franklin and Andrew Carnegie were real people; their life stories were tales of hindrances and helps, defeats and victories. That's reality. Sometimes things work out and sometimes they don't, but the person of character can find a way to deal with almost anything. Jurgis Rudkus was defeated because it suited Upton Sinclair to describe defeat, not because things always work out that way in the real world.

Sinclair, though, was not interested describing the real world. He wanted to get even with it. The son of an alcoholic and raised in an often divided household, his childhood circumstances had shifted frequently, suddenly, and without warning between moderate comfort and abject poverty. His earliest experiences were of the helplessness and resentment he described in his book; The Jungle's descriptions of poverty and fear came from his own memories. But not all of these tragic memories had been inflicted upon him. Some of them were his own doing. In the winter of 1904-5, for example, his refusal to seek nonliterary employment had brought terrible suffering to his sick wife and young son. But he blamed the world for his troubles, and his books were his way of striking back.[11]

Early in his career he had tried his hand at writing stories similar to those of Horatio Alger, but he never had much luck with them. His first big success was a well-planned hoax. In 1903 he published The Journal of Arthur Stirling, which was represented as the autobiography of a bitter young poet who had recently committed suicide. It was in fact the product of Sinclair's vivid imagination and his unique capacity for the description of heartbreak and tragedy. One of his friends inserted accounts of the "death" into the New York papers and let the publisher's literary adviser in on the secret. The book gathered a good deal of attention, and reviewers were as taken in as the public at large. One of them described it as "at once an authoritative document, a heart-searching appeal, and tragic entertainment."[12]

So much for "realism." Sinclair's concern for honesty and a fair presentation of the facts is apparent also in the research he did for The Jungle. It took him all of seven weeks. The time was short because he knew exactly what he needed to find. He was working under an assignment from *Appeal to Reason* (yes—surprise, surprise!—the same social-istic magazine that brought peace to Jurgis Rudkus at the end of *The Jungle*). Its editor had offered Sinclair five hundred dollars for serial rights to a novel dealing with "wage slavery" (i.e., the heinous practice of requiring people to work for a living) as effectively as one of his earlier novels had dealt with chattel slavery. Sinclair was by this time a member of the Socialist Party, but he used the money for the very unsocialistic purchase of private property (a farm) and set off for Chicago.[13]

The Jungle's success was due only in part to Sinclair's capacity for engaging the reader's emotions with a tale of undeserved suffering. More important was the appeal he made to popular prejudice with his unflat-tering portrayal of the meatpacking business. In 1905 the Chicago stock-yards were a new and frightening institution, about which people were more than willing to believe the worst. This was especially true because by operating efficient enterprises and distributing their products over wide areas, the meatpackers put many small-town butchers out of busi-ness. There had been, in addition, a scandal about the army's purchase of "embalmed beef" during the Spanish-American War. Local experi-ence and recent history had conspired to prepare readers for Sinclair's descriptions of unsanitary conditions in the preparation of canned meat.

There undoubtedly were (and are) many unsavory things about the process in which live animals are converted into food for the dinner table. But what Sinclair said about the stockyards would apply equally well to the operations of a small-town butcher. At the beginning of the twentieth century the leading figure in the meatpacking industry was Philip Armour, who offered this challenge: "As for sanitation, go visit your local village slaughter-house and then come see the way I do it."[14]

The legislatures of Colorado, Minnesota, and Indiana passed meat inspection laws designed to protect the butchers among their constitu-ents from national competition. The fact that such laws completely failed to destroy the big meatpackers suggests that people were not afraid to buy their products and therefore that Armour was right about the com-parative cleanliness of his operations.

But his words came at a time in history when readers had become willing to distrust everything said by a man who had achieved real and practical success. This was another thing that contributed to the popularity of *The Jungle.* Reports about "unfair" practices on the railroads, stories about the Homestead strike, and news of antitrust actions against men like Rockefeller spoke to an emerging conviction that exceptional success was the result of dishonesty. Earlier generations had admired the achiever; Americans were now beginning to envy and distrust him. When they read Sinclair's description of the man who owned the packing plant as a person "who was trying to make as much money as he could, and did not care in the least how he did it,"[15] they were ready to believe it. When they read about how this man demanded hard work from his employees, they wrote him off as greedy and insensitive.

It never crossed their minds to think that his concern for profit was the result not of dishonesty, but of his need to offer his products at a competitive price, attract investors, and meet his payroll. They never stopped to think that as producers and consumers they were themselves the primary beneficiaries of his efforts. Armour tried to tell them. To the farmers he said, "You get more for your produce today than you did before I showed up on the scene; and you get your money on the minute, without haggle or question." To the consumer he said, "I supply you with regularity, and I give you a price more advantageous than your local butcher can command."[16]

But it was to no avail. Better prices for farmers, lower prices for consumers, and the readier availability of meat were sufficient evidence of Armour's malicious intentions. The jobs he provided proved once and for all that in the meatpacking industry there was no place where (as Sinclair put it) "a man counted for anything against a dollar."[17] The age was ready to believe a novelist who wrote from his imagination, but not a businessman who spoke from experience. Even today students submit papers in which *The Jungle* is described as a reliable presentation of life in the Chicago stockyards.

George Babbitt

In the widespread prosperity of the 1920s, commercial enterprise enjoyed a fleeting popularity. The same Ida M. Tarbell who had once vilified John D. Rockefeller now displayed the weathervane morality of popular journalism by becoming big business's biggest fan. Muckraking was a thing of the past, but the businessperson was still fair game. If nothing else, writers could use the products of their imagination to agree with Upton Sinclair in affirming that there was no connection between personal character and practical success.

This was the central thrust of Sinclair Lewis' novel *Babbitt*. George Babbitt is a real estate salesman, "nimble in the calling of selling houses for more than people could afford to pay."[18] The Protestant Ethic idea of a calling as the highest use of one's life has degenerated in Lewis' usage to mere cleverness. Babbitt's concern with the wise use of time is limited to his pride in being the owner of an alarm clock. His interest in innovation is limited to his desire to be in on all the latest trends—in tires, in cigarette lighters, in men's underwear, in water-coolers, and of course in cars. In the place of persistent effort we find a faith in "hustle."

As regards honesty, George Babbitt admires Charley McKelvey because the man has made a fortune as a contractor without bribing any more members of the city council than was "absolutely necessary."[19] Leaving for the office, Babbitt says he's going to "sting a few clients."[20] And sting them he does, listing houses for twice their real value on the assumption that his prospects will try to talk him down—and then resisting their efforts to talk him down. He is developing the Glen Oriole subdivision and takes pride in the fact that it has a complete sewage system, while that of another real estate developer offers only septic tanks. The downside is that his sewage system does not have an adequate outlet, and the filth accumulates. He has covered his tracks by paying health inspectors to look the other way.

Although he takes pride in his individualism and for one brief moment does manage to have an opinion of his own, George Babbitt is anything but an individualist. The only ideas to which he can give spontaneous expression are those he holds as a Republican, a Presbyterian, and a real estate broker. Half the houses in Floral Heights are exactly like his, and they are all decorated in exactly the same way. George Babbitt loves tall buildings, busy streets, and Babe Ruth. He has mixed feelings about the study of Shakespeare and anyone who can read a foreign language. He hates reformers, labor unions, socialists, Communists, Bolsheviks, Lenin, and every businessman who thinks he's too good to join the Chamber of Commerce.

What we see in the behavior and thinking of George Babbitt is the direct opposite of the Protestant Ethic. His is anything but the unified personality implied by the word "character." He is a mass of contradictions. He strongly supports Prohibition but does not hesitate to purchase bootleg liquor. He believes in personal morality but looks longingly on the young women with whom he does business, hopes briefly for an affair with his secretary, and eventually has one with a woman closer to his own age. Incapable of self-discipline, he stops smoking twice a month.

Previous "realistic" literature had described successful businessmen as aggressively evil monsters who came straight from the depths of hell. George Babbitt, though, is less a demon than a ninny. Upton Sinclair had described the owner of the meatpacking plant in *The Jungle* as deliberately wicked; Lewis describes George Babbitt as unintentionally ridiculous. Lewis' protagonist is not different from those of previous writers because he is less dishonest or less selfish. He is merely less intelligent and less successful. The message is clear: not only the giant of industry but even the local entrepreneur is a threat to those around him.

Babbitt was an immediate best seller. Reviewers loved it. One of them praised it because it described life in America as "dehumanized by indifference or enmity to all human values"; he said it demonstrated the hypocrisy of the belief that "business knavery is social service."[21] He failed to mention that the society he was complaining about was the most prosperous on the planet. In spite of its supposed "enmity to all human values" it was providing its citizens with a greater abundance and a wider range of choices than any other society in history. He failed also to note that this prosperity was in large measure the work of entrepreneurs who (except for their greater honesty and reliability) were very much like George Babbitt.

But never mind the facts. H. G. Wells, who was as prominent a socialist as he was a literary figure, thought the book was a great accomplishment. "I wish I could have written *Babbitt*," he said.[22]

Well, really, he almost had. Lewis had begun reading Wells while he was still at Yale. His first successful novel and the most direct of *Babbit*'s intellectual ancestors was entitled *Our Mr. Wrenn*, the central character of which came less from any of Lewis' actual experiences than from the fiction of H. G. Wells. Something of this kind could be said of all Lewis' writing: he seldom relied, said Carl Van Doren, on his own experiences; he preferred instead "to work out large projects for what ought to happen."[23] Another critic described Lewis' writing as "the accomplishment of a foreknown task."[24]

And the foreknown task was always that of giving expression to his own unhappiness. Miserably homely, he had spent a solitary childhood in the shadow of a dictatorial father and a handsome, gregarious older brother. By the time he got into preparatory school he was a sarcastic, caustic loner. At Yale his classmates nicknamed him "God Forbid" and said that he could "fart out his face."[25] Years later, one of these classmates, now chairman of the board at U.S. Steel, would observe that Lewis rebelled against the world because he failed to attain the social acceptance he so desperately craved.[26] Even as a best-selling author at the height of his powers, Lewis was described by acquaintances as a man without inner certainty, balance, or serenity.[27] He was an alcoholic, divorced twice, and alienated from both of his sons.

Like many another lost soul, Lewis gave expression to his own misery by condemning the world. He railed against Christianity and capitalism and went on endlessly about the tragedy of poverty in America, but the real problem had nothing to do with theology or economics. The real problem was Sinclair Lewis. George Babbitt's dishonesty was Lewis' dishonesty. George Babbitt's failures as a father and a husband were Lewis' failures as a father and a husband. George Babbitt's unhappiness was Lewis' unhappiness. George Babbitt's need for acceptance and approval was Lewis' need for acceptance and approval.

Lewis could write about George Babbitt because he was George Babbitt. In his mind he was a great rebel: over his signature in a letter to Jack London he wrote, "For the Revolution,"[28] and he wrote essays about the passing of capitalism. In practice he was the perfect conformer, dressed in the latest style, perfectly groomed, always playing the role of

George Babbitt, as Ernest Boyd wrote, "an aggressive, forwardlooking, up-standing citizen, a sales promoter of ability, a key man and a live wire."[29] When he went to a reunion at Yale, he drove a Cadillac to impress his former classmates. Boyd's conclusion: "This, then, is 'the significance of Sinclair Lewis', that he has burlesqued himself and gotten away with it."

Thinking back to the terminology described in the first chapter, we can see that *Babbitt* is a book about a man whose dominant motive is his need for affiliation. He wants above all else to belong, to feel liked and accepted. To this end he joins clubs, dresses like those around him, and mouths popular ideas. He seeks not objective measures of actual accomplishment but the feeling of being admired by his acquaintances, and so he engages in conspicuous consumption, drives a nice car, lives in a nice home in a nice part of town, and buys his clothes in the best stores. The appearance of upward mobility is a means to the feeling that one is rising in the opinions of others.

The reading public of the 1920s may have enjoyed Lewis' story because it gave them a chance to laugh without fully realizing that they were themselves the source of their amusement. George Babbitt was very much the kind of person many of them were becoming. By 1925, according to McClelland, the need for affiliation was beginning to replace the need for achievement as the dominant American motive. One's standing in the eyes of others was becoming an acceptable alternative to practical accomplishment. There were some who, without the benefit of hindsight or McClelland's terminology, noted this change even as it was occurring. Summarizing the work of thirty leading scholars in his preface to *Civilization in the United States*, Harold Stearns had commented on it a year before *Babbitt* was published.[30]

Lewis' book is important because it tells us how Americans were beginning to feel about themselves. Fifty years and a hundred years earlier, personal independence and practical success had been regarded as worthy goals. The route to what was best in life went through self-reliance, honesty, effort, original thinking, and deferred gratification. In the 1920s and in the sad case of George Babbitt, the only open road was that of conformity and deception. Success was an empty show, a matter not of what you accomplished, but of how others felt about you. People saw themselves in George Babbitt, and what they saw were leaves in the whirlwind.

The New Priesthood

According to Mark Schorer, the novels of Sinclair Lewis, particularly *Babbitt*, were important because they popularized the ideas of the economist Thorstein Veblen.[31] A prominent Marxist, Veblen was critical of America's mass culture and the economic system that made it possible. The goals of individualistic businessmen, he said, were directly opposed to the good of the community; driven by a desire for money and power, such persons sought to create economic disturbances in order to profit from them. Veblen looked forward to the appearance of a world in which management would free itself from the greedy materialism of existing business leaders and function according to the logical dictates of industrial efficiency.[32]

The great obstacle to the realization of this vision was the fact that people do not usually live according to the dictates of logical efficiency. Left to their own devices, people tend to behave like individuals, to think their own thoughts, and to work on improving their own lives. The solution is obvious: don't leave them to their own devices. Auguste Comte, the great nineteenth-century prophet of authoritarian socialism, emphasized the importance of public opinion as a means of social control. The mass mind, he said, must be reshaped by a new intellectual hierarchy of priests, philosophers, and sociologists. The popular media, as Ortega y Gassett would later say, must submit to the guidance of an intellectual elite.[33]

This new elite began to appear during the 1910s and 1920s in the form of management consultants and educational experts.

Scientific Management

The way was paved by a man named Frederick W. Taylor. Taylor was like Elbert Hubbard in that his opinions about life were formed in the world of practical experience. He passed Harvard's entrance exams with flying colors but decided against college and took an apprenticeship as a pattern worker and machinist. He got a job at Midvale Steel and rose rapidly. He enrolled in a home study course and earned a degree in mechanical engineering without attending class except to take the exams. By the beginning of his seventh year he had attained the rank of chief engineer.[34]

Taylor made the move from industrial employment to consulting because experience had led him to the conviction that workers should be treated and rewarded as individuals. As long as they were treated like the members of a herd, he said, they had no incentive to do their best. Assigned, furthermore, to work for which they were suited by neither temperament nor physique, they were not really capable of doing their best. The solution was to give a person a job to which he was suited and then show him the best way in which to perform it. Thus selected and trained, the average worker would become a "first class man" and earn a first-class paycheck. This was the system to which Louis Brandeis would later apply the term "scientific management."[35]

Taylor's ideas were the direct descendant of the old Protestant Ethic belief that each of us has a unique calling and will find the best life can give by pursuing it with faithfulness and diligence. Like the old-time Calvinists, he emphasized the careful use of time and resources and was constantly on the lookout for better ways to do things. He was as concerned as Andrew Carnegie about expenses, and his system provided for constant feedback. Applied at Bethlehem Steel, it reduced labor costs from $.072 per ton to $.033 per ton; workers' wages, meanwhile, increased by an average of 60 percent.[36]

Labor unions depend upon the demand for standardized rules and working conditions as a way to maintain group solidarity, so labor leaders were less than enthusiastic about Taylor's ideas for individual incentives. In 1911 his method was tried at the Rock Island Army Arsenal, and the unions began a campaign against it. There were congressional hearings in October of the same year. At the head of the investigating committee was William B. Wilson, a former official of the United Mine Workers. (He was at the time chair of the House Labor Committee and would later become Woodrow Wilson's secretary of commerce.)

"Is it not true," Wilson bellowed, "that a man who is not a good workman and who may not be responsible for the fact that he is not a good workman has to live as well as the man who is a good workman?"

"Not as well as the other workman," Taylor replied; "otherwise, that would imply that all those in the world were entitled to live equally well whether they worked or whether they were idle, and that certainly is not the case."[37]

The notion that the more productive worker was entitled to earn more than the less productive worker did not sit well with Mr. Wilson. He also took issue with the term "first-class man." Taylor tried to explain that with training and persistent effort almost anyone could become a first class man, but the committee did not want to hear about it and voted against letting Taylor define his terms. There was no evidence that Taylor's methods had been the source of any abuses or that there was a need for remedial legislation. Congress nevertheless passed a resolution against its further use in military agencies. Senator Henry Cabot Lodge (heir to a textile fortune) said it was a victory for those who wanted to end "the days of slavery."[38]

The members of the intelligentsia, always suspicious of ideas about individual effort, were every bit as happy as the unions about Taylor's defeat. They regarded the quest for economic efficiency as indicative of greed and dishonesty, and they wanted to have done, as Walter Lippmann would write, with the "cesspool of commercialism."[39] John Dos Passos portrayed Taylor as an efficiency monomaniac. Joseph Wharton had begged Taylor to stay with Bethlehem Steel, but Dos Passos represented him as having been unceremoniously fired. Taylor, he said, died with a stopwatch in his hand.[40]

Mary Parker Follett

Opponents of individualism found nothing to fear in the next generation of management consultants. The first of these, as the beneficiary of a substantial inheritance, was 31 years old before she ever did anything other than go to school and write.

Mary Parker Follett studied at Radcliffe and Cambridge, and her favorite thinker was the German philosopher Johann Fichte. The importance of this lies in the fact that, as Frederick Copleston observed in his eight-volume *History of Philosophy*, Fichte was a major contributor to the intellectual foundations of Hitler's National Socialism.[41] The freedom of individuals, said Fichte, must be subordinated to the demands of the state; an individual personality was best understood as no more than one element of a greater whole: the social, or better, the national personality.

This was the doctrine Follett preached in her book *The New State*. She liked terms such as "togetherness," "group thinking," and "the collective will." The person's "true self," she said, "is the group self"; "man can have no rights apart from society or independent of society or against society"; and chillingly, "the theory of government based on individual rights no longer has a place in modern political theory."[42]

Ms. Follett did not subscribe to the notion that an exceptional individual might be uniquely qualified to direct the operations of a business enterprise. She taught instead that all decisions should be group decisions: "The best leader does not ask people to serve him, but the common end."[43] She left unanswered the question of how the common end was to be determined. She apparently believed that Pittsburgh's potential steelworkers could have been relied upon to meet, decide on the creation of an industry, and divvy up the tasks. Their orders would not have come from a network of authority centering on a creative genius like Carnegie; instead, everyone would have obeyed "the orders given by the situation."[44]

All this, remember, came from someone who had never started a business, had never met a payroll, had never managed anything, had never even had a job, had never done anything but go to school, read, write, and talk. It seems curious, looking back on it, that anyone would have given her a second thought, but somehow she caught on. Her book on *Creative Experience* became popular with business leaders, and the Bureau of Personnel Administration called her to New York to deliver a series of talks to groups of executives.

She was popular because she spoke to the changing value orientation of those who read her books and listened to her lectures. Robert and Helen Lynd published their famous *Middletown: A Study in Con-*

temporary American Culture in 1929. In it they noted that among business leaders, individualism was on the decline; a need to belong and conformity were on the rise.[45] Perhaps, having reached financial security at the top of the social ladder, these persons were seeking the emotional safety that accompanies the surrender of one's own unique ideas. Is that not what had happened to George Babbitt?

Those who were still climbing, it might be added, tended to believe in the old individualism. The Lynds found that blue-collar workers remained insistent upon making their own way in the world. Their interest in being able to measure their progress was evident in their unenlightened tendency to think in terms of financial status. They showed very little interest in joining unions.[46] The members of the new priesthood, though, were anxious to find collectivist longings even in this last bastion of achievement motivation. That is the story of the Hawthorne studies.

Elton Mayo

These began as an exercise in scientific management. The theory was that people would work better if the illumination were improved. So the management at Western Electric's Hawthorne plant turned up the lights. Productivity went up. Cool. Just what they had expected. Some curmudgeon turned the lights back down, though, and productivity perversely rose still further.

Social scientists, as we have already observed, are always prepared to deal with situations of this kind. When new facts don't fit the old theory, they offer them as incontrovertible evidence for the truth of a new theory. But the managers of the Hawthorne plant were not social scientists, and so they had to call one in. Actually they called in several, but the front-runner turned out to be a Harvard professor named Elton Mayo.

Mayo had a big advantage over the competition because, long before he arrived at or had even heard of the Hawthorne plant, he already knew what he was going to find. His study of the French sociologist Emile Durkheim had helped him devise the term "pessimistic reveries" as an explanation of what went wrong in industrial settings. "Pessimistic reveries" are what a person has when he is thinking about his own goals and problems. They are produced by our consciousness of individuality, and they disappear to the extent that we experience ourselves as the members of a group. Changes in the level of illumination, Mayo said, made workers aware of the fact they were the subjects of a scientific experiment. This awareness created a new sense of group solidarity, a decline in pessimistic reveries, and an increase in productivity. In a series of experiments, he "proved" that group influences were vastly more important than individual motivation.[47]

More careful examinations of the data have since demonstrated that most of Mayo's conclusions were bogus. If changing the lighting had an effect, it was probably because the workers knew someone was paying attention to them. Their productivity increased because they felt someone was aware of them of them as individuals. Mayo said individual financial incentives were unimportant, but when one of the workers was asked about why productivity was higher in an experimental situation, she said it was because the pay was better.[48] Bogus or not, the conclusions became popular because they spoke to a declining faith in the importance of individual motivation and initiative.

John Dewey

Will Durant's *The Story of Philosophy* was originally published in 1926. It became a best seller because it spoke to the mind of the time, and in the mid-twenties many were ready to agree with Durant (who barely even mentioned Ralph Waldo Emerson) in thinking of John Dewey as the quintessential American philosopher.

Dewey made a name for himself primarily with his ideas on the subject of education. He thought that the nineteenth-century ideal of a liberal education was antiquated. He did not think, as his forebears had, of education as the means by which the human mind could be awakened from its dogmatic slumbers and see the world for what it is. The proper purpose of an education, he said, was that of adapting the individual to the demands of an industrial society. Thought itself was not a means to the knowledge of external reality but an instrument of adaptation. The individual is better conceived of as a product of his environment than of his own goals, effort, and thought. And it is foolish to think in terms of absolute right or absolute wrong. We are better advised to think in terms of good and better, and under the guidance of a wise philosophy to move constantly toward the latter.[49]

Dewey's attitude toward religion offers a key to his thought. He did not think much of religion. Science, he said, had made it obsolete: biology, for example, cast doubt on the doctrines of sin, redemption, and immortality.[50] But even the most casual critic can see that biology does not attempt to address these issues. Dewey insisted that it did because his problem with religion had nothing to do with science. His problem with religion was its emphasis on the importance of the individual. The thing he did not like about religion was its view of humanity and personal freedom. Religion insists upon the human being as a center, not of adaptation, but of eternal value. Religion (or at least Christianity) recognizes the tremendous importance of environmental influences but puts the emphasis on what a person can do in the face of them. And the religious mind does not see the world and human behavior as a continuum of ever-increasing goodness; it thinks in terms of right and wrong.

The traditional Christian emphasis on the individual as the locus of value and moral responsibility, however, was beginning to fade. In its place, people like Follett, Mayo, and Dewey would argue, as Follett put it, "Man discovers…his true freedom only through the group."[51] Leading theologians, the proponents of the "social gospel," nodded their heads in agreement and argued, in place of the old insistence on personal character, that the real need was for social reform. Look at the sad cases of Jurgis Rudkus and George Babbitt, which obviously proved that the individual as such meant nothing and character was irrelevant.

Under Dewey's leadership, the Progressive movement in education thought not in terms of developing character but in terms of fitting the child into the group. Peer socialization was to replace parental influence. Groups, in particular small groups, were seen as the panacea for individual adjustment. The new emphasis was not on personal achievement but on "personal participation in the development of a shared culture."[52] The keys were getting along and being accepted, not personal effort. What was important was not what you thought of yourself but what others thought of you.

It turns out that George Babbitt wasn't a fool, after all. He was a role model.

Conclusion

The first three decades of the twentieth century witnessed a declining faith in the value and power of the individual. The "realistic" trend in literature described an ordinary man like Jurgis Rudkus as helpless in the face of greedy individualism. Lewis helped people laugh at the deluded buffoon who insisted on believing that he really did have some ideas of his own. Follett, Mayo, and Dewey insisted that one must think in terms of group membership rather than private accomplishment. Lacking any idea of character as the means to overcoming difficulties and the medium through which personal motivation could be translated into a social good, they agreed in thinking of the isolated individual as dangerous, helpless, and foolish.

The people who took this fear-filled approach to life seem for the most part to have been people who had little experience of it. Those who had actually gone out into the world and accomplished things were more optimistic. Consider the case of Elbert Hubbard: like Benjamin Franklin, he owed much of his success to his writing; also like Benjamin Franklin, he earned his living as a printer. He published over ten thousand articles and essays but never described himself as a writer. He always thought of himself as a businessman, and he said he admired the person who could "look a payroll in the eye."[53] Frederick W. Taylor had also formed his opinions on the basis of his practical experience in the world of business. Sinclair, Lewis, Follett, Mayo, and Dewey never tried their hands at much beside thinking and writing; their knowledge of the world came primarily from books.

Those who base their estimate of our human existence on actual experience will have no difficulty in finding things about which to lament. Their own lives have taught them the lessons of obstacles, hardship, and undeserved suffering. But their lives have taught them also about the strength to overcome obstacles, discipline in the face of hardship, and patient perseverance in the midst of suffering. They have seen their share of defeat, but they have also seen some victories. Philosophers seek the logic in things, novelists look for a plot, and "social scientists" search for predictability. The person who refers to actual experience understands that these are what life always denies us. Life is good and bad, hard and easy, exciting and dull, fair and unfair, and one never knows what will happen next. The power to deal triumphantly with both the sun and rain is the power of personal character.

That is the lesson of experience, and it was the dominant message of popular American literature for most of the nineteenth century. Buoyed up by the faith that the power to see it through lay deep in their own souls, the people of the United States survived the Civil War and the depressions of 1873–77 and 1893–97. Their descendants would be less fortunate. Having come to believe that life was impossible and personal character was irrelevant, they found themselves unequal to the challenge of the 1930s, began to look around for someone to take care of them, and took the first steps toward surrendering their freedom. We turn now to tell that story.

Chapter 8

THE GREAT DESCENT

I am the proud father of four exceptionally fine children, two boys and two girls. When it came time to tell the boys the facts of life, I dutifully shouldered the responsibility. Six-year-old Paul accepted the training with good-humored resignation. When his turn came two years later, six-year-old Ben was horrified. "But Dad," he protested, wide-eyed, "you don't HAVE to do that when you get married, do you?"

Having assured Ben that it was not as awful as it sounded, I believed I had done my share and it was now up to my wife to inform our daughters about the way of a man with a maid. I did, however, take it upon myself to teach the girls the fundamental principle of relations between the sexes. Amy and then Alaina, each in her turn, learned to repeat the words on cue: "Boys are dirt."

For as long as they were little, the girls had no difficulty in seeing the truth in this statement. Their every experience with boys at school and their brothers at home served to reinforce it. As they grew older, though, they seemed to be forgetting this vital lesson, and it became necessary to expand. "Boys are dirt—they only want ONE THING and they will say ANYTHING to get it."

It is assumed that the reader already knows about the ONE THING boys want. As an example of the ANYTHING they will say in order to get it, consider Arthur's bragging to Guinevere at the time of their first meeting in the musical *Camelot*. He tells her that laws have been passed (presumably under his wise leadership) against the extremes both of summer's heat and winter's snow. Winter, furthermore, cannot begin until December, and it has to end no later than the first of March. There are legal prohibitions against rain during the hours of daylight, he boasts, and the morning fog has to be gone by eight. All in all, his laws have created a wonderful place, and he is certain she will enjoy it.[1]

How could she help but be impressed?

But in making his excessive claims, Arthur was displaying more than just the traits of an amorous male. He was displaying also the traits of a politician. Nothing is more common among politicians than their professed faith in the power of law, legislation, and regulation to do things for which law, legislation and regulation are entirely unsuited. Arthur seems either (a) to have believed that laws really could control the weather or (b) to have hoped at least that Guinevere would believe it.

Between the Middle Ages and the beginning of the campaign against global warming, politicians gave up the claim that they could use laws to create a favorable climate. Early in the twentieth century, though, they began to claim they could use laws to create material prosperity. Late in the 1920s they began to preach it and to run on platforms that promised it. Whether they actually believed any of this remains in doubt. What is absolutely certain is that they hoped the voters would believe it.

It is sad to say that many voters did. They elected leaders who claimed the power to do for them what they should have known they could do only for themselves. And in choosing such leaders, they took the first steps toward surrendering control over their own lives.

The Great Depression

It is improbable that anyone will ever be able to explain to everyone's satisfaction everything about the Great Depression. Of all the explanations, however, the least satisfactory is that it was somehow the result of the stock market crash of 1929. The only notable economic historian who ever took this explanation seriously was John Kenneth Galbraith, who liked it primarily because it fit so well with his socialistic inclination to blame the wealthy for the problems of everyone else. The more common view is exemplified in the opinion of Robert Heilbroner, who said that both the Great Crash and the Great Depression were manifestations of the same underlying problems.[2]

If that is true, however, the primary underlying problems were those growing out of Washington's new powers for, and its new insistence upon, manipulating the economy. By the middle of the 1920s the Progressives were seeing their dreams come true. The federal government had begun at last upon a program of social engineering…and the first thing the new engineer did was run the train off the tracks.

It began with the creation of something without which no advanced society can survive, namely organized crime. In 1919, by means of both a law and an amendment that made the law constitutional, it became illegal to produce, sell, or transport "intoxicating liquors." This did not, of course, reduce the consumption of alcoholic beverages. H. L. Mencken observed that there was no place in the country where someone who wanted a drink would be unable to get one. Walter Ligget noted that even in Kansas, which had already been "dry" for half a century, he could go to any town he wanted and get a drink within fifteen minutes of his arrival.[3]

This confirmed the Progressives' suspicions about personal character: if you looked deeply enough, they believed, everyone was a little dishonest. The real lesson was that moral standards are effective only as a person imposes them on himself. An attempt to impose them by law is worse than useless. That great ethical philosopher George Babbitt summed up Prohibition like this: "It's a mighty beneficial thing for the poor zob that hasn't any will-power, but for fellows like us it's an infringement of personal liberty."[4] But the "poor zob" that hadn't any willpower was as resentful of the law as anyone else. The demand for alcohol actually rose during the decade and criminals organized themselves to supply it. A study done by the Justice Department in the 1970s identified Prohibition as the starting point for virtually all of America's crime families.[5]

With this great victory under its belt, Washington turned next to the first of its many wars on poverty. Herbert Hoover's campaign promise was "A Chicken for Every Pot" and "Wages, Dividends, Progress and Prosperity,"[6] and he was not about to let inevitable fluctuations in the business cycle keep him from making good on that promise.

Economic ups and downs go back at least to 1500 BC, when Joseph said the pharaoh's dreams meant that seven years of plenty were to be followed by seven years of famine. Secretary of the Treasury Andrew Mellon recognized this, and when business activity began to fall off late in 1929 he advised Hoover to leave things alone. There had been a severe downturn in 1920; the Harding administration had done nothing, unsound businesses had failed, sound businesses had survived, wages and prices had fallen to their natural level, and by the end of 1921 the twenties had begun to roar. If Hoover had taken Mellon's advice, the story of 1929 would have been similar. Instead of chapters on the Great Depression, our history texts would have a paragraph on the severe recession of 1929–31.

But his Progressive upbringing and his training as a mechanical engineer had rendered Herbert Hoover incapable of allowing things to run their natural course. In the Soviet Union, Stalin was using the skills of engineers to divert great rivers from their natural courses, and Hoover intended to do the same thing with the American economy. He began one month after the Great Crash to hold a series of conferences with industrial leaders, in which he secured their promises to maintain wages at the existing level. He cut taxes. He launched a series of public works projects, including the San Francisco Bay Bridge, the Los Angeles Aqueduct, and (of course) the Hoover Dam. His Reconstruction Finance Corporation and Agricultural Marketing Act were aimed specifically at the distribution of federal funds.[7]

Hoover's bumbling attempts at intervention made things worse, not better. His high-wage policies (real wages actually rose) in a time of economic contraction meant that there would be fewer jobs. He demanded an investigation of the stock exchanges, thus discouraging private investors. He tried to save failing businesses, thus hindering the flow of funds to more efficient enterprises and prolonging the final agonies of those that were already doomed. He weakened bankruptcy laws in order to protect insolvent debtors and thus helped ruin the banks.

The fate of the banks, in fact, is central to the story. An important part of Woodrow Wilson's Government Expansion Program had been the Federal Reserve Act of 1913. Twice in the two decades before that Washington had mismanaged America's finances so badly as to bring the nation to the verge of crisis. It never set well with the Progressives that in these times of extremity the government had been forced to ask J. P. Morgan ("the Money Trust") to set things right.[8] The Federal Reserve was designed to manage the nation's economy and in the process save politicians from the necessity of calling upon individual businessmen to bail them out.

A federal agency, alas, is only as good as the individual who is at the head of it. The Federal Reserve managed the economy without making any obvious blunders for as long as Benjamin Strong was its most influential member. With his death in 1928 there began something that is not altogether uncharacteristic of a political agency, namely a political struggle. As a result of this struggle and in an attempt to exert its influence, the Federal Reserve began to contract the money supply in 1930.[9]

The task of explaining the grisly details will be left to economists. It is enough for now to point out that if there is less money in circulation, you will have more difficulty getting your money out of the bank than you would if there were more money in circulation. Assurances from the teller that, "Oh, no, you don't need to worry; your money is quite safe; it's just that you just can't have it" do not sit well with the average depositor. A bank failure is what happens when a lot of people decide they all want their money NOW. The bank's loans may be perfectly sound and backed by adequate collateral. It may be well and honestly managed. Its collection of interest and principal payments may be right on schedule. But if it does not have enough cash on hand to pay all the depositors who want to liquidate their accounts, it will go belly-up.

This is exactly what the Federal Reserve was intended, and failed, to prevent. Banks began to collapse in the autumn of 1930. When the Bank of the United States closed its doors on December 11, it was the largest commercial bank failure in the history of the United States.[10]

By now the crisis had become severe, and in Washington there was a raging debate over what to do about it. The government would later resort to its standby cure for everything from poverty to the decline of family values: increase taxes and expand the federal bureaucracy. The first step, however, was a tax on imports, the Hawley-Smoot Tariff. The idea was to make foreign products so expensive that Americans could not afford to buy them and thus encourage the purchase of things made by citizens of the United States. Unfortunately, this also made it impossible for the people of other nations to sell their products in this country and thus earn the money with which to purchase American products and repay their debts to the United States. Other side effects included a rise in the cost of living, the encouragement of inefficient production, and the reduction of American exports, especially trade in agricultural surpluses.

Over a thousand economists petitioned Hoover not to sign this legislative masterpiece.[11] Oswald Garrison Villard, editor of the *Nation*, said nothing in the world could be more perfectly designed to make things worse. Mr. Hoover put his name to it, though, saying that, "It was undertaken as the result of pledges given by the Republican Party at Kansas City...Platform promises must not be empty gestures."[12] The political rule of thumb seems to be that campaign promises will be honored only if they will do some real damage.

Financial panic swept Europe, foreigners dumped their American securities in order to raise cash, and both the economy and the markets slid even farther. The Dow Jones Industrial Average, which had stood at 381.17 on September 3, 1929, fell to a low of 41.22 on May 26, 1932, and even that was only after the *Wall Street Journal* had replaced the eighteen worst performing stocks to hold the average up.[13]

Unemployment, which had been 1.25 million in 1929, reached twelve million by the end of 1932. Charitable organizations ran out of funds with which to help the jobless. Unable to collect rents, landlords were incapable of paying their taxes and city revenues dried up. Driven from their apartments, many families moved to vacant lots on the outskirts of town, where they would improvise dwellings out of sheet iron and packing cases.[14] Joseph Kennedy, founding father of the famous family, made millions with stock market manipulations, but his experience was a rare exception. Few profited. Many were lowered to destitution.

The Great Despair

The malign and impersonal forces in which Upton Sinclair so fervently believed had been unleashed on the American people by the farsighted planning of a wise and benevolent government. A dim awareness about the source of the problems is evident in the new vocabulary that emerged. The newspaper that an unemployed worker used to cover himself as he lay down to sleep on a park bench was a "Hoover blanket." A pocket pulled out to show it was empty was a "Hoover flag." The shantytowns that arose on empty lots were "Hoovervilles."[15]

But people were less aware of the source of their woes than they were of the Depression's implications for their faith in themselves. Prior to this, said E. Wright Baake of Yale, they had believed that a person was responsible for his or her own failure or success. They had believed in the value of individual effort and in the possibility of raising yourself by your own bootstraps. With the coming of the Great Depression, he said, this idea fell by the wayside. Some idea of the change that occurred between the beginning and the middle of the century may be taken from the fact that Baake himself, writing in 1945, referred to the older convictions as "folklore."[16] Ideas about the power of the individual, he meant, were not merely a thing of the past. They were a myth.

Baake was right about the change in thinking. His own opinions bear witness to it. But he was at least partially and perhaps even entirely mistaken about the cause and effect relationship between this change in thinking and the events of the 1930s. By the 1920s, as we observed in the previous chapter, the potential and perhaps even the existence of the independent and responsible individual was being called into question. Jurgis Rudkus is a signpost; George Babbitt is a mile marker. The stories about these men made for best-selling books because many Americans felt the stories somehow mirrored their own. They were beginning to think of themselves as persons who had no control over their own lives and as the members of a crowd rather than distinct individuals. Their long-standing faith in personal character and achievement was giving way to a desire for belonging. John Dewey's dream was coming true: Americans were beginning to think of themselves not as adults who were in charge of their own fate, but as children playing under the watchful eye of a teacher.

This transformation was far from complete on Black Thursday. Still, it is clear that the change in thinking came first. The decline in business activity, the stock market crash, and the bumbling government intervention that turned them into a depression came afterward.

It is worth considering the possibility that a people who still thought in terms of shaping their own fate by means of their own effort would have laughed at a politician foolish enough to promise "A Chicken for Every Pot." Nor would they have cried out for him to "do something" at the first sign of trouble. They would have expected him to stay out of their way, they would have asked for their neighbors' assistance, they would have given whatever help was in their power, and they would have done what they could. A few gifted minds would have come up with answers, free persons would have selected from among these answers the ones that appealed to them, and the economy would have recovered, just as it had so many times in the past.

This is not far-fetched speculation. No less a historian than Samuel Eliot Morison pointed out that the Depression of 1893 was every bit as severe as the Depression of 1929.[17] In the 1890s, though, Americans still thought in terms of taking personal responsibility for their problems, and they put an end to the Depression of 1893 in less than four years. Events followed the course they did in the 1930s because by the time of the 1929 stock market crash the age of self-reliance was already a thing of the past.

The Great Depression did not create Americans' doubts about themselves. It confirmed them. In the prosperity of the twenties they had been able to hold these doubts at bay, as George Babbitt had, with new clothes, new cars, new homes, new fads, and the illusion that they were rising ever higher in the opinions of those around them. When conspicuous consumption was no longer possible and upward mobility had become a pipe dream, their uncertainty about themselves moved from the wings to the center of the stage. People looked around them and saw that the events of their time were telling them what they already believed.

The New Orientation

Americans once thought of themselves as independent achievers; they admired and liked to read about people who did things. By now they were beginning to think of themselves as members of a crowd, and they were more inclined to read about how to get along. The self-help best-seller of the Depression years was Dale Carnegie's *How to Win Friends and Influence People*, a book that owes very little to the spirit of *Poor Richard's Almanac*. Benjamin Franklin had said that the road to success led through self-control, hard work, a clear conscience, the careful use of time, frugality, and constant improvement. Carnegie said that it led through good human relationships. Franklin had understood the importance of good human relationships; he studied them and displayed such skill that Carnegie often used him as an example. For Franklin, though, the points of emphasis were self-discipline and practical accomplishment, not interpersonal harmony.

Sinclair Lewis referred to Dale Carnegie as "the Bard of Babbittry." America in the 1930s needed heroes like John D. Rockefeller and the characters described by Horatio Alger. It studied instead the habits of George Babbitt. It needed individualism, achievement, and productivity, but it told itself that what was called for was conformity, affiliation, and consensus. Two of the decade's leading management consultants were James Mooney and Alan Reiley. In *Onward Industry!* they enjoined business leaders to alleviate human misery through "the efficient coordination of relationships."[18] An age that needed Andrew Carnegie was asking for Dale.

The affiliation-oriented personality does not venerate exceptional personalities or remarkable accomplishment. It thinks in terms of belonging and reduces everything to the lowest common denominator. Dale Carengie and management consultants like Mooney and Reiley gained an ear not because they addressed their time's most pressing needs but because they said what people were ready to believe.

This tendency is evident also in popular fiction. Nineteenth-century America had idolized the entrepreneur as an expression of achieving individualism. In the literature of the period between 1900 and 1930, the businessman was likely to be portrayed as fool or a villain, but he was still a recognizable individual. In the literature of the 1930s and 1940s he became a nonentity. Of the "owner men" he described in *The Grapes of Wrath*, John Steinbeck wrote, "All of them were caught in something greater than themselves. Some of them hated the mathematics that drove them, and some were afraid, and some worshipped the mathematics because it provided a refuge from thought and from feeling."[19] What we have here, observed William G. Scott, are not distinct or proactive personalities, but an impersonal, or better a depersonalized, "they," not individuals who do things, but debris carried in the tide.[20]

The Grapes of Wrath now belongs to the centuries. "A Cool Million" is more of a period piece. In it, Nathaniel West describes the fate of a man whose very name breathes hopelessness and despair. Lemuel Petkin sets out like a Horatio Alger hero to become a great industrialist. Beginning with a great faith in himself, he is gradually dismembered by forces beyond his control and then murdered. His friend Shagpoke Whipple later becomes the dictator of America and turns Petkin into a martyr for the cause of National Socialism because the man had believed in the spirit of capitalism and free enterprise.[21]

People read books about hopelessness and despair when they have themselves become hopeless and despairing. Books about how to fit in become best sellers only if large numbers of readers are acutely aware of their need to belong. During the 1930s, said Erich Fromm, people became more and more willing to surrender their sense of individuality and to conform to the demands of the group.[22] The strength that it took to stand alone deserted them and they gave up their right to self-determination. The need for affiliation was already beginning to replace the need for achievement when the 1930s began; fifteen or twenty years later its triumph was almost complete. The old self-confidence was disappearing. In its place there was a demand for help from the outside.

The Great Liar

This change in Americans' dominant psychological orientation was associated with a new kind of leadership. The difference between Herbert Hoover and Franklin D. Roosevelt was not that the first was a laissez faire capitalist and the second believed in government control of the economy. Hoover had a great faith in government intervention and was quick to try his hand at it. At the Depression's outset he put in motion a series of relief measures upon which, as Walter Lippmann observed at the time and Roosevelt's right-hand leftist Rex Tugwell admitted forty years later, the New Deal did no more than expand. Historian Paul Johnson has gone so far as to say that the New Deal really began not with Roosevelt, but with Hoover's Reconstruction Finance Corporation of 1931.[23]

Roosevelt had if anything less conviction than did Hoover about the value of government involvement in the economy. Roosevelt's policies are sometimes described as an application of Keynesian economics, but the plain fact is that Franklin Delano Roosevelt did not know the first thing about economics. He would have been incapable, as Allan Nevins once observed, of grasping the disciplined and mathematical logic of a man like Lord Keynes.[24] FDR was simply, as Walter Lippmann said during the 1932 presidential race, "an amiable man...who, without any important qualifications for the office, would very much like to be president."[25] The legislation he rammed through Congress during the early months of his presidency served only to make the Depression worse. If these were, as Nevins describes them, "four of the most brilliantly successful months in the history of American government,"[26] their success was limited to the government itself. Roosevelt's proposals kept Congress busy and helped create additional jobs in the halls of Washington, but it was hard on the already-strained economy. Unemployment in 1934, at 26.7 per cent, was worse than it had been in 1932.[27]

Like Hoover, Roosevelt was a bumbling interventionist; like Hoover's, his policies made things worse, not better. The difference between the two men was a difference of style, not of substance. Roosevelt was a new kind of leader for a new age in American history.

Roosevelt was, in the thinking of political scientist James McGregor Burns, the very best kind of leader, a "transformational" leader. (Three of the other great democratic figures upon whose heads Burns places this crown are Hitler, Lenin, and Mao.)[28] A leader who wants to deal with the issues is merely "transactional," and that's all right if it's the best he can do, but the truly great leaders, Burns says, deal with emotions. A transformational leader helps his followers forget about themselves as individuals and turns their minds away from their personal concerns. He calls them from the "pessimistic reveries" that concerned Elton Mayo and enables them to feel that they are a part of something greater than themselves.

A transformational leader, in short, is exactly the right kind of leader for a people among whom the need for affiliation has become the dominant psychological tendency. A person who is driven by the need for achievement is more concerned with facts than with feelings. When trouble arises, this individual wants to do something. In the same situation, the person who is high on the need for affiliation wants to be a part of something.

Transformational leadership appeals to the need for affiliation, so it is heavily dependent upon the leader's ability to create the feeling that he and his followers are joined in a spirit of camaraderie. This is an ability that the dour Hoover completely lacked. His chipper, smiling, joking successor had it in spades. Roosevelt made effective use of this ability not merely in his public presentations but also and perhaps more importantly in his famous "fireside chats." By means of the radio he was able to enter homes, where people gathered to hear their compassionate fellow traveler talk about the journey upon which they were embarked. "My friends," he began, or "My fellow Americans,"[29] and they sat transfixed. They felt they belonged: "We're all in this together."

The need for achievement turns one's mind toward the outer world. It is always searching for some*thing*. The need for affiliation turns toward persons; it is always looking for some*one*. In times of difficulty, transformational leadership needs therefore to create an awareness of enemies. There must be someone to blame. Hitler blamed the Jews.

Roosevelt blamed the American economic system, "the evils of the old order," as he described it in his inaugural address,[30] incarnate in the persons of bankers and business leaders. Hope for the future lay not in dealing with the objective facts, but in driving "the money changers from the temple."[31]

The Great Tyranny

Foremost among the said money changers was former Secretary of the Treasury Andrew Mellon, who had suggested that the best thing the government could do about the economic downturn of 1929 was keep its hands off. He was a symbol of the prosperity the United States had enjoyed during the 1920s. Through his charitable work in founding and endowing the National Gallery of Art, he was also a significant contributor to America's public culture. Roosevelt hated him and sent the IRS to drag him through the courts on charges of tax evasion. Even after a grand jury had refused to indict him, Roosevelt demanded that the government proceed with a civil case, which dragged on until Mellon's death.[32]

This example is but one of many. Roosevelt had a long list of enemies, and he sent the IRS after as many as he could. It was very much in the spirit of the times. In 1934, Matthew Josephson published *The Robber Barons*, raising once again the old myth that the great capitalists were sinister figures working behind the scenes to ruin the lives of everyone else. The nonreading public got a similar message from the programs of the "radio priest," Father Coughlin, who claimed to have thirteen million listeners; he said that the Depression had been caused by the wicked machinations of bankers.[33]

Achievement-oriented individuals of exceptional ability, the very persons whose efforts the United States most desperately needed, were regarded with suspicion and contempt. There was a widespread feeling that, far from setting them free to express their talents, arrangements should be made to rein them in. Capitalists who disagreed with the government's plans, wrote Henry Harriman, "would be treated like any maverick…roped and branded and made to run with the herd."[34]

The words give almost perfect expression to the political sentiments of the affiliation-oriented personality. It seeks the safety rather of numbers than of actual solutions, and it fears originality because originality always disturbs the comfortable consensus. It does not see that in denying freedom to the creative individual it is denying itself the salvation that might come with a new approach. It does not see that if one person's freedom can be legally restricted, no one's freedom is safe.

The evidence was all around, if anyone had cared to look. The New Deal was an experiment in social engineering, and the only available models of social engineering were those of the totalitarian regimes. In 1934, Roosevelt's National Planning Board studied the examples of Japan, Italy, Russia, and Germany. The last of these, as Reinhold Niebuhr wrote in his widely read *Moral Man and Immoral Society* (first published in 1933), was regarded as the country "where all the social and political forces of modern civilization have reached their most advanced form."[35] When Mussolini said that Italy's restrictions on individual freedom were the inevitable consequence of the advanced stage its civilization had assumed, many Americans nodded their heads in agreement. Franklin Roosevelt believed to his dying day that the Soviet Union was truly a "people's democracy," that Joseph Stalin was a peace-loving democrat, and that anyone opposed to communism was a paranoid reactionary.[36] (Eleanor Roosevelt would later visit the labor camp where Alexander Solzhenitsyn was imprisoned and describe it as a humane institution for the rehabilitation of criminals.)[37] What had "worked" in the European dictatorships ought also to be tried in America.

"There is just one thing to do," said Roosevelt's photogenic Stalinist Rex Tugwell. "Take incomes from where they are…and place them where they need to be."[38] His choice of words is revealing. He did not say anything about the redistribution of existing wealth. That was the last thing in which the Roosevelt administration had any interest. The Roosevelts were old money. The family had been rich and prestigious for so long that no one even thought about where the money had come from. Roosevelt said he wanted "fifteen or twenty youthful Abraham Lincolns from Manhattan and the Bronx"[39] to assist in implementing the New Deal, but the fact is that virtually none of those who worked for him came from poor families. Alumni of Harvard, Yale, Princeton, and other Ivy League law schools, they were predictably biased against taking from those who were already rich and giving to the poor. Their fine phrases notwithstanding, what they really wanted to do was hinder the rise of achieving individuals who might become part of the *nouveaux riches*. It was not wealth but the creation of wealth that they regarded as shameful.

This takes us back again to ancient Greece and to the struggle between the old propertied classes and the rising merchant class. It takes us back to the stories in which Hermes is represented as depriving Apollo of his position in society by means of treachery and clever deceit. It takes us back to Aristotle's insistence that if a man could not be taught to refrain from accumulating additional wealth, he should be forcibly restrained from doing so. It takes us back, in short, to the eternal desire of those who are at the top of the social structure to retain what they regard as their rightful place as the arbiters of society.

The one point at which the new regime took deliberate action to deprive the wealthy also tells us much. There had been an inflationary scare in the 1890s, and since that time bond indentures had come to stipulate that creditors could demand payment in dollars of the same gold weight as they had lent. In 1934 the currency was devalued and these gold clauses were declared null and void. Debtors' burdens were thus relieved and creditors' assets were diminished by act of Congress. Bondholders crowded the courts, claiming that that this amounted to the legalization of theft. In *Norman* v. *B.&O. Railroad Co.* (1935), the Supreme Court ruled that the government's sovereign power to define and redefine the value of its money took precedence over contracts between individuals.

"The guarantees heretofore supposed to protect against arbitrary action," said dissenting Justice McReynolds, "have been swept away."[40] Justice McReynolds saw better than the court majority the implications of their decision. If the court could make arbitrary choices about which contracts were binding and which were not, the rule of law in America was on its way to being a memory. The Constitution, which had been designed to free individuals from uncertainty about the behavior of the government, was no longer the supreme law of the land.

In its place would be the fluctuating intentions of politicians who wanted to reshape America according to what they perceived to be the demands of the moment. One of the intellectuals who assisted Roosevelt was Raymond Moley, who said that although future historians might be able to discern some guiding principle in FDR's policies, he could not.[41] Roosevelt himself said that his programs were like the decisions of a quarterback who "called a new play when he saw how the last one turned out."[42] The adoring Allan Nevins, looking down from the high clouds of academia, regarded this approach as highly virtuous. He did not understand that if nothing is predictable, if neither the law nor even the ruler's will can be relied upon, individuals will not make the long-term commitments necessary for economic progress.

But the new regime took no thought for the importance of individuals. It saw prosperity as something that the government conferred upon people rather than something they created for themselves. It did not see rights as the unoffending citizen's freedom to be left alone. It saw them instead as something to be conferred by the power of the state. These assumptions remained implicit until Roosevelt's State of the Union Address of January 1944, in which he specifically outlined a new bill of "self evident" economic rights. Among these were the right to a well-paying job, "adequate food, clothing, and recreation," medical care, retirement income, and protection from the dangers of unemployment.[43]

The authors of the Constitution had aimed to set individuals free to pursue not merely these things but anything else that appealed to them. Understanding the wide variety of human aspiration, they would never have suggested anything so narrow as a promise of economic security, which could be offered only by requiring one citizen to pay for the upkeep of another. Set people free, they believed, leave them alone, and they will take care of themselves and everything else as well.

But ideas like that were going out of style. Gunnar Myrdall's report to the Carnegie Foundation was published in 1944 as *An American Dilemma*. Myrdall was a Swedish socialist, and his book was directed superficially at the problem of race discrimination in America. It was at a deeper level an attack on the inadequacies of democratic government. Legally elected representatives, Myrdall said, could not be relied upon to create a truly "just" society because they were beholden to the voters. Judges, who were wiser than the electorate, needed to step in and correct the failures of Congress. This was in perfect accord with the emerging school of "legal realism," which argued that sociological approaches to the law should take precedence over the "original intent" not merely of specific statutes but even of the Constitution.[44] Judges were an enlightened elite, and they should make decisions on behalf of the ignorant masses, who obviously could not be trusted to make choices for themselves.

By the end of 1920s, as we have already seen, Americans were beginning to see themselves not as independent and responsible adults, but as children playing in the schoolyard under the watchful eye of a teacher. By the middle of the 1940s their government was prepared to treat them that way.

The Great War

It was not the New Deal but the Second World War that restored health to the American economy. The stock market, which had begun its slide on September 3, 1929, began to revive exactly ten years later on news of events in Europe. American industry was soon busy with supplying arms and matériel to the combatants, and employment soared.

The Second World War also opened the door to social engineering on a scale that would have been unimaginable in peacetime. It was a more believable crusade than the attack on the institutions of capitalism, more effective in eliminating Americans' traditional tendency to think and act like individuals, and more useful in establishing once and for all the mechanisms of a powerful and intrusive government.

This is not the place to take up the debate about whether Roosevelt wanted to involve America in the war or could have done anything to prevent it. A few things are clear. For one, the New Deal was dead in the water by 1938. The economy had not recovered. The Supreme Court had heard nine cases on New Deal legislation and had found in seven of them that the laws were unconstitutional. In response, Roosevelt had tried unsuccessfully to "pack" the court with the addition of justices who were ready to do his will. Finally, he had been unsuccessful in his attempts to get an income tax that would "soak" the wealthy. As long as the nation remained at peace, the executive branch of the government had neither the authority nor the legislative backing it needed to impose sweeping changes on American society.

It has become popular in recent years, if not to argue at least to imply, that the United States' involvement in World War II was the result of a widespread desire to stop the Holocaust. This would be wonderful if it were true. Unfortunately, it is not. If America had cared about the plight of Hitler's victims, the ready solution would have been to allow them to immigrate. The results of German antipathy toward the Jews, though less horrendous than they would later become, were already in the news by the middle 1930s, but Jewish applications for immigration visas were denied by the millions. Even after there were Allied armies in Europe, Roosevelt was unwilling to divert military resources to prevent the horrors that field commanders were frequently reporting. If there was anything that stimulated American desire to get involved in the war, other than Pearl Harbor, it was the newsreel reporting of Edward R. Murrow from the streets of London during the blitz, not the needs of the Jews.

The United States, some tentative steps like Lend-Lease notwithstanding, never volunteered for World War II. Once it had been drafted, though, first by the attack on Pearl Harbor and a few days later by the German declaration of war, the Roosevelt administration moved swiftly to impose a program of widespread social control. FDR finally got a revenue bill he liked, with provisions for a tax rate as high as 90 percent on personal incomes and an "excess profits" tax on businesses. By 1943 government agencies were telling Americans how far they could drive and what they could manufacture. Laws spelled out their rights to change jobs, raise rents, eat beef, and stay on the streets at night. Federal bureaucracies built housing and tore it down, created new companies, and withheld truck tires from firms that hauled such objectionable items as booze, cigarettes, and Orange Crush. In Oklahoma, which remained a "dry" state even after the end of Prohibition, the Office of Price Administration required speakeasies to post ceiling prices on bootleg whiskey.

Two elements of the new intrusiveness were particularly ominous. First, Congress turned every employer into a tax collector. The tax rate increases of 1942 raised the question of how many Americans would be willing to file tax returns in 1943. Beardsley Ruml of the Federal Reserve suggested that henceforward businesses could withhold a portion of each employee's wages and send the money to Washington. That way workers would not develop the unfortunate habit of thinking the money they had earned was their own. The new plan was sold to the public by offering tax amnesty for the previous year. The war was a national crisis, and although there were some protests, most Americans consented to the new system.[45] It worked so well that fifty-five years later their children and grandchildren and great grandchildren would accept it unthinkingly, and if by chance they owed no additional taxes on April 15, they would say, "Well, I didn't have to pay anything this year." They were in fact paying at rates high enough to finance a war.

The other ominous thing was the appearance of regulatory lobbyists and professional regulators. These were first seen in connection with the Office of Price Administration's attempts to police the economy. With more people working but fewer consumer products available during the war, inflationary pressures were strong. Rather than allowing prices to rise to market-clearing levels and thus encourage careful spending, Washington instituted a system of rationing. The inevitable results were shortages and the appearance of black markets. Prices were of course much higher in the black markets, and people resorted to them only when there was no other way to get things like cigarettes, butter, or silk hosiery. It was not unlike shopping at Saks Fifth Avenue because you have found that Wal-Mart doesn't carry the item you need. Everybody did it once in a while. Nobody thought much of it.

Well, not quite nobody. The one element that took wartime regulations seriously consisted of those who were employed in writing the regulations and in lobbying for regulations or exceptions to regulations. After the last shot of the war had been fired and the last soldier had come home, these regulators and lobbyists remained. Now part of the alphabet soup of government agencies, they began to weave the detailed, complex, and contradictory spider's web of codes that would still be interfering with life in the United States at the dawn of the twenty-first century.

The Great Tragedy

The new world in which Americans would now have to live had important implications for personal character. Before the war, people had regarded the incomes they generated by means of their own thought and effort as their own, and out of these incomes they paid such taxes as they might rightfully owe. After 1943 the first claims on their incomes would be those of the federal government. The relationship between work and income, between cause and effect, began to disappear. It was not simply that chance might step in and prevent one from enjoying the rewards of one's labor. The effects were now systematic. The results of one's efforts were not one's own. They belonged first to the political authority, and out of its surplus that authority would allot the individual such resources as it deemed appropriate. The feedback loop essential to the need for achievement was being cut.

The new method of collection had appeared because the political authority did not believe citizens could be trusted to pay their taxes. This distrust was evident also in the new and rapidly expanding body of regulatory law. The older faith had been that people could be relied upon to look after themselves, and that the courts were available if one person's exercise of freedom interfered with the freedoms of another. The new assumption was that people needed to be told what they could and couldn't do. In fact, they even needed to be told what to do. The old faith had been that people were responsible adults. The new conviction was that they were disobedient or perhaps even deviant children, who needed constant attention.

We have already noted F. A. Hayek's observation that the most important change produced by government controls is a change of character: the old spirit of independence gradually disappears; the willingness to take responsibility for one's own life falls into disuse. This chapter and the previous one have argued, conversely, that the door to government control was opened by a change in character. Still, there is an important truth in Hayek's statement. People adjust to the demands of the environment. If it gets cold, they put on coats. If it begins to rain, they take out their umbrellas. They will become in time as helpless or as untrustworthy as the social system in which they live assumes them to be. The decline of traditional American values opened the door to political change, but once it was open, once Americans began not merely to tolerate but to expect and perhaps even to demand governmental intrusions, the decline was accelerated.

At the end of the eighteenth century, the authors of the Constitution had made a bet on the character of the American citizenry. Now that bet was off. The old assumptions remained strong in the hearts of many, but a powerful countertrend had been unleashed, a trend that would in time create a culture opposed to almost all of the Founding Fathers' most heartfelt beliefs. That new culture is the subject of the next two chapters.

Chapter 9

THE LITERATURE OF CRISIS

Consider a recent and insidious threat to public safety: road rage. According to an article in the *Los Angeles Times*, it was "an exploding phenomenon across the country." Much later in the article, however, one discovered that the number of deaths actually attributable to angry drivers during the years from 1993 to 1998 came to the staggering total of five.[1] That's one a year. In other words, if you are looking for an interesting way to get killed, don't bet on this particular "exploding phenomenon." You have a better chance of being struck by lightning.

But here's the cool thing about road rage. It creates an opportunity for political outcry. Road rage, unlike lightning, is something we can "fix." We can pass laws against it, and we can hire policemen to enforce the new laws. Perhaps we could set up a sliding scale of penalties, requiring officers to issue a $100 ticket to the driver who is mildly irritated, a $200 ticket to the driver who is angry, a $500 ticket to the driver who is furious, and so on. Never mind that the laws we already have against drunk driving, which kills far more people than road rage (or "guns," for that matter), are poorly enforced. We can handle this one. Just pass the laws. Hire the cops. Nip it in the bud. Make America a safe place to live. And Mr. President, Mr./Ms./Mrs. Congressperson, thank God for you and your interest in our well-being.

In the years since the Second World War the United States has become a crisis-oriented society. The cycle has been repeated countless times. It begins when someone raises public awareness about something that, with sufficient imaginative effort, can be seen as boding ill for the future. Interest groups coalesce around the "crisis," some politician arises with a "vision" that can be realized by passing a law and creating a bureaucracy to administer it, and the public submits because of widespread ballyhoo about the danger. The issue itself is never resolved, but it becomes familiar and uninteresting, and soon public consciousness-raisers call us to something else that demands "immediate attention."

The cycle was first seen with the outcry following the publication of *The Jungle* and the creation of that wonder of regulatory efficiency, the Food and Drug Administration. It occurred again in the aftermath of the stock market crash of 1929. In the years since World War II, it has become the mainstay of popular culture and political life. In this chapter we will look at how the crisis mentality has evolved. In the next we will consider its relationship to the decline of character and the disappearance of personal freedom in America.

Growing Up Absurd

First published in 1960, Paul Goodman's *Growing Up Absurd* described American culture as a soul-destroying wasteland, conformity to which left its youth "apathetic, cynical, and wasted."[2] This dark portrait, observes Roger Kimball, does not square up with the reality. The 1950s, he says, were in fact a time of confident prosperity, and they offered Americans the greatest economic, social, and intellectual freedom they had ever enjoyed.[3]

Kimball is undoubtedly correct about the prosperity. He may be incorrect about the confidence. In the years between the end of the Second World War and the beginning of the 1960s, Americans came to see their world as very much the kind of place Goodman said it was. They learned somehow to see themselves as "trapped" in easy, well-paying jobs and a comfortable lifestyle.

Consider the sad case of Tom Rath, the protagonist (not the "hero") of *The Man in the Gray Flannel Suit,* which was made into a movie starring Gregory Peck.[4] He wants only two things, enough (but not "too much") money and security. To get them, he compromises and conforms as necessary. His only notable virtue is his devotion to his family, which stands in sharp contrast to his boss's primary vice, his devotion to his business. Rath performed well, almost bravely, as a young officer during the war but now has settled into a comfortable rut and has no interest in the new or unknown. He just wants to fit in, and he hopes his world will remain as it is.

Consider, again, the life of Charley Gray in *Point of No Return.*[5] He is held captive by family responsibilities and obligations under a variety of monthly payment plans. Thinking about the possibility of being promoted to a new position, he begins to question the value of it all, but this upsets his wife. The promotion, when it comes, turns out to be no more than an opportunity to conform at a higher level. Charley is unlike Tom Rath in that he is smart enough to know he is trapped and to be unhappy about it, but he is still trapped. He has arrived, as suggested by the title, at the point of no return.

The central characters of this literature are nothing like the heroes of a Horatio Alger novel or even the more modest figures in the *McGuffey's Reader.* They have neither the desire nor the opportunity for anything daring, no daunting obstacles to overcome, not even an occasion for the display of notable virtues. They are dependent employees rather than independent achievers, and their "heroism" amounts to nothing greater than a willingness to conform and toleration for grinding mediocrity. In a 1957 article in the *Saturday Evening Post,* Howard Upton tried to put a good face on it, but his description was far from encouraging. "The real hero," he said, "is the fellow you see there with the briefcase, waiting to catch the night plane to Houston to see what he can do about sacking up that big double-threaded pipe order."[6]

Ideas of this kind do not become popular because people see themselves as set out on a quest for great victories. They become popular, upon the contrary, because large numbers of readers (and moviegoers) see something of themselves in the stories. In the midst of the widest abundance the world had ever seen, with a range of opportunities their ancestors could not have imagined, Americans had somehow contrived to see themselves as trapped and dependent. "Once people liked to think, at least, that they were in control of their destinies," wrote William H. Whyte Jr. in 1956, "but few of the younger organizational people cherish such notions. Most see themselves as objects more acted upon than acting—and their future, therefore, determined as much by the system as by themselves."[7] They had come to think of their security as depending almost entirely on factors other than their own thinking and behavior, and so of course they were ill at ease.

Continual news about one form or another of world "crisis" played to and accentuated this sense of insecurity. The Roosevelt administration had never paid much attention to warnings about the extent of Communist activity within the American government. The Truman administration was more vigilant, but it was taken by surprise when Senator McCarthy announced that he had a list of 205 Communist Party members at work in the upper echelons of the State Department. McCarthy did not know the first thing about the issues he raised; he was interested in nothing higher than his own political career. But the press loved it, and news of the McCarthy hearings filled the headlines. Books like Elizabeth Dilling's *Red Network* and Richard Whitney's *Reds in America* enjoyed a wide popularity.[8]

In this case the danger was real, even if the 205-name list was bogus. The next crisis was the product entirely of media hype and political opportunism. Beginning in the early 1950s, there was news of a "jet bomber gap." The Russians, it was said, had more jet bombers than we did and were preparing to bomb us back to the Stone Age. Schools showed movies about what to do in the event of a nuclear attack and conducted drills. I remember my mother setting up an air raid shelter in one room of our basement. The Civil Air Patrol had a Ground Observers Corps, whose duty it was to keep an eye out for enemy planes; members received a manual of photographs and silhouettes of military aircraft. No one bothered to mention that if there were an attack, enemy bombers would be flying at altitudes of over thirty-five thousand feet and could barely be seen, much less identified, with the binoculars available to a ground observer.

In fact, the only crisis was the one that had been generated in the public mind. As the 1950s began, the United States was at least four years ahead of the Soviet Union in its bomber technology, and at the height of the "bomber gap" had several times as many jet bombers.

At the end of the decade, John F. Kennedy played to public fears with another fabrication of the same kind: the missile gap. He said the Eisenhower administration had allowed the Russians to get ahead of America in the number of their intercontinental ballistic missiles. This was a lie, and he knew it. Asked about the issue after he had been elected, Kennedy laughed and asked, "Who ever believed in the missile gap anyway?"[9]

The fact that he knew it was a falsehood did not keep him from appealing to Americans' uneasiness about our military preparedness. In 1961 he published a *Life* magazine article in which he urged families to build backyard fallout shelters and provided do-it-yourself plans for their construction.[10] By 1970 the danger was real because politicians had been too busy with the creation of a welfare state to deal with it. Kennedy's article, though, at the time he wrote it, was merely an attempt to arouse public anxiety.

But the press was thrilled to have something about which Americans liked to hear, and the press loved Kennedy, and media moguls loved the love affair because crisis sold advertising. People who think of security in terms of factors external to their own thinking and acting want to know about every possible threat to the sources of that security. Next to "information" about a "crisis" that would spell an end to their way of life, Americans found a full-color pitch for the latest trend in consumer products. Next to news about the bomber and missile crises one generation would find ads for the new, filtered Camel cigarettes and the Chevrolet 409. Next to news about the crises of teenage smoking and global warming because of engine emissions, later generations found advertising for cholesterol-laden junk food and condoms. Juxtaposed to the advertising of the future they will probably find news about the crises of obesity, heart attacks, and the spread of venereal diseases against which condoms are useless.

There was nothing original in *Growing Up Absurd*. It was, as Roger Kimball has observed, no more than a clever recycling of received wisdom. But the book's title points to important facts about the American mind at the end of the 1950s. It is absurd that the members of the most successful society in history had arrived at adulthood believing they had a right to complain about the small disciplines associated with their easy jobs and comfortable style of living. It is absurd that the citizens of the most secure nation on the planet had grown to believe they had to live in constant fear. And it is absurd that they would buy and read in large numbers a book telling them their young people were being stifled by the greatest abundance and the widest range of opportunities the world had ever seen. They enjoyed the world's highest standard of living, and they thought of it as oppressive.

Still, the old values seemed to hang in the back of their minds. The popularity of books by authors like Norman Vincent Peale attests to some awareness of the connection between goals, self-discipline, individual accomplishment, and the good life. But the elements of the achievement cycle were no longer seen as tightly linked. Submerged in the depths of large organizations, surrounded by the cushions of company benefit plans, and calmed by the guarantees of the emerging welfare state, Americans were becoming less inclined to see the relationship between their own effort and their own lives. They were becoming less inclined to think in terms of achievement and more inclined to think in terms of belonging. They were beginning to believe in a magic that would provide them with whatever they needed and to live in fearful resentment of anything that might break the spell.

The Greening of America

Robert Bork assigns the weight of the responsibility for the cultural revolution of the sixties to the pampered generation that came of age (one hesitates to say "arrived at adulthood") during that decade.[11] He may be correct in doing so. Still, one does well to remember that the apple rarely falls far from the tree. Already in the thinking of the 1950s there was a disconnect between effort and achievement. The belief that one was entitled to a life without challenges, difficulty, or personal responsibility was something that the youth of the sixties had learned at mother's knee. It is not surprising that they were unhappy when they learned that they had been lied to.

Americans' problem with the war in Vietnam was never, as Jane Fonda and her ilk would scream, that it was immoral; the agonies of the Vietnamese after America left them to their fate showed that the worst suspicions about Communist intentions were more than justified.[12] The real source of the war's unpopularity lay in its suggestion of obligations associated with the privilege of living in America. Protestors wanted to deny that there was a price attached to the advantages they enjoyed as citizens of the United States. The Johnson administration encouraged this belief with its half-hearted conduct of the war and its wholehearted efforts to expand the range of benefits Americans could expect to receive from the government without having to pay for them.

One of those who professed outrage at American policy in Vietnam was Susan Sontag. The war gave her an opportunity to specifically condemn both the values associated with the achievement motive and the blessings these values had conferred upon the world. She said that the West's industrial, cultural, and political accomplishments were insufficient to make up for its crimes. (She failed to include in this list of evils the freedom of speech that allowed her to run her mouth without fear of reprisal.) She said that America's wealth should in justice be taken away from it. (She graciously consented, though, to delay the day of reckoning until after she had claimed some of that wealth—in the form of numerous grants and awards—for herself.) The great problem with capitalism, she said, was its failure to "satisfy the appetite for exalted, self-transcending modes of concentration and seriousness."[13]

The poor dear. She didn't realize that opportunities for "exalted, self-transcending modes of concentration and seriousness" have been offered by very few of history's societies or economic systems. "Very few" as in "none." The United States and the capitalism about which she complained came closer than most. But the real source of Ms. Sontag's unhappiness was not America or capitalism. What she didn't like was reality. What she didn't like was the fact that even after the comforts and the freedom conferred by American industry and American values, the world remained a hard place in which to live. She was protesting, not against the war in Vietnam, but against life's inevitable difficulties, discomforts, and delays. She seems to have believed that life ought to be easy. When she discovered that it wasn't, she raised her voice in righteous indignation.

A glimpse of her magical thinking is evident in her claim that no writer in Castro's Cuba had been put into jail or was even failing to get his work published.[14] A world without rejection slips: the perfect world of every writer's fondest dreams! That's all the sixties protestors were asking for: the perfect world of their fondest dreams. Lauding the spirit of the decade, Duke University's Professor Jameson wrote of the "widely shared feeling" that "everything was possible,"[15] the feeling, in other words, that the world really was as you felt it "ought" to be, the feeling of freedom from the constraints of space, time, and limited resources. It was the feeling of being free from the hard necessity of difficult choices. There was no need to set priorities, no need for patience, no need to delay present gratification for the sake of long-term goals.

The disciplines and sacrifices and choices associated with personal achievement were seen as unnecessary or even irrelevant. All you had to do to get what you wanted was ask. Or more precisely, demand. "Satisfy our demands," said Jerry Rubin, "and we've got twelve more. The more you satisfy, the more we've got."[16] This is the attitude of a badly spoiled child. It is the feeling that a tantrum is the most efficient means to one's ends. The vision of John Dewey was becoming a reality. A generation of Americans had come to think of themselves as children playing in the school yard under the kind observation of a benevolent supervisor. Dewey hadn't realized, though, that they would throw rocks at the teacher when she tried to call them in from recess.

Religion and those who took their religion seriously were not much in favor among the mouthpieces of an age that believed there was no need to face up to the difficulties of personal life. Such persons were not interested in the solace of religion because they lived in a world of their own creation and in the expectation of a utopian future. They had no patience with the disciplines of religion because they thought only in terms of momentary pleasures. They bitterly resented the ideas of Christians who took God seriously, affirmed His right to make demands upon us, and believed His will could be found in the pages of the Bible. Sixties radicals agreed with the sentiments of the Beat Generation's William Burroughs, who described Christianity as "the worst disaster that ever occurred on a disaster-prone planet." Devout Christians, he said, were "a menace."[17]

The atheism, hedonism, and impatience of the sixties were summarized in Charles Reich's *The Greening of America.* The book is important primarily because of the role its author played (as we shall see in the next chapter) in the process that caused the decade's magical thinking to move into the mainstream of American political conviction. Reich himself was pitiable. An attorney and later a professor of law at Yale, he was externally successful but inwardly tortured. The sources of his worries changed constantly, he said, but he never had a moment without fear. He worried about his work, his clothes, criticism from his partners, flying, and hotels, but mostly about "the discovery and exposure of my secrets."[18] He reached the age of 43 before having sex, and then it was with a thirty-five-dollar prostitute, who was a man.

All in all, he was not the sort of person we would hope to find the country looking to for intellectual leadership, but *The Greening of America* was an immediate success, a best seller, and the object of critics' adulation. Among its many deep truths: life and work are pointless; every choice is the right one; tests are a form of violence; each of us should build his own philosophy from scratch; the concepts of individual excellence and comparative merit are outmoded; bellbottoms are a rejection of competition and authority.

Reich recognized that there would be many who would not accept these truths. Such persons, he said, were Consciousness I types, small businessmen, for example, and farmers. But Consciousness II types were just as bad, maybe worse. They had been open to the New Deal revelation that government should assume responsibility for the life of the citizen but were unable to move to the next level of political thought because of their insistence upon rationality. What the world needed, he said, and was then emerging, was Consciousness III, "a new way of living—a new man."[19] Consciousness III rejected logic, time, schedules, authority, power, status, and tradition (but apparently not sexism, as is evident in Reich's use of the summary term "man" rather than the politically correct "man and/or woman").

What Reich rejected was everything associated with achievement motivation; what he embraced was everything associated with the need for affiliation. Everyone is equally excellent, each in his or her own way, and that without the slightest personal exertion, so there is no need for effort. Work is meaningless. Experience is irrelevant. Schedules are oppressive. Self-control is obsolete. Rational thought is evil. In the place of those who had paid homage to such obsolete notions, he said, was appearing a generation that thought only of "closer, warmer, more open, more sensitive" relationships.[20]

Reich's book was popular because there were many who wanted to believe it. This is not to say that everyone bought into his vision. Even among the rising generation there were large numbers, perhaps even a majority, who still believed in self-control, effort, and purposeful living. But in the sixties and seventies they kept their opinions to themselves. They worked hard, went to church, saluted the flag, served in the military, started families, and made plans for the future. They recognized the insanity around them for what it was and waited for the mood to change: "This, too, shall pass."

The Endless Crisis

Unfortunately, it didn't.

The mind of the 1960s lived on to infect the rest of the century and the beginning of the next. There was a brief respite in the eighties. With the Reagan administration, there was a return to traditional values, traditional faith in the power of personal character, traditional distrust of big government. Americans reaffirmed their faith in individual creativity and enterprise by making best sellers of books like *Wealth and Poverty* and *In Search of Excellence*. The success of M. Scott Peck's *The Road Less Traveled* testified to the existence of a public that still believed in the value of self-restraint, hard work, and purposeful living. Patriotism came back into fashion. And for just a little while it looked like the United States might be back on course.

But ideas have a gestation period. It is not when they are planted but when they come to maturity that they have their real impact. Someone has observed that what you believe when you are twenty leaves a permanent stamp on your view of life. Journalists and politicians who went though their twenties in the two decades between 1960 and 1980 came into positions of recognition and authority during the 1990s and began to preach what Paul Harvey has called a "round the clock warning."

The New Crises

Ronald Reagan threatened to use America's financial and technological superiority to develop weapons so advanced that the Soviet Union could not possibly counter them. Russian leaders realized they had been beaten, gave up the arms race, and briefly relaxed their stranglehold on the lives of their people. So the military crisis was laid to rest. In its place appeared, among others, the environmental and consumer crises.

The first had been looming in the background ever since the beginning of the twentieth century, but it really got off the ground in 1962 with the publication of Rachel Carson's *Silent Spring*. According to Ms. Carson, a 1956 article in the *Journal of Agriculture and Food Chemistry* showed that birds exposed to DDT produced fewer offspring. In fact, the article had found virtually no difference between birds that had been exposed to DDT and those that had not. The only exceptions were pheasants, and in their case the birds exposed to DDT produced *more* offspring than did the control group. Later suggestions that DDT caused cancer in human beings were also shown to be bogus. Opposed to such false claims were the certainties that DDT made American farms the most productive in the world and that it had eradicated malaria in places where the disease had once been a scourge.[21]

But environmentalists didn't care about the facts. They wanted to be done with DDT, and in 1972 American politicians obliged them. William Ruckelshaus had said in 1970 that there was no evidence for the harmful effect of DDT on either humans or birds, but as head of the EPA in 1972 he banned the use of DDT.[22] This turns out to have been good for another "crisis," namely overpopulation, because without DDT large numbers of Third World children die from malaria.

The consumer crisis began with the publication of Ralph Nader's *Unsafe at Any Speed*, which "proved" that the rear-engine Chevrolet Corvair was dangerous. No one stopped to point out that it would hardly be in General Motors' best interest to produce a car specifically designed to kill its customers. Mr. Nader's book said it had, and that was good enough for most readers. Later research showed that the little car was as safe as any other car its size and a good deal safer than its nearest competition, the rear-engine Volkswagen Beetle, about which Mr. Nader had (mercifully) failed to write a book.

The Corvair was admittedly less safe than the huge gas guzzlers of the 1950s and 1960s, which were essentially four-wheel Sherman tanks with tail fins. But Mr. Nader didn't like those either. The Corvair was not in fact much of a danger to anyone, least of all its passengers. By the time that was shown, however, the crisis had been forgotten, the car had gone out of production, and a "consumer protection" lobby had entrenched itself in Washington, where it now generates a never-ending list of new consumer safety crises.

The oil crisis of the seventies was the result as much of bungling federal market interventions as of anything OPEC did, but it was a made-in-heaven opportunity for dire predictions. The Carter administration issued a highly publicized *Global 2000 Report*, which predicted that by the year 2000 the dangers of overpopulation, pollution, and diminishing resources would finally overtake us. The only hope, according to yet another government study, was more action by the government.

That study came in the midst of a recession, and there were many who believed it. Fortunately there were even more who believed Ronald Reagan, who said a recession was evident in the fact that your neighbor had lost his job, a depression in the fact that you had lost yours, and a recovery in the fact that Jimmy Carter had lost his. Mr. Reagan was elected, markets were allowed to operate, people began to conserve, oil prices fell, and the energy crisis died down.

And as far as the year of doom is concerned, 2000 seems to have

come and gone without much comment. In response to the widely publicized Y2K crisis and being my mother's son (remember the air raid
shelter), I got stocked up. The fact that nothing happened was a big
letdown. I had eaten most of my food reserves by the end of February,
but I still have eight gallons of bottled water in the pantry. You can't be
too careful.

There remains the looming threat of global warming. In a way I
ought to feel relieved. When I was a teenager the great fear was global
cooling. (I am hoping that the two ominous trends will cancel each other
out.) Global cooling was a "serious concern" for quite some time. As
recently as the mid-seventies, Robert J. Ringer could tease about it (he
called it the "iceball theory") as an example of an uncontrollable trend
about which it did not do the slightest good to fret.[23] But global cooling
has passed into memory and perhaps even out of it, and today the "serious concern" is global warming. In 1997 world leaders, apparently
motivated by memories of King Arthur's promises for climatological
perfection in Camelot, met in Kyoto to sign a treaty that would prevent it.

It seemed not to bother them that global warming (if there really is
such a thing) is a trend that has nothing to do with human behavior.
Arthur and Zachary Robinson, chemists at the Oregon Institute of Science and Medicine, say that in the last three thousand years there have
been at least five extended periods when it was warmer than it was at
the end of the twentieth century. An extremely cold period, to which
scientists refer as the Little Ice Age, came to an end about three hundred years ago, and temperatures have been rising ever since (except,
one assumes, during the period of "serious concern" about global cooling). None of this has anything to do with the carbon dioxide emissions
against which the Kyoto treaty was supposed to "protect" us. It is the
result of cycles on the surface of the sun.[24] According to the University
of London's Philip Scott, "The idea that we can control a chaotic climate governed by a billion factors through fiddling about with a couple
of politically selected gasses is carbon claptrap."[25]

But never mind reality. What Gregg Easterbrook has described as
"the politics of instant doomsday" demands a crisis. Having completely
failed to deal with any of the problems for which they have promised

solutions, politicians need something additional about which they can pass laws, and so they look for crises. As the twentieth century came to an end, people were living longer and healthier lives than at any other time in history, abundance was more widespread, and by every objective standard the future seemed bright with promise. In the midst of this good fortune, said Paul Harvey, politicians have nothing better to do than call for "drastic remedies" for such problems as still remain.[26]

Mr. Gore has been particularly eloquent. There is a need, he said in an impassioned appeal to the environmental lobby, for "sacrifice, struggle, and a wrenching transformation of society."[27] He did not go on to say that it would be taxpayers who would have to sacrifice and struggle. All he planned to do was turn the wrench. One hopes that his defeat in the Battle of the Dimpled Chads will encourage Mr. Gore to put his toolbox back in the closet.

The Politics of Crisis

But even if he is kind enough to join it there, America's destiny will remain to a large extent in the hands of politicians who came of age during the cultural revolution of the 1960s and 1970s. Our elected leaders disagree about a great deal, but they agree in affirming the central tenets of sixties orthodoxy: there is something radically wrong with the United States; Americans are held captive by ideas that have become obsolete and cannot be trusted to deal with the issues of the times. The only hope lies in the work of farsighted politicians who, although not one of them can give any details about what the "vision" is, qualify as guides because they believe in themselves and can get people to vote for them.

This distrust of the average citizen, disrespect for traditional America, disdain for anything specific, and disregard for anything but feelings were the trademarks of student radicalism. And many of our current leaders first began to hone their political skills by doing their part for campus protest. Senator Clinton, for example, was a law student at Yale when nine members of the Black Panthers were tried for torturing and killing a black man named Alex Rackley. When two Panthers in the visitors' section were charged with contempt of court, student radicals protested that the trial was unfair. Hillary joined forces with Bill Lann Lee (who would later head the Civil Rights Division of Mr. Clinton's Justice Department) to use the legal system in supporting the Panther's cause. She seems to have been very much in sympathy with the sentiments of the Panthers' Doug Miranda, who said, "We're going to turn Yale into a police state."[28] That seems also to be what she would like to do with the United States. Perhaps her opposition to smoking is the result of the fact that burning cigarettes were among the instruments used to torture Alex Rackley.

Persons like Senator Clinton do not have much of an affinity for facts or the law. All that is important to them is feelings. Campus protestors were unhappy with events at Berkeley and Yale and Cornell and a hundred other schools, so they firebombed buildings; members of the Clinton administration were unhappy about their successors, so they looted and vandalized the White House. The common denominator is a refusal to submit one's behavior to judgment by external and objective standards. If it feels right at the moment you do it, that's enough. We are in the midst of a crisis. There is no time for thought or reflection. Just do something! We can worry about the ethics of it and the consequences at some time in the future. "Why don't we just strike tonight," asked a Jonathan Edwards College co-ed who is today about the same age as Senator Clinton, "and we'll decide tomorrow what we're striking for!"[29]

This is just what we would expect from a person in whom the need for affiliation has become the dominant motive. The central issue is not what it would be for the achievement-oriented personality. Achievement motivation inclines one to think in terms of cause and effect, obstacles and resources, problems and solutions, acts and consequences. The affiliation-oriented individual, on the other hand, is interested primarily in the feeling of being accepted by others, being a member of the group, a part of something. Ways and means are irrelevant. "Why don't we just strike tonight," that is, join together, affirm our unity, share the warm experience of mutual acceptance? That's good enough for now. The question of precisely what needs to be accomplished is one that can entertain us at some other time.

Leftist politicians appeal to the affiliation-oriented personality by asking everyone to "get involved." The facts of the matter, the issues at stake, the consequences of involvement—these are glossed over with catchphrases like Senator Clinton's famous "politics of meaning." One of my students skipped Friday classes during the fall of 2000 so that she could drive to Nashville and make phone calls on behalf of Mr. Gore. Asked about why she favored his policies, she told me it was because he wanted to "invite everyone to the table." She was irritated when I asked her what that meant and how Mr. Gore's ideas would advance such an obviously noble cause. "I'm only twenty-one," she said, "I can't know everything." Or even very much: she knew nothing about American history or the Constitution; even the year (or for that matter, the decade) in which the Declaration of Independence was signed was quite beyond her. All she could remember was that Mr. Gore said the United States was 240 years old.

She is exactly the kind of person the activist politician loves: intelligent (GPA, 4.0), attractive, and motivated. Give her a place to stand and she will move the world. Why it needs to be moved or where we're going to put it are questions that have never crossed her mind. She just wants to be involved. She is sure of three things: there is something wrong with the United States; whatever it is, it demands immediate attention; the issues at stake are far beyond the grasp of the ordinary citizen. Given these premises, there is no need to think about costs or consequences. The fine phrases with which her chosen politician describes his "vision" guarantee its viability. Never mind the sad and unintended consequences of the last great "vision." This one will work because it feels good.

The wine that the fathers drank has intoxicated the children. The radicalism of the sixties has become mainstream political orthodoxy. What once seemed sensible is now treated as extreme. Any politician who can come up with a "crisis" and a "vision" is likely to get some attention. He or she does not need to be from the lunatic fringe: Mr. Gore, obviously, is the condensed essence of dull sobriety. But people from the lunatic fringe are more likely to devise and believe in crises. So the lunatic fringe has moved to the center of American thought.

The Voice of Crisis

Not, however, without the willing assistance of the media.

Not only leftist politicians, but also many of our "intellectual leaders" (I use the term for want of a more accurate expression) are still preaching the doctrines of sixties radicalism. They, too, are convinced that our society is in the midst of a crisis, a crisis for which traditional American values offer no solution. Writing in 1998, Arthur Marwick said, "The good society which lies just around the corner can easily be attained if only we work systematically to destroy the language, the values, the culture, the ideology of bourgeois society."[30]

The appearance of the good society, in other words, depends upon the destruction of everything associated with achievement motivation. What needs to be destroyed, "the values, the culture, the ideology of bourgeois society," is precisely the ethic that arises in connection with a widespread need for achievement. Marwick calls upon us to do away with belief in the value of the individual, to stop insisting on the importance of goals, work, and deferred gratification, and to quit stressing the need for creativity, experimentation, and persistence. He calls upon us to destroy the moral foundations of material progress.

Only a few people read writers like Marwick, but many are bombarded every day with the messages of the mainstream media. Richard Lowry of The *National Review* has observed that members of the media tend to sit enchanted as they listen to the rant of leftist "intellectuals" who talk about our duty to "remold" American society. Journalists align themselves with extreme feminism and multiculturalism because, like the radicals of the 1960s and activist politicians, they have fallen for the idea that feelings are more important than facts. John Leo of *U.S. News & World Report* was hissed and booed by an audience of journalists when he talked about the need for objectivity.[31] Facts (except such unassailable truths as global warming and the need for gun control) are treated as merely subjective interpretations.

Members of the media, from whom most Americans get their opinions, are not well prepared for critical thinking or balanced consideration. I have advised students at two universities. At neither of them were journalism majors required to take so much as a single course in statistics or economics. This is important because statistics and economics are the things upon which reporters and pundits are most likely to base their wise pontifications. Yes, journalism majors have to take a course in psychology as well as a few courses in English literature and at least one in public speaking (so they'll know how to act in front the camera). But courses that would train them to speak wisely and see events in perspective, courses in history and philosophy, and especially courses in economics and statistics—here the journalism curricula are sadly lacking.

This is the training of the people who tell us about the world. It's like getting advice about your car from a beautician. We listen to them and believe them nonetheless, just like the lady who is getting her hair fixed gives credence to the opinion of the person who is putting in the curlers, and for about the same reason. We listen to them because they're there. Harvard's Peter Gibbon has estimated that there are 81 television sets for every 100 Americans. There are over 100 channels. In the average home the television is on for six hours a day.[32]

And what we see on television is never "news" in the sense of objective information about what is happening in the world. Dan Rather and Peter Jennings and Hugh Downs and Barbara Walters wouldn't stand a chance against reruns of *Caroline in the City* if all they did was hand on the facts. Advertisers wouldn't like that. So television news has to be a crowd-pleaser. Professor Marianne Jennings of Arizona State University reminds us that when NBC's *Dateline* did an investigative report on problems with the gas tanks in GM trucks, it used incendiary explosives to stage dramatic crash scenes. It was not until after the editor of a popular car magazine had exposed the scandal and GM had spent $2 million on an investigation that NBC admitted to any wrongdoing. NBC president Michael Gartner insisted even then that the program had been "fair and accurate."[33]

In mediaspeak, "fair and accurate" means "entertaining," and the whole truth, alas, seldom meets that criterion. But "crisis" is interesting. "Crisis" sells advertising. In 1999, *People* magazine did a profile of Chief Justice William Rehnquist, reporting that the covenants on his house and vacation home included clauses forbidding their sale to members of certain racial and ethnic minorities. The obvious implication was that the man was a racist. Reporting on this, Professor Jennings (the author of a widely used textbook on real estate law) pointed out that there are very few properties in the United States without a such a covenant somewhere in their history. All such covenants were declared unconstitutional back in the 1950s, but it would be prohibitively expensive to go back and physically remove them, so they remain on the books.[34] Even as I write this chapter, some ambitious journalist is probably preparing to use the very existence of these clauses as evidence for the "crisis of racism among American homeowners," probably excluding the non-WASPs who now own the homes whose ownership the clauses were originally intended to regulate.

I cannot resist the temptation, at this point, to address "the crisis of racism." I live in the Old South. I joined a friend at her (upscale) church to enjoy the performance of a famous boys' choir. About a third of the attendees were black, and there was a lively interchange between black couples and white. As I waited in line at a fast food restaurant, a group of workmen came in the door. The black and white members of the group were smilingly insulting one another (this is how men express affection); they sat down together and continued the banter over lunch. Three old black ladies were cooing to a white baby.

I am quite certain that the people in the scenes I have just described knew the color of their skin was different from that of those with whom they were interacting. That does not make them "racists." It is not our awareness of differences, but our attitude about the appropriate response to these differences, that puts us in such categories. During a break from her studies at Georgia Tech, my twenty-one year old had a part time job waiting tables in a local restaurant. A large black family came in for a birthday party. "Girl, you are so white!" the mother exclaimed (Alaina has very fair skin). "You are so white! That's all right. You just be who you are." They laughed and joked with her as she brought their food, gave her a piece of the birthday cake, and left her a good tip. I think it all comes down to an old rule of thumb: if you treat people with courtesy, you will be treated courteously.

This is not to say there are no idiots in the world. Even if the great and overwhelming majority of us act as we know we should, there will always be a few who attempt to enhance their self-image with offensive behavior. I am familiar with the case of a teacher whose students told her they didn't have to pay attention to her because she was white. And there are undoubtedly white people who insist on referring unkindly to persons of other races. Isolated instances of prejudice, however, do not add up to a crisis in race relations.

Members of the media seem to be incapable of grasping this distinction. There is a place in Plato's *Republic* where one of the speakers observes that people quickly learn to parrot whatever their rulers tell them. There are many individual Americans who have learned to see through political fabrications, but when it comes to members of the press, Plato was right. Most members of the press have learned to repeat verbatim the opinions of anyone who thinks the United States is facing some kind of a "crisis" that calls for heavy-handed political intervention.

Anyone who believes America is still the greatest country on the earth or speaks out for traditional values or (as in the case of Kenneth Starr) sings hymns is referred to as a "right-wing extremist." Those who defer to the desires and methods of autocracy are treated as if they speak with the voice of reason. Interviewing the lawyer of Elian Gonzales, Diane Sawyer was clearly hostile to the notion that the boy's welfare should be placed ahead of bureaucratic policy. The crowds who wanted to keep him in America were described as lawbreakers and hypocrites. A woman who voiced an opinion in favor of sending him back to the deprivation awaiting him in Cuba was treated like a hero. Clearly there was no thinking going on here. Members of the press tell us that the loss of even one life to "road rage" is too many, but they willingly consent to ruining the life of a small child for reasons of state.

Conclusion: Crisis and Character

The achievement-oriented individual, as we observed in the first chapter, needs to have a sense of control over the central issues of his life. The need for achievement cannot become widespread within a society if most of its members are convinced that the primary responsibility for their lives lies in factors external to their own thinking and behavior.

This is not to say there will be no high achievers at all. Now and again in almost any society we will find the combination of personal talent and early self-reliance training that have prepared particular persons for remarkable accomplishment. But these persons will be fewer and farther between to the degree that the dominant belief of their time places an emphasis on belonging and individual helplessness rather than individual achievement. A society with a comparatively small number of high achievers, in turn, cannot advance as rapidly or respond to the demands of change as effectively as a society rich in them. A society in which the need for achievement has become rare is on the verge of stagnation.

The crisis mentality bodes ill for the future of America because it bodes ill for the future of achievement motivation. People who believe they are surrounded by the portents of some inevitable doom will not see much point in creative problem-solving or long-term goals. People who believe their hope for a better future lies primarily in the work of politicians will not see much point in self-reliance. People who have lost their faith in individual excellence and comparative merit will not see much point in planning, patience, or personal effort. Having ceased to believe that they are capable of caring for themselves or that they should have to, they will begin to act like dependent children. They will become, as Jerry Rubin proudly said of the sixties generation, "permanent adolescents."[35]

But adolescents need more than care. They also need to be supervised. We will address that issue in the next chapter.

Chapter 10

THE ADMINISTRATIVE SOCIETY

One of the time programs (*60 Minutes* or *48 Hours* or *Dateline*) did a show on the high cost of medical insurance and the increasing number of Americans who cannot afford to buy it. One of the couples they interviewed had a business of their own, were getting along without medical insurance, and hoping against hope that they would never need it. Poor souls—put in a situation like that by the unjust healthcare system, greedy doctors, and rapacious HMOs!

What was not asked about was the large boat parked on one side of their driveway. Did the expenses associated with that have anything to do with their inability to buy insurance?

We don't know because the question never came up. The interviewer would probably have been embarrassed to ask it. Such a question might have been taken to imply that these people had some responsibility for their own lives, a very un-American implication. It would be unfair to ask them to give up a luxury for the sake of a necessity. In our affluent society no one should be forced to make choices of that kind. We should all be provided with life's necessities so that we can enjoy as many luxuries as we can afford.

This is an illustration of the attitude described at the end of the last chapter. Americans once read *Poor Richard's Almanac*, the *McGuffey's Reader*, and the novels of Horatio Alger because they believed the world was a place in which one could gain a reasonable level of comfort and security by means of persistent effort. They now pay attention to media messages of pending disaster because they regard life as a succession of unpredictable crises and the individual as incapable of self-sufficiency or significant accomplishment. They have come in large measure to think of themselves as helpless children, whose continued happiness depends upon resources other than their own. They think someone else should provide for them.

The dangers of this attitude are obvious. There is first the matter of arithmetic: the more there are who ask to be provided for, the fewer there will be to do the providing. The next question will be with regard to who should be helped and who should supply the assistance. As long as a person was regarded as responsible for his own life and entitled to whatever level of comfort his talents and efforts could create, questions of that kind never came up. Nineteenth-century America produced an abundance of charitable institutions: there was never any shortage of achievers who were willing to help the few who really could not help themselves. But a society that regards most of its members as victims is compelled to deal with the question of who should be taken care of and whose resources should be used to offer the care. If the ruling majority can demand its upkeep at the expense of the minority, we are returned to the arithmetic difficulty with which this paragraph began.

There is then the matter of administration. Andrew Carnegie believed, as we have seen, that one could prove he had the ability to distribute money wisely by accumulating the money in the first place. Recent generations have been willing neither to wait on such a demonstration of practical ability nor to rely upon the virtues of the person who displays it. They have insisted that the government take charge of the matter and entrust the tasks of administration to civil servants, whose professional training combines with legal guarantees to insure fair treatment for everyone involved.

Charles Reich, with the wisdom we would expect from the author of *The Greening of America*, wrote, "Government should gain no power by reason of its role as a dispenser of wealth."[1] But the ability to dispense wealth *is* power. Such power is very limited when it is divided up among a large number of private individuals, each of whom is managing only his own property. Concentrated in the hands of public officials and backed by the coercive authority of the state, it is pervasive and inescapable.

This is the problem facing Americans at the dawn of the twenty-first century. We have demanded that "society" take care of everyone and everything, and we have concentrated power in the hands of a vast bureaucracy, from whose decisions there is no escape. We have refused to accept the duty of meeting challenges with the inner disciplines of personal character and personal choice, and we now find ourselves at the mercy of external regulations and government officials. "We expect bureaucrats to protect us from all of life's contingencies," writes Herbert Schlossberg, "which they cannot do, and we leave ourselves defenseless against our protectors."[2]

This chapter describes the rise of bureaucracy, the decline of freedom, and disappearance of personal character in the last decades of the twentieth century.

The New Wealth

Robert Caro wrote that if he could witness any historical event of his choice, he would like to see the young Lyndon Baines Johnson conferring with Franklin Roosevelt as the latter ate breakfast in his wide mahogany four-poster.[3] (Considering the two men's shared propensity for philandering, a bedroom was probably the right place for their meeting.) Roosevelt always looked upon the young man as his natural successor and predicted that Johnson would become the first twentieth-century president to come from the South. In 1944 he made an illegal and unconstitutional use of his executive authority to keep Johnson from going to jail on charges of criminal tax fraud and the illegal use of campaign contributions.[4]

His faith in the young man turned out to be justified, for Johnson picked up where Roosevelt left off. It was under Johnson that the financially irresponsible welfare state finally fastened its grip on America. Truman had expanded very little upon Roosevelt's policies. Eisenhower used deficit financing in fighting the recession of 1958, but he was opposed to any permanent expansion of federal commitments and usually ran a balanced budget. He put a premium on holding down inflation because he believed the only reliable form of "social security" was price stability. Eisenhower's worst nightmare was exactly what Johnson, with the aid of a compliant Congress, managed to create: a combination of excessive spending on defense and a welfare system gone mad.[5]

The Welfare State

Johnson thought that Kennedy's plans for expanding the welfare state, the so-called "New Frontier," were too timid. When at last the reins were in his hands, Johnson set out to take Roosevelt's beginnings to their logical conclusion. His presidency soon ran up a peacetime record for imposing new laws on the American people and charging them for the privilege of being thus imposed upon. The war in Vietnam led to a massive increase in defense spending, but the costs of the welfare state outstripped even defense. The tax increases of 1968 were so great as to create a $3.2 billion federal budget surplus for fiscal 1969, but that was soon spent.[6]

The expansion of federal spending on older Americans was already well underway when the "War on Poverty" began. The government had assumed responsibility for retired people with the Social Security legislation of the New Deal. This was from the first, as Ronald Reagan said, an "inter-generational Ponzi game." Young people were not taxed to accumulate a fund for their own retirement; they were taxed to pay for the retirement of their elders. Beginning in 1950, Congress passed more than a dozen laws increasing both the size of benefits and the number of people who were eligible to receive them. Wilbur Mills' index-linking act obligated the federal government (meaning taxpayers) to make sure Social Security benefits kept up with inflation. The Consumer Price Index consistently overestimated the rate at which prices were actually increasing, so the real income of Social Security recipients (and the tax burden on workers) increased steadily. By the mid-eighties Social Security benefits were providing the average recipient with a purchasing power of more than five times what the individual had paid into the system.[7]

The Johnson administration's "war on poverty" worked like Social Security: it taxed some to provide for others. But it didn't really have much to do with poverty. Roger Kimball has described the cultural revolution of the 1960s as "a revolution of the privileged, by the privileged, and for the privileged."[8] This was true also of the war on poverty. Although represented as being for the benefit of the "less fortunate," it worked out in practice to provide primarily for the more fortunate. The chief beneficiaries of government programs, as Rose and Milton Friedman have observed, are the people who administer the programs.[9] College educated and from comfortable backgrounds, they seek job security, decent paychecks, annual raises, good working conditions, and the promise of early retirement. People of this kind now swarmed into federal positions.

Director's Law, as we observed in chapter 6, states that people with high-flown plans for saving the world through the power of government always find a way to turn the plans to their own advantage. Intellectuals and bureaucrats set themselves up as a new class, whose high ideals justify their maintenance at the expense of the taxpayer. This is exactly what happened with the war on poverty. William Simon observed that the *increase* in federal welfare expenditures between 1965 and 1975, divided by the 25 million people who were officially defined as poor in the latter year, should have provided each family of four with an annual income of $32,000.[10] (This was a very handsome sum in 1975, about twice the income of a captain in the army, one of which I—with a family of five—happened to be at the time.) Disadvantaged families received far less than that because, as Congressman Ron Paul estimated in 1980, only about 20 percent of social welfare expenditures actually went to "the poor." The remainder was consumed by fraud, waste, and the costs of administration.

The costs of administration: this refers to the salaries and benefits of the bureaucrats who administer government programs. Federal "aid to the poor" is a system that takes money from the productive elements of society and gives it to the nonproductive elements. The welfare state takes money from those who earn it by making something or providing a service and gives it to those who do nothing for which others would willingly pay. It works only because, thanks to tax withholding, the money of those who are profitably employed is taken away before they get into the habit of calling it their own.

Some of this money goes to retired people. Some of it goes to those who supposedly cannot help themselves. A large part of it goes to those whose jobs depend upon government programs, intellectuals and bureaucrats, who justify their comfortable existence by pointing to the constantly expanding number of people who need to be cared for and the increasing magnitude of the crises facing America.

The Redefinition of Property

We met the worried, anxious, fearful, neurotic Charles Reich in the previous chapter, where it was observed that he was not the sort of person to whom America should look for intellectual leadership. He would have been particularly unfit as a legal scholar, because he did not believe in a rule of law. For him the important thing was feelings. "To observe duties toward others," he wrote, "after the feelings are gone, is no virtue and may even be a crime."[11] This does not seem to be the kind of thinking that would be of much use in the definition of property rights. It was nevertheless exactly the kind of thinking that would guide court decisions at the dawn of the twenty-first century.

Reich was already hard at work on The *Greening of America* in 1960, when he left private practice and became a law professor at Yale. His article on "The New Property" was published in *The Yale Law Journal* in April 1964. Here he argued that those who receive government benefits should be regarded as having a right to them. More than that, government benefits should be treated as the property of those who receive them, "not much different from the absolute right of ownership that private capital once invoked."[12] In 1970 and in *Goldberg* v. *Kelley*, the Supreme Court specifically adopted Reich's position: welfare benefits, it said, met the constitutional definition of property.[13]

This was an interesting turn of events. The authors of the Constitution believed in natural rights. Students of John Locke, they believed that a person was entitled to whatever he had honestly created by means of his own thought and effort. He was not entitled to what someone else had created. He might obtain it by means of a voluntary exchange or as a gift, but he had no right to it. He had a right only to the results of his own productivity. If he did not consume all that he produced, he had a right to set it aside for future consumption or the expansion of his personal fortune.[14] The way to wealth lay in working and saving, and therefore in personal character, for both working and saving are expressions of character.

Reich and the Supreme Court turned Locke on his head. They said a person was entitled to what someone else had earned. Wealth was created, not by thought, effort, and self-control, but by an act of Congress. The welfare recipient was entitled to an income, and so were the people who administered welfare benefits, not because they provided anything of value, but because the government said they were. Reich was quite open about it: property, he said, "is the creation of law"; it "is not a natural right but a deliberate construction"; private property is like government largesse in that it "comes from the state, and in much the same way."[15]

The IRS agreed with Reich and the courts. The vast system of federal largesse rested on the back of the taxpayer who provided something of real value in exchange for his income: the private employer, the private employee, the small entrepreneur. These persons could not, in the new scheme of things, be regarded as having a right to what they had earned. Internal Revenue Code provisions that allowed an individual to keep a portion of his earnings now described him as the beneficiary of a "tax expenditure" or an "implicit government grant."[16] His income, in other words, was not his own but something that the government granted him by not taking it away.

If wealth is the result of a government grant, the most direct route to it does not lead through productive activity. It leads through political involvement. Unlike their forebears, modern Americans do not seek freedom from government intrusion. They seek, on the contrary, to have the government intrude on their behalf. They have adopted the standard of 1960s radicalism and expect to get what they want by demanding it rather than by working for it. They are less interested in individual accomplishment than in being a part of some group that can make a case for itself as entitled to some form of special assistance.

What was once represented as an effort to help retired people and "the disadvantaged" has thus become a legislative free-for-all in which lobbyists from the competing groups press their demands upon Congress and the presidency. The old distinction between "liberal" and "conservative" has become meaningless. Political contests were once about different philosophies on the role of government. They are now battles over who will gain the greatest benefits from the process of redistributing earners' incomes. Ronald Reagan decided in 1980 that New York City and the Chrysler Corporation should be added to the welfare roles. Twenty years later, George II paid some of his political debts with measures to protect the American steel industry from foreign competition, thus raising prices for consumers and transferring extra dollars into the pockets of steel industry executives.

The New Morality

There was a time in history when Americans would have raised their voices in protest against a system of this kind. There was a time when it would have been recognized as ruinous to the character of everyone involved in it. It discourages the achiever by taking away the fruit of his effort. It eliminates incentives for the nonachiever by guaranteeing his security without demanding anything in return. It ruins the spirit of charity by replacing voluntary sacrifice with a system of forced payments. It replaces the stimulus of free-market competition with backroom political deals.

It is damaging even to those who administer it. John Stossel says that visitors to Moscow used to note the blank look on the faces of its citizens: they looked this way because their every act had to comply with the petty details of bureaucratic rules. He adds that the same dead-eyed look can be seen in Washington, DC, and in the faces of those who work for the EPA.[17] The excitement of real accomplishment cannot be found apart from the freedom, risk, and individual effort that lead to it. Peters and Waterman described the high-ranking civil servants with whom they consulted as "demotivated towards work"; to add some interest to their lives, most of them had part-time businesses on the side.[18]

But by the 1960s, Americans were no longer concerned with the issue of character. Politicians could not have created the welfare state without a nod of agreement from the electorate. Peter Drucker, who had to flee his native Austria when Hitler look over in the late thirties, said that not even a totalitarian regime could impose its will on a people who were determined to challenge it.[19] The Nazis could not have committed their crimes against the Jews and the churches without a measure of consent from the German population. And American politicians could not have created a system of forcible confiscation and redistribution without a measure of consent from American voters.

Voters' consent to a change in policy is always traceable to a change in values. By the middle of the twentieth century, Americans had begun to subscribe to what Ayn Rand called the "the tribal premise." This is the primitive notion of a person as no more than an appendage of the tribe, a tool to be used or discarded according to the whim of tribal chiefs.[20] It gives political voice to the need for affiliation. For as long as the need for achievement was their dominant psychological orientation, Americans thought of the individual as free, independent, and self-sustaining. They now thought of individuals as "national resources," in the same category as coal and forests. What a person accomplished had no value in itself. It was important only to the extent that it served the needs of the tribe, which in practice meant whatever leaders defined as the "national purpose."

Few of the justifications for the new system were this direct. Appealing to the mentality of the 1960s, Robert Heilbroner wrote, "The resolution of the crises thrust upon us can only be found through political action."[21] Arthur Schlesinger Jr. said that American affluence had left us with a "spiritual disquietude." We could not solve our spiritual problems, he said, or find our way to "the promised land" except through the action of the government.[22] In May 1962, John F. Kennedy told a press conference that the problems facing America were "beyond the comprehension of most men,"[23] (but presumably not beyond the comprehension of JFK and his Ivy League advisers). They all agreed that the man on the street was too stupid to take care of himself. He needed to be taxed so that the politicians would have enough money to save him.

There was also an appeal to "social justice." For most of the nineteenth century Americans believed that this term described the elimination of artificial barriers to personal achievement: the person who was willing to work and save should be allowed to rise as far as his talents and opportunities allowed. By the second half of the twentieth century Americans were learning to view exceptional accomplishment with suspicion. One of the characters in B. F. Skinner's widely-read *Walden Two* said that a person could accomplish a great deal in the economic sphere only "at the expense of poverty, disease, and filth for many more." Earlier in the book the same character said it was impossible to make a fortune "without making a few paupers in the bargain."[24] If one accepts that premise, "social justice" refers to legal devices for preventing achievement and making it less desirable. According to Christopher Jencks, there should be laws to reduce both the rewards of success and the costs of failure.[25]

This profound observation brought American social thinking all the way up to the fourth century BC and to Aristotle's observation that those who will not voluntarily restrain their economic ambitions should be legally hindered in the pursuit of them. But it all seemed new and insightful in the sixties and seventies. Legal scholar Ronald Dworkin said, "A more equal society is a better society even if its citizens prefer inequality":[26] achievement bad, mediocrity good, and damn the fool who wants to make the sacrifices necessary for exceptional accomplishment. Theologian Joseph Fletcher used the terms "microethics" and "petty moralism" to describe the old idea that a person who was doing well should use his personal resources to assist those who were genuinely needy. What the twentieth century called for, he said, was "macroethics," which would endorse higher levels of taxation for the sake of "a wholesome investment balance and socially sensitive social balance."[27]

This kind of thinking, observed Herbert Schlossberg, raises confiscation and redistribution to "the pinnacle of moral rectitude."[28] The notion of morality as matter of personal honesty and trustworthiness had become passé. Americans were learning to pride themselves on a sensitive "social conscience" and to ignore the weightier matter of individual responsibility. They were learning, as F. A. Hayek once said, "to be unselfish at someone else's expense."[29] They forgot the difference between demanding that political leaders "do something" and taking responsibility for doing the right thing themselves.

They also failed to realize that, in giving the government authority to make impositions on the person who had achieved a great deal, they were giving it the authority to impose on them. This point would soon be pressed home to them.

The Bureaucratic Stranglehold

Bureaucracy expands in response to demands for solutions to the latest "crisis." Having accepted the notion that the individual as such is neither significant nor capable of dealing with large issues, Americans ask the government to take care of them. The response always comes as a new law with a bureaucracy to administer it. Each "serious concern" generates a new Act, and each Act creates or expands an agency. The Air Quality Act was passed in 1967, and the Clean Air Act (just to make sure) was passed in 1970. The Occupational Health and Safety Act and the Environmental Protection Act were passed in 1971. The Federal Water Pollution Control Act of 1972 mandated an end to the discharge of pollutants by the end of 1985. (How are we doing on that one?) Each of these Acts and a hundred like them added to the alphabet soup of regulatory agencies.

These agencies, however, seldom do much about the "crisis" they were created to solve. In 1972 and in response to the furor over *Silent Spring,* the Environmental Protection Agency was assigned the task of reviewing about six hundred pesticides and determining which of them should be removed from the market as hazards to human health. The EPA put over a thousand people to work on the job and agreed to report back in three years. As of the mid-nineties, they had passed judgment on only about thirty of the 600 pesticides. The Occupational Health and Safety Administration, with over 4,000 detailed regulations and more than 2,000 inspectors, has had virtually no effect on American workplace safety.[30]

Philip Howard uses cases of this kind as examples of government inefficiency. He is missing the point. OSHA and the EPA have been inefficient in carrying out their assigned responsibilities but tremendously efficient in carrying out their real purpose. The primary goal of every organization is self-preservation, and this is as true of regulatory agencies as of any other organization. As long as the "crisis" they were supposed to deal with has not been solved, Congress has a reason for keeping them on the books. Instead of a means to the solution of problems, they become a part of the federal landscape.

Federal agencies can be effective in carrying out their real purpose only by means of inefficiency with regard to their stated purposes, and this inefficiency contaminates everything they touch. Two-thirds of funds involved in developing a new drug are spent on meeting FDA requirements. One pharmaceutical company said it spent "more on forms and paperwork than it did for all research on cancer and other diseases."[31]

Afraid of approving a drug that might have unknown side effects, the FDA puts unnecessary roadblocks in the path of every new therapy. Such delays would be excusable if they sprang from a genuine concern for risks to the patient; they seem in fact to spring merely from a desire to avoid bad press. People die because the FDA seeks to preserve itself by maintaining good public relations. John Stossel tells of a press conference at which the FDA announced its long-awaited approval of a new beta-blocker. It predicted that the new drug would save 14,000 lives a year. This means, Stossel observes, that the FDA killed 14,000 people by not approving the drug a year earlier.[32]

Inefficiency, though, is the least of the evils the bureaucracy inflicts upon us. The greater problem is tyranny. Government agencies' independence from the political process gives them the power to operate without concern for the outcome of elections. They can generate as many rules as they wish and administer these rules as they see fit. Paul Harvey has observed that for every law passed by Congress, the federal bureaucracy cranks out 18 regulations.[33] During the Clinton administration, half a million pages of detailed regulations were added to the Federal Register.

These regulations tell us how to live. They tell us what kind of car we can drive, where we can work, who we can hire, what kind of house we can live in, what kinds of materials we can wear, and what medicines we can take. They tell banks what rate of interest they can charge, and they tell manufacturers what they can make. "You've got so much power here that it's unbelievable," a congressman told the chairman of the Consumer Product Safety Commission. "You've got life or death over whether consumers have anything to consume."[34]

Detailed regulations are an invitation for the abuse of power. Philip Howard has described how bureaucrats use the provisions of the Resource Conservation and Recovery Act (RCRA) to blackmail large companies. The RCRA requires companies to keep a record of when hazardous materials are received, when they are disposed of, and where each container is located. When federal environmental agents discover in a surprise inspection that records on the location of every barrel are not up to the minute, they threaten a criminal indictment if the company does not pay a large fine.[35]

One of Mercer's MBA students a few years ago was a registered nurse. Her paper for my class in business ethics included a horror story about a run-in between her hospital and the Justice Department. The hospital administrator received a letter that began, "It has been determined that your institution should be civilly prosecuted" in connection with the False Claims Act.

False Claims Act? When did Congress pass that? During the Civil War. It was intended to frighten army contractors into honest billing practices with the threat of a substantial fine plus triple damages for every false claim. The federal bureaucracy knows about things like this because legal minutia are its bread and butter. Its knowledge of every fine point gives it an advantage over taxpayers, who are self-interestedly attending to their own business.

In the present case the hospital was accused of incorrect bills in the amount of $7,998. If it defended itself in court and lost, its penalty would have been $153,576, in addition to its legal expenses. It settled out of court for a fine of $12,557. This $7,998 example of "fraud and abuse" came to less than 1 percent of 1 percent (that's not a typo: as a decimal, the figure is .0001) of the hospital's Medicare billings for the period in question. An institution that does things correctly 99.99% of the time is doing pretty well, probably a lot better than the Justice Department. But the bureaucrats knew the details of the laws, and the hospital did not, so the government's act of extortion went unchallenged.

But it isn't just hospitals. It isn't just businesses. Bureaucratic regulations touch every area of our lives. Howard also has a story about California homeowners whose homes were engulfed by fire. They were not allowed to prevent the fire's spread by using a disc to turn under the dried grass because their area was the habitat of an endangered species, the Stephens kangaroo rat.[36] (The results were burned homes, insurance claims, and roasted rats.)

The Dangerous Apathy

Americans are not up in arms about all of this for three reasons. First of all, stories about it seldom get into the news. The press busies itself with spreading the word about the "crises" government bureaucracies are intended to solve but rarely gets around to reporting on their complete failure to solve them. The media go on endlessly about how businesses restrict our freedom but have little to say about how government agencies are stealing it.

A second factor is the political power of the bureaucracy itself. By providing a large number of government jobs, politicians have created a massive special interest group for the support of candidates who want to continue or expand existing programs. Suggestions that all these programs impose an unreasonable demand on the profitably employed taxpayer are greeted with cries of horror. The person who wants to keep what he has honestly earned is described as a selfish individualist. The bureaucrats who want to live at his expense are every bit and perhaps even more self-interested, but they prefer to think of themselves as public servants engaged in a quest to save America from selfish individualism. They will contribute to the cause of any politician who will aid them in the quest and guarantee their jobs in the process.

There is at least one other reason that most Americans do not speak out against the spread of bureaucracy. We do not speak out because our ideals have changed. We no longer admire or strive to imitate the independent achiever, who is trying to accomplish something of practical economic value. We admire instead the person who holds a comfortable position in an agency or institution. We seek not the challenges associated with personal accomplishment, but the certainties of tenure. Our ancestors asked for freedom. We ask for security. We think we're entitled to it.

The Disappearance of Character

At the foundation of what has come to be called "the entitlement mentality" is a conviction that the first line of defense for our lives is the responsibility of someone other than ourselves. This is probably less widespread among the poor to whom it is often attributed than among well-educated and well-paid wage earners. They once accepted it as high doctrine from the hands of their college professors and now see it in the record of their own experience. Their existence has been comparatively sheltered, and they have survived many of life's challenges at least in part through resources supplied by someone other than themselves. Large numbers of them continue even as adults to receive financial assistance from their parents, a situation to which Professors Thomas J. Stanley and William D. Danko refer as "economic outpatient care."[37] They have a predictable monthly paycheck and a panoply of benefits, but they feel stretched thin even with these. Many live in fear that their employer might go under. If that were to happen, they would be doomed.

This makes them susceptible to the news about the latest "crisis," to the assurances of the welfare state, and therefore to anything that encourages them to focus on the present. We are capable of giving our attention to the future only to the extent that we believe we have some control over it. If what happens to us is entirely the result of powers other than our own, there is no point in exercising our own powers. We will not work or save or plan or sacrifice for that which is the result of something other than our own working and planning and saving and sacrifice.

If there is no future for which to defer gratification, we will seek it in the present. For a dozen years I earned my living as a financial planner. One couple stands out in my mind as an example of many with whom I worked. Between the two of them they made a lot of money, but they spent it faster than they made it. When I cautioned them about what this implied for the future, the response was, well, one can't be sure about the future. The important thing was to be happy right now. "We can't enjoy ourselves without going into debt," the wife told me.

The baby boomers were the first generation of Americans to be raised amid news of constant crisis and the assurances of the welfare state, and they became the most self-indulgent adults the United States had ever seen. I have in my notes for the year of 1985 the remarks of Kenneth Rosen, a real estate professor at the University of California. He said the baby boomers (the oldest of whom were then in their late thirties) wanted to live in houses like those their parents had been able to afford only toward the end of a long career. They didn't want to work and wait and save for these homes like their parents had. They wanted them right now. A study published at about the same time found that over half of the young professionals surveyed said they would rather spend right now than save for retirement. Another study found that among the half of the baby boomers who saved anything at all, the majority saved only for short-term purposes: a car, a vacation, or something else to improve their present standard of living.

Tendencies of this kind became stronger with the passage of time. In the first quarter of the year 2000, consumer spending rose at a rate described by David Orr, chief economist at First Union Corporation, as "almost beyond comprehension." In spite of the fact that consumer confidence was declining, spending increased much more rapidly than personal income.[38]

This means that modern Americans go on spending even in the presence of considerable doubt about their ability to pay the debts they are accumulating. As the nineties evolved, there emerged an ever-greater willingness to renege on one's financial obligations. Personal bankruptcy rose to an all-time high. The majority of these bankruptcies were not the result of health problems or job loss. They were simply cases of well-paid individuals (most credit card debt is held by persons who earn over fifty thousand dollars a year) who let their desires run away with them. When it became difficult to meet their obligations they declared bankruptcy, under lenient laws got to keep most of the things they had accumulated, and before long went out on another spending spree.[39]

At the beginning of the twentieth century people looked with contempt on the man who ran up his debts or tried to renege on bills that he could have paid. By the end of the century no one thought anything of it. We once thought of the good life as something that was earned. We now think of it as something to which we are entitled. If we cannot provide for it ourselves, either the government or our creditors (and maybe both) will step in to fill the gap.

The tendency toward a focus on the present is related also to moral relativism. A belief in moral absolutes, after all, is simply a belief that our actions have predictable consequences. The moral absolutist is a person who believes in a long list of undesirable future occurrences that can be avoided by means of honorable behavior in the present. Ralph Waldo Emerson, the seventeenth-century Puritan, and the medieval monk would have disagreed about many things, but they would not have disagreed about that. They all believed that actions have consequences, either in time or in eternity.

Modern Americans, though, are disinclined to think in terms of consequences. *Sports Illustrated*'s survey of a thousand athletes found that 54 percent said they would take a drug that guaranteed a victory at the Olympic Games even if it meant certain death in five years. Lutheran Brotherhood conducted a survey of eighteen to thirty-four year olds. The question was, "Are there absolute standards for morals and ethics or does everything depend on the situation?" Seventy-nine percent expressed a disbelief in absolute standards. They said that it all depended upon the situation.[40] Such a response means simply that they see no need to think in terms of more than the present moment. Their lives are not in their own hands, so they feel no obligation to the future…

Destroying the Future

...Or for raising their own children. A 1997 Census Bureau survey discovered that 55% of new mothers return to work within one year of giving birth.[41] Some of the babies involved are put into the care of grandparents or relatives, but most are left in day care centers. American parents, that is to say, are willing to entrust paid strangers with the formative years of their children's lives.

When the Clinton administration proposed a $21.7 billion package for the expansion of day care, it offered the support of findings by the National Institute for Child Development and Health. The study, trumpeted by *USA Today* with the headline "Day Care Not Harmful to Growth or Bonding," had come to the amazing conclusion that good day care was better than bad day care. It was not mentioned that the study had also found a negative correlation between the amount of day care and the relationship between a mother and her child. (This was most true, it should be added, in nonpoverty situations.) Nor was mention made of earlier studies, which had found that children raised in day care centers were more likely to be emotionally maladjusted, aggressive, and withdrawn.[42]

But how can parents be expected to take account of such things? If we are all victims of forces that we cannot control, how can people be held responsible for raising their children? We shake our heads in pity at the plight of young families, pressed as they are by credit card debt, mortgages on beautiful houses, and car payments. It would be nice if a mother could stay at home with her little ones, but with all the other obligations she has, how can she do it? And anyway, hasn't she the right to a "fulfilling career" outside the home?

The "socially responsible" attitude on this issue is wonderfully expressed in a popular bumper sticker. "Have you hugged your child today?" it begins to ask but then changes its mind. "Your" is crossed out and replaced with "a." What remains is the very impersonal "Have you hugged a child today?" The implication is that we should all go out, grab the next child we see, and give him or her a big squeeze. Modern parents are too busy to raise their own children, so we should all help shoulder the load. Maybe the mother who left her baby at a day care center in the morning can even the balance by hugging someone else's eight-year-old over the lunch hour. If we all pitch in we'll all be fine.

Aside from the risk that repeated acts of free-floating fondness might land you in a jail cell, this bumper sticker misses an essential point. Children's need for predictability is at least as great as their need for affection. Bullying from a familiar sibling is preferable to a hug from a stranger. Consistent discipline is preferable not only to random discipline but even random rewards. The small child for whom the same people display every day the same personality traits, repeated habits not merely of affection but also of irritability, learns to see the world as orderly and as a place to which one can adapt. The child who experiences life as a series of random events (in the frequent turnover of employees at the day care center, for example) grows up with the conviction that the world is out of control.

This conviction is confirmed by what he sees on television. As soon as a child moves beyond *Sesame Street*, there is a world of conflict, violence, and perversion to learn about. Material aimed specifically at the youthful audience seeks to gain an advantage over the competition (as for example in *South Park*) with disturbing content and borderline profanity. Evening television, which children watch even if it is not "intended" for them, is a series of programs about parties, the over-consumption of alcohol, constantly changing lovers, and criminality. And of course as soon as they get home from school there are the afternoon talk shows, Jerry, Sally and all the rest, whose favorite topics are dishonesty, abusive relationships, infidelity, and sexual deviance.

Not to say that what they got at school is much better. American public education is a failure story. In a series of exams administered to high school seniors in 21 countries in 1995, American students scored 19th in general math, 20th in advanced math, and dead last in physics.[43] A record number—about one-third—of our high school students have 4.0 (that is, straight A) grade point averages, but on the Iowa Tests of Basic Skills, students who should be scoring at the nineteenth percentile barely make it into the seventieth.[44]

It has thus become possible to get good grades without learning anything. In California as many as nine out of ten of the students entering college have to take remedial courses in English or math. Most students entering community colleges in New York do not score high enough for placement in even the remedial courses.[45]

But not to worry. If American schools are not educating our children, they are at least "preparing" them for the horrors of life on planet earth. As early as kindergarten there are warnings about safe sex, drugs, and smoking. Children learn to feel guilty about slavery, the "genocide" (an ever-popular term) of Native Americans, and the oppression of women, this last presumably because the mere fact of the children's existence may put some restraints on their mothers' career opportunities.

Educators build "self-esteem" by congratulating students on their answers even if the answers are wrong and at the same time describe for them a world so vast and confused that it will stymie their best efforts. The messages of the day care center and television are confirmed. Even if a sense of self-worth could be created in the absence of real achievement (which it cannot), it is of little value to make children feel good about themselves and then teach them that the world into which they are going is a chaos.

But this trend in education is nothing new. Marie Winn commented on it as early as 1981, by which time it had become the established practice. In her book *Children Without Childhood*, she pointed out that our society was seeking not so much to protect its children as to "prepare" them.[46] Thus "prepared," children who were raised in the seventies, eighties, and early nineties are now the adults upon whose moral relativism we have already commented, the same adults who are ready to renege on their financial obligations, the same adults who believe that "society" owes them something. And they are the same adults who are now reluctant to accept responsibility for raising their own children.

Conclusion

"Poverty, chastity, obedience." Adapting the ancient monastic rule to the needs of their own time, seventeenth-century Puritans insisted that a person live within his means, adhere to a rigid moral code, and do the best that was possible within the limits of life's inevitable frustrations and delays. This was the central theme of American literature and education from the publication of The *New England Primer* in 1690 until the last *McGuffey's Reader* rolled off the press two centuries later. And the authors of the Constitution assumed the existence of a citizenry that subscribed to these values.

Beginning about 1900, though, the existence of such a citizenry began to be doubted and the values themselves were called into question. Gradually there arose a government and a literature based on different assumptions, a government and a literature that appealed not to the virtues of the population but to its fears. We will consider the probable consequences of this change in the final chapter.

Conclusion

CHARACTER AND THE FUTURE

Whenever I have more to do than I can get done in the time available, I always begin by doing something else. It doesn't advance my primary obligations, but it helps because it gets my mind off them. When I should have been writing my dissertation, for example, I spent long hours reading old aviation magazines. They didn't have anything to do with the dissertation, but at least they kept me from worrying about it.

As a result of some very bad planning, I found myself one weekend with 30 essay exams and a promise to have them all graded and returned on Monday. In situations of this kind, I like to browse through the rack on which the Mercer University librarians display recent additions to their catalog. Barry Glassner's *The Culture of Fear: Why Americans are Afraid of the Wrong Things* was irresistible. For one thing, the title seemed to suggest a thesis similar to the one I developed in chapter 9, and for another, I had all those tests to grade.

The selection was fortuitous. It quickly convinced me that my time would be better spent grading tests. I began to realize this when, early in the introduction, Dr. Glassner made it a point to say that he was a "social scientist."[1] I am one of those people myself, and I can tell you from painful experience that it is nothing to brag about. With a few exceptions, there is no group of people who are less scientific or more willing to hitch their wagon to what seems to be a rising star than those who describe themselves as "social scientists." Our training has taught us how to find exactly what someone else has told us we should be looking for.

Ruth Benedict, to cite a notable example, in her book *Patterns of Culture*, praised the Zuni Indians for their noncompetitive culture, their devotion to religion, their sobriety, and their sexual self-control. Later anthropologists said this was nonsense: the Zuni were ambitious, anxious, suspicious, hostile, sexually promiscuous, and usually drunk.[2] It is possible that by the time the second set of anthropologists got to them, the Zuni had read Dr. Benedict's book and had perversely decided to confuse things by changing their ways. It is more probable that either Dr. Benedict or her successors or perhaps both skewed their conclusions to meet criteria that had nothing to do with the study itself.

Disciplines dealing with human affairs, said F. A. Hayek, are easily turned into the factories of official myths.[3] It seemed to me, as I read Dr. Glassner's book, that he had fallen into this trap. His presentation of the facts is impressive. Much less so is his complete inability to present them with anything similar to objectivity. No matter what he talks about, his knee-jerk response is to offer it as support for the liberal agenda. He displays an almost Freudian originality in twisting things around to make them fit preconceptions that are not even really his own but something he has picked up from some political campaign.

He says, for example, or at least implies that there is nothing to fear from the complete breakdown of morality and even civility in America. What should be a source of concern, he says, is that there are more "poor" people in America than ever before, and the gap between "rich" and "poor" is widening. This is what "we" need to "do something" about.

He fails to point out that the number of "poor" is increasing because the income level at which a family is defined as "poor" is adjusted every year according to the CPI, and that for more than thirty years the CPI has significantly overestimated the actual rate of inflation. He fails to point out that America's "poor" are the richest "poor" on the planet, enjoying a standard of living far better than even the moderately wealthy of many other countries. In 1995, 41 percent of America's "poor" owned their own homes (750,000 of of them with values in excess of $150,000), 70 percent owned a car, and 97 percent owned a color television. The average "poor" American lives in a place with a third more living space than the average Japanese home and four times as much as the average Russian home. As for nutrition, the average "poor" kid of 1995 was one inch taller and 10 pounds heavier than the average soldier in the Normandy invasion of 1944. Most of today's "poor" Americans enjoy a standard of living that would have been considered luxurious at the beginning of the twentieth century. The rich may be getting richer, but so are the "poor."[4]

Dr. Glassner somehow manages to miss this. Perhaps that is because he has not taken the time to examine his assumptions. Like so many other "social scientists," he seems to begin with the assumptions of political orthodoxy and to judge everything in that light.

My Assumptions

I have taken another tack, but that does not mean I have made no assumptions. I lay no claim to being a disembodied intelligence who can describe the world without passion or prejudice. I believe my analysis has been correct precisely because of the facts I have chosen to emphasize, but I do not pretend that my personal convictions did not affect my choice. This book began with the story of a successful prediction, and the temptation to conclude it with another prediction is irresistible. My prediction, however, will be no better than (in fact, probably not even as good as) the assumptions on which it is based. So before I go any farther, I am going to lay my cards on the table.

The Individual and Society

I have assumed that "society," as Ayn Rand observed, is a foggy term. If it is used to refer to something other than the individuals of whom the "society" is composed, it serves only to cloud our thinking. "Society" does not think; individuals do. "Society" does not devise solutions; individuals do. "Society" does not accept responsibility; individuals do.

"Society" does not work or plan or save except through the working, planning, and saving of the individuals of whom it is composed. As soon as we begin to suggest that "society" can accomplish things except through the creative efforts of individuals, we have begun to talk nonsense.

It is true that every society faces problems, in the sense of issues that are threatening to most or perhaps even all of its members. But no "society" has ever yet devised a solution to these problems. That has always and without exception been the work of individuals. "Society" did not come up with an answer to the problems implied by the isolation of family farms and the transportation needs of a scattered urban society. That was the work of Henry Ford. The only "society" (Hitler's Germany) that attempted to provide a similar solution (the Volkswagen, "people's car") never delivered a single automobile to a single buyer, in spite of the fact that many workers had paid for them in advance under a government-sponsored system of installment payments.[5]

Late in 1993 an old woman froze to death while sitting on a bench in front of the Department of Housing and Urban Development. Speaking at her funeral service, Mr. Clinton's HUD secretary Henry Cisneros said, "Something is not right" (well, duh!) and made a pledge to spend $250,000 for temporary beds in Washington, DC. When the Reverend Lester W. Allen gave the eulogy, he said, "I'm convinced that those in positions of authority are sincere...but you don't mind if I tell you the truth now, do you?...Beloved, they have never solved our problems."[6]

No, of course not. "Society" does not solve problems. That is the work of individuals, either alone or in concert with other specific individuals. Persons who are intent upon accomplishing things find ways to climb over the obstacles before them, and in so doing they open a path for their neighbors. A society filled with people of this kind will advance by the conquering of one problem after another.

It is not the duty of "society" to take care of the individual. Even those in need of some special assistance will receive better treatment from other individuals than from "society." They will be better cared for through the benevolence of compassionate individuals than through the services of bureaucrats who define their jobs as the management of "entitlements," do everything according to the "rules," and regard their wards as "cases" rather than as human beings. A nursing inspector said that rules and regulations had almost nothing to do with making a nursing home a decent place. The critical factor was the charge nurse: "If she's competent and cares about her job, the place will be alright; otherwise, forget it."[7]

Even those who really need special help are best entrusted to the care of specific individuals. But in an advancing civilization, the number of people who regard themselves as in need of assistance is comparatively small; the number of those who regard themselves as independent problem solvers is comparatively large. As this balance shifts, the civilization begins to decline: it has proportionately more problems and proportionately fewer people who are intent upon devising creative and original solutions to them.

The Meaning of Character

I have assumed that the people who devise these solutions do so because they regard it as in their own (not "society's") best interest to get the problem solved. They may want to solve it for themselves, because they believe they can benefit by solving it for others, or both. The lives of those around them are improved by means of their efforts, but their first motivation is not a desire to improve the lives of those around them. Their first motivation is the challenge of the problem itself. It may be a problem with a scientific discovery, an invention, the marketing of that invention, or the management of the workforce who produce it for the consuming public. Whatever the problem, achievement-oriented individuals feel that their own lives are incomplete until they get it solved.

The person who claims to live without any desire for personal rewards is both self-deceived and a deceiver of others. Adam Smith observed that none of us has any deficiency of self-interest.[8] We differ in the way we define and pursue our self-interests, but we are all self-interested. The more vehemently a person insists that he or she is simply the disinterested and loving servant of humanity, the more certain we may be that this person has a hidden and self-interested agenda. College professors, "social scientists," rock musicians, inventors, presidents of corporations, factory employees, local merchants, entrepreneurs, union members, and (especially) politicians are in it for themselves. The starving artist sets aside wealth and fame in order to experience creative ecstasy (and hopes for wealth and fame). There may be a precious few, Mother Teresa for example, who are seeking primarily the good feeling they get from helping others or serving God, but even they are pursuing their own best interests according to their particular definition of what those interests are.

The person of character is not the person who claims to live without self-interest. He is rather a person who habitually entertains a very refined conception of where his best interests lie. Immanuel Kant (who was raised in the traditions of Scotch Pietism)[9] was famously critical of the tradesman who was honest because "honesty is the best policy" rather than because it was his duty to be honest.[10] For the Puritan, Mennonite, Baptist, Quaker, and Methodist, honesty was the best policy precisely because it was one's duty. Such persons became successful because they had learned to think of personal success as an expression of something Eternal in their lives. They thought of human existence as a challenge, not as a vacation. They believed that God had given them great things to do, they were determined to be about their Father's business, and they were insistent on doing it in ways that would be pleasing in His sight.

The heirs to this tradition loosened their grip on the details of their faith, but they never doubted that it was in their best interest to abide by its principles. The pithy maxims of *Poor Richard's Almanac* were not intended to suggest that Franklin's readers should stop seeking their own best interest. They were assembled, rather, to point out the most efficient ways in which to pursue it. "These are well-proven," Franklin was saying. "Follow them in spite of your leanings to the contrary and you won't go wrong." Self-reliance, honesty, effort, persistence, saving, innovation: all are associated with short-term discomforts and long-term rewards. The *McGuffey's Reader*, Emerson, and Horatio Alger agreed. Life's pains have a meaning in them, they said, but you cannot find it unless you shoulder them bravely; think in terms of personal progress rather than personal comfort, and you will find both.

The present work has examined values of this kind in connection with a thoroughly studied psychological tendency known as the need for achievement. In every case that has been studied, societies whose members have agreed in defining self-interest in terms of creative problem-solving have agreed also on placing a great deal of responsibility on the shoulders of the individual. They have insisted at a minimum on self-reliance, work, innovation, and the careful use of both time and money. In every case that has been studied, advancing societies have had a value orientation of this kind. And in every case that has been studied, the disappearance of that value orientation has been associated with social decline.

The Roles of Literature and Government

I have assumed and attempted to demonstrate that we can gain an insight into a nation's value orientation by examining the literature (and in recent times the media messages) to which its people give their attention. We learn what they believe by studying what they read and watch and listen to. Americans did not begin to distrust free market business enterprise because they read *The Jungle*. They would not have turned Sinclair's book into a best seller if they had not been semiconsciously searching for a justification of the distrust they already felt. The book was the confirmation of an existing belief, not the revelation of a new one. It was popular because it gave expression to convictions that were becoming widespread at the time of its appearance.

The old convictions had emphasized the power and potential of the individual. The new convictions emphasized his weakness and fallibility. Americans learned to distrust others at precisely the moment they began to distrust themselves. Even as the first copy of *The Jungle* rolled off the presses, conscientious public librarians were dutifully removing Horatio Alger's novels from the shelves:[11] they did not want to encourage children with ideas that were out of touch with the new "realism." Americans took the first step toward seeing themselves as victims on the day they stopped seeing themselves as Alger heroes.

With the new sense of helplessness came a new cry for institutional guarantees. Americans' doubts about themselves were displayed in a distrust of their neighbors and an insistence that something be done to reign them in. Legislatures are rarely in a hurry: the publication of *The Jungle* was followed so quickly by the Pure Food and Drug Act only because it released a long pent-up demand. Americans were beginning to think they needed someone to take care of them. The welfare state was just around the corner.

Popular literature gives expression to popular values. As their values change, people modify the institutions that govern them. Constitutions composed in days gone by offer no guarantees because they have become irrelevant. The "original intent" of those who composed such documents is stretched, pulled, twisted, and deformed by the reasoning of courts, the actions of legislatures, and the decisions of executives who think with the mind of their time. A nation that emphasizes heroism will create institutions to set people free for the doing of great things in the world. A nation that emphasizes helplessness and distrust will create institutions to hedge its people in on every side, to protect them, and also to control them.

The Age of Descent

I have assumed, finally, that sooner or later every nation begins to crumble and fall. The evidence of history, even if we cannot provide a detailed record of character for every case, is that civilizations do not go on rising forever, ascending endlessly from one peak to the next. The story has been told more than once: Egypt, Babylon, Assyria. In the three hundred years between 1200 and 1500, Spain became one of the world's strongest nations. By 1610 its age of ascendancy had passed. Today it is one of the poorest countries in Western Europe. Before Spain, Rome rose from weakness to become the dominant force in Mediterranean civilization, enjoyed about two centuries of almost unchallenged mastery, and then began its precipitous decline.

And before the grandeur that was Rome, there was the glory that was Greece. At almost exactly the point where the forces making for ascent began to give way to the forces making for decline is Plato. His work is now a piece from the ancient world, dead, abstract, and far removed from the realities of life as we know it. In his own time, though, he was much talked about and part of an ongoing discussion about the proper ordering of a society. An examination of his ideas may therefore be of value in helping us understand the dominant beliefs of a civilization that has passed its prime.

Plato was successful because he said things the "right" people wanted to hear: his school, the Academy, was set up with the specific intention of shaping statesmen and rulers.[12] He could never have become popular by saying things that were genuinely new or radical. If Plato had learned nothing else from the fate of Socrates, he had at least learned that. He could appeal to his students' imaginations only by revisiting ideas with which they were already familiar. It is dismaying to find that these ideas were very similar to those of modern Americans.

Attitudes Toward Achievement

The Greece of Plato's day was a place in which the desire for economic success was likely to be equated with a tendency toward unethical behavior. In the *Gorgias* we find Callicles describing the opinions of those who defined dishonesty as a desire for exceptional accomplishment in the world of business.[13] He observed that people who want to disguise their own inability or laziness describe the achieving individual as a malefactor. The nobler natures, he said, are enslaved and brought down to the dull average by those who fear that the challenge of fair competition will demonstrate their own inferiority. And at the dawn of the twenty-first century we find Ralph Nader, who has done nothing with his life except complain, and whose contributions to charity have been less than remarkable, attacking Bill Gates, who has created one of America's greatest businesses and given a fortune.

Plato, indeed, demonstrates an eminently Naderite attitude toward everything having to do with economic achievement. He dislikes the commercial classes, merchants and shopkeepers, who are described in the *Laws* as men of "unfaithful and uncertain ways."[14] He recognizes the importance of economic progress but suggests at the same time that the best government will prevent the appearance of a prosperous commercial society. In the *Republic*, he says the economy needs to be managed so as to insure a "just" distribution of wealth. There must be, in particular, strict limits on how successful a person is allowed to become, and anyone who gains more than four times the average amount of wealth must surrender the excess to the state.[15]

Plato's audience liked the *Republic*, and they would have loved our modern graduated income tax system. They would have applauded Mr. Daschle, who complained that tax reform would provide the greatest benefits for those who are taxed at the highest rates. (The top 1 percent of American earners pay 25 percent of America's income taxes.) Plato's readers and listeners would have been strongly in favor of any system that hindered a person from doing too much with his life or getting too far ahead of his less ambitious neighbors. "When I was a boy," said Isocrates [the fourth century teacher of rhetoric, not the fifth century philosopher], "wealth was regarded as a thing so secure and admirable that almost everyone affected to own more property than he actually possessed... Now a man has to defend himself against being rich as if it were the worst of crimes."[16]

And this hostility toward practical achievement, remember, became widespread among the people of Athens at the very point at which their civilization moved from its period of ascendancy into its age of decline.

The Ruling Classes

Plato's *Republic* is, if not quite the first, at least a very early attempt at social engineering, and Plato was like other social engineers in his contempt for those who wanted to live their own lives in their own way. He especially disliked those who preferred to spend their time in the practical activities of daily life. In describing the process by means of which his "philosopher kings" are selected to rule, Plato says that those who fail the test of intelligence will be assigned to the economic classes. They will be men of business, factory workers, clerks, and farmers, competent for not much more than the fulfillment of animal wants.

There is no point in expecting much from such dolts. They will need to be managed. But they may not see that. We therefore need to eradicate their dangerous tendency to think for themselves. They must stop seeing themselves as capable of meeting the great challenges of their time. Plato says they must be taught the myth of the metals: most people are made of brass or iron and are fit only for obedience; others, fewer in number, are made from silver, and are meant for the military; a tiny minority are made from gold and should be the rulers.[17]

We cannot review these ideas without thinking of the attitudes that characterize the government of modern America. In September 1999, Representative Tom Coburn announced his decision not to run for another term in Congress. He had made himself unpopular with the leaders of both parties by insisting that the House live up to its 1997 promise to accept some limits on its spending. The problem with these limits, in the eyes of most congresspersons, was that they restricted the members' ability to do special favors for their special interest groups. It was far more important to them to be reelected than it was to honor their word. Representative Coburn decided that Congress was suffering from an incurable disease called "careerism," and he wanted to get out before he was infected.

"Congress no longer represents the majority of Americans," he said to a high school audience in Mounds, Oklahoma. "Congress represents special interests and itself. It's an elite ruling class."[18]

An "elite ruling class." Yes. Plato's gold class, with a perfect right both to tell the incompetents of the bronze and iron classes how to live and to spend their constituents' money in such a way as to keep themselves in power. The "fire-breathing" Republican Congress of 1994 made a "Contract with America" to downsize government and make it responsive to the demands of the voters, but someone took a fire extinguisher and hosed them down. In 1998 they signed a budget deal in which all pretense of reform was abandoned. Their promises had been forgotten. All that was left was their desire to remain in power by appealing to the special interests that had elected them in the first place.

Their success in doing that has been impressive. In the elections of 1998, for example, over $1 billion was spent on campaigns. Political action committees gave between seven and eight times as much to incumbents as they gave to challengers, and money was the deciding factor in 95 percent of the contests. The winner in 98 percent of the contests for seats in the House was the person who already held the seat. Of 401 incumbents, 395 were reelected. In the Senate, 26 of the 29 incumbents won, for a 90 percent rate of success.[19]

Democratic victors were beholden to the trial lawyers association and now would do the bidding of that organization. Loral chairman Bernard Schwartz gave the Democrats a quarter of a billion dollars, and his company received a technology-sale waiver from the Clinton administration. And it is no coincidence that the leader of the senatorial hounds baying at the heels of Bill Gates was Orrin Hatch, one of whose Utah constituents was Novell, creator of a word-processing package that Microsoft had blown out of the water.[20]

"Power corrupts," observed Lord Acton. "Absolute power corrupts absolutely." He was talking about Louis XIV, but the words are as true for elected rulers as for a hereditary monarch. To the extent that anyone has power over the lives of others but is not accountable for the way in which that power is used, he is quickly corrupted. Government leaders go to great pains both to create detailed legislation that will police the morality of others and to protect themselves from being held responsible for their own behavior. A college professor or business executive caught in a scandal like the one swirling around the name of Monica Lewinski would certainly have lost his job and would probably have gone to jail. Mr. Clinton got off scot-free because he wanted to get back to "what he had been elected to do."

But it isn't just Mr. Clinton. The members of Congress also think of themselves as an elite ruling class, and they hold themselves above the law. They have left themselves free to do as they wish with regard to such things as job safety, freedom of information, fair hiring, and civil rights. The only people in America who are completely without protection against job discrimination are those who work for the members of Congress.[21] Congresspersons have routinely insisted that administrators of federal agencies like the Economic Development Association ignore the law and channel funds to dubious local interests. "Mr. Gates," intoned Wisconsin senator Herb Kohl, "no one, no matter how powerful, is above the law."[22] Except Mr. Kohl and his congressional cronies.

Elected leaders think of themselves as the members of an elite ruling class, Plato's gold class. One of the responsibilities of the governing class, Plato said, was to banish every piece of literature that was harmful to public morality. This would mean in practice that the gold class would first arrive at a definition of morality and then impose it on the citizens. In modern America, we observe the curious phenomenon of Hillary Clinton, who has lived rather well at the expense of the taxpayer, complaining that modern advertising sends out "a relentless, unstopping, message of consumer, materialistic pleasure." She is extremely unhappy that the First Amendment protects advertisers from having to accept directives from the government.[23] Popular culture, she whines, makes people think of themselves as "consumers" (that is, individuals who make their own choices and work to pay for the things they want). She wants us to think of ourselves as "citizens" (that is, people who use what she allows us to get the things she thinks we should have). She belongs to the gold class, she believes, and understands better than we what we should be allowed to read and how we should be allowed to think.

Beginning with the Children

The trouble with the "myth of the metals," Plato saw, was that people might not believe it. Adults in particular, with memories of success in the management of their own lives and observations on the incompetence of those who claim to be a ruling elite, might be hard to convince. Although willing to admit that Plato was a great thinker, a skilled artisan might also have noted the man's incapacity when it came to the practical matters of everyday life. A shopkeeper might have said that he had no doubts about Plato's intelligence and then have added a wish that this intelligence would somehow aid the philosopher in remembering to pay his bills on time. Mrs. Plato would doubtless have chimed in at this point with unflattering remarks about her husband's skills as a bargainer in the marketplace. Theories are one thing, these people would have agreed, and daily life is something else. "We will be glad to try your plan," they may have told the great teacher, "and we'll certainly make use of it if it works. But let's see if it really does work before we talk about turning it into a set of rules for everyone to follow."

Well, obviously this would never do. A plan won't work if people can refer to their own experience in offering reasons for disobedience.

(Robert Heilbroner, a great believer in government planning, complained that new policies were frustrated by people's attempts to go on living as they always had.)[24] There was no hope if one began with the society of adults. It would therefore be necessary to begin with the education of the children.

During their great age of growth, the Greeks emphasized the importance of strong families; Plato wanted to do away with them. Get the children out of the home, he said, where they are exposed to the perverse ideas of their parents, and into a public program, where they can learn what the authorities think they should know.

This is exactly what is happening in modern America. Parents take a constantly decreasing part in the raising of their own children, shuffling them off to day care centers, then to preschool, then to kindergarten. At school the children are not so much educated as indoctrinated. They learn to be politically correct and they are trained in helplessness. Reading, writing, and arithmetic have become passé. In their place students learn about scarce resources, pollution, and ecological apocalypse. They never hear a word about the greater and more immediate dangers earlier generations faced and conquered by means of courage, effort, ingenuity, and persistence.

That would require a realistic examination of history, but such a study has become taboo. Everything has been twisted to fit the demands of those for whom feelings are more important than the facts. The authors of the Constitution, to take one example, would never have allowed the executive as much power as they did if they had foreseen a president like Mr. Clinton. The Second Article of the Constitution allows the president a wide discretion because its authors believed George Washington would be president.[25] Both his personality and his successes in the Revolutionary War showed that he could be trusted. A best-selling textbook, however, *The United States: In the Course of Human Events*, represents him as a failure. The authors would prefer, apparently, a more Clintonesque Washington, a man whose heart was (or seemed to be), in the words of Thomas Jefferson, "warm in its affections."[26] The same textbook ignores famous American religious leaders but makes a great deal over the pre-Columbian Toltecs.

American public schools indoctrinate. They do not educate. A recent International Math and Science Survey, which tests the students of 42 countries, found that one-third of American high school seniors could not compute a 20 percent discount on the price of a $1,250 stereo. On a more personal level, one professor has told about helping her eighth-grade daughter (a straight-A student) with algebra. The girl had not the vaguest notion of how to calculate 10 percent or 25 percent of something. "Are the other kids this dumb?" the mother asked. "Oh, they're much dumber," her daughter replied. The same girl, on a tour of historic sites in Boston and after listening to the tour guide's story of Paul Revere, asked, "What side was he on?"

"What exactly did you do in the advanced placement U.S. history class you just completed?" her mother responded.

"I made a great many charts," her daughter said, "and I did a lot of little projects with painting."[27] Anyone who has sent a child to a public school in recent years can testify to similar experiences.

The members of the gold class want to save their own children from this kind of thing, and so they send their children to private schools. As much as possible they do what they can to deny bronze and iron-class children a similar opportunity. A voucher system would allow any parent to send a child to the school of his or her choice, but Mr. Clinton and Mr. Gore, along with the Democrats in general, repeatedly turned thumbs down on it. And George II, in spite of his campaign promises, has done nothing to improve the situation. These people send their own children to the best schools and force others to send their children to the worst.

Their lackeys in the liberal press, meanwhile, cheer them on. "By putting the selection of schools firmly in parents' hands," writes David Brewster of the *Seattle Times* (note the implied denigration of parents), "you interfere with the way pluralistic public schools traditionally help children escape from a smothering family culture."[28]

Yeah, right. You might also interfere with the way "pluralistic public schools" fail to the teach the children about anything but "pluralism." Someone has said that if Chelsea Clinton had gone to the public schools of Washington, DC, she would not now be aspiring to a career as a professional. Her highest goal would be to read at an eighth-grade level.

Greek Values at the Beginning of the End

Only a small proportion of ancient philosophy has survived. Even of Plato's works we have only a part. Some works were preserved and others were destroyed because of events that were random and unpredictable. But a good part of what we now have has survived because certain groups wanted to protect it and hand it on as an expression of their own deep convictions. The ideas we have just reviewed were once held by many people. And as we have seen, they seem to have been frighteningly similar to many of the ideas held by modern Americans. Hostility toward the achiever, glorification of an elite ruling class, the denigration of parents, an emphasis on political correctness at the expense of education: these things are not unique to twenty-first-century America. They were also in the minds of upper-class Athenians as Greece slid into her age of decline.

If that is true, and if it is also true, as we observed in chapter 2, that a civilization's rise and fall can be predicted on the basis of its dominant values, what does the future hold?

America: Renewal or Decline

There seem to have been several occasions on which people asked Jesus about the future. He always said that he couldn't tell them a thing and added that nobody else could either. It's shrouded in mystery. We know that there will be wars and tumults, floods and famines, terrors on the earth, and signs from heaven, and that's about all.

If Jesus (who as regards the future may be said to have had what stockbrokers call "inside information") refused to predict anything specific, the scholar in his study would be a fool to make the effort. The following paragraphs are no more than tempting speculations, and the reader is advised not make any decisions on the basis of them. You should not liquidate your bonds, buy gold, take your money out of the bank, or sell short on the stock exchange. What will be, will be. I am going to use historical ratios, and historical ratios are notoriously unreliable. If it turns out that any of this can someday be interpreted as having been correct, it will be because of a lucky guess rather than any special insight.

On the Verge of Decline

Ancient Greece's age of growth lasted approximately four and a quarter centuries, from 900 to 475 BC, and its age of ascendancy spanned just a little over a century, from 475 to 362 BC. The age of ascendancy, that is to say, was slightly over one-fourth (26 percent, to be more precise) as long as the age of growth.

By comparison, the first lasting colony to be planted in what is now the United States was Jamestown, which was founded in 1607. As I showed in chapter 8, by 1930, America was a mature civilization: it was turning from its historic emphasis on individual initiative to government planning of the kind endorsed in *The Republic.* That is 323 years. If the Greek ratio holds, it would mean the American age of ascendancy should last about 26 percent of 323 years, or 84 years. Our age of ascendancy, in other words, is now coming to an end, and we can expect to see the evidence of decline by 2014.

This is pure speculation. The only thing that gives it any credence is the similarity between the values the Greeks held as they entered their age of decline and the values that seem to animate the life of modern America. If I am mistaken in pointing to such a similarity, the rest of my argument falls as well. Even if I am right, there is nothing sacred about my selection of a date. One might also select 1919, when the United States was first recognized as the world's most powerful nation, as the beginning of American ascendancy. The calculation would then produce the year 2000 as the beginning of decline. It may be that future historians will tell the story of federal thugs breaking into a Miami home to steal a child and send him off to a life of deprivation, note Americans' passivity, and mark it as the beginning of the end.

The Hope for Renewal

Is there any hope?

If there is, it is not in the political process. It is important to be careful about the way you vote, because the way you vote is an expression of your own personal values. But that is exactly the problem. Political outcomes are more the result of voters' values than the cause of them. Apart from a change in values, things are destined to go from bad to worse.

That is the record of Greece in the fifth and fourth centuries before Christ. Citizens came to despise the independent achiever, forgot about self-reliance, and gradually learned how to vote themselves an income from the public purse. As they did, their civilization came apart at the seams. Political processes sealed the doom that had been foreordained by the decline of personal character. "Death thus raged in every shape," Thucydides tells us,

> And as usually happens at such times, there was no length to which violence did not go; sons were killed by their fathers, and suppliants were dragged from the altar or slain upon it…Revolution thus ran its course from city to city, and the places where it arrived last, from having heard what had been done before, carried to a still greater excess the refinement of their inventions…and the atrocity of their reprisals.[29]

Jesus wasn't kidding when he talked about wars and tumults, floods and famines, terrors on the earth, and signs from heaven. Even the calm wisdom of such a careful observer as Robert Bork allows that we might be headed in exactly this direction. Given the decline of the values that make for civility, it seems increasingly probable.

History suggests only one alternative. As we have seen, England seemed at the dawn of the eighteenth century to be beginning on an age of decline. It had seen a revolution, a counterrevolution, and yet another revolution to counter that. Some tensions had been resolved, but others were emerging. Corruption was widespread and morality was at a low. There is no way an unbiased observer, writing in 1700 or 1725, could have predicted the great age of achievement that was about to come.

But something happened to change the character of the English people. It did not touch all of them, but it touched enough of them to change the course of history. Many things played a part in bringing it about, and it is unlikely that we will ever understand them all. If we were to pick a single location as the place where it began, however, the place would be a chapel on Aldersgate Street in London. It was here, in the evening of May 24, 1738, that young John Wesley felt his heart "strangely warmed." And from here he set out to begin a religious revival that transformed both England and America. Paul Johnson, probably the greatest living historian, has gone so far as to argue that it is impossible to understand the American quest for liberty and independence except against the background of that revival.[30]

This has been a book about character. I have barely touched upon the subject of religion. It is extremely difficult, however, to separate character from religion. It is quite true that we can always point to a few persons who, although not Christians, are exemplars of character. In cases of this kind, we usually find that somewhere in the recent past these persons have been exposed to the influence of religion. As an adult, Andrew Carnegie was an avowed atheist, but as a child he breathed the air of Scotch Calvinism. It is impossible to understand the person he became or what he did with his life except against that background. A civilization, similarly, with religious faith in its recent past, may continue for a while to live on its accumulated moral capital. As its age of faith recedes into memory and the capital is wasted, that civilization begins to break down.

We have examined the philosophy of Plato as a clue to ideas popular in Greece as it began to slide from its grandeur into the shadows. In addition to resentment for the achiever, the denigration of family life, and a glorification of the ruling classes, late-fifth and early-fourth-century Athens was troubled by the decline of its ancient faiths. Even the most superficial examination of Plato leads quickly to the conclusion that among the problems with which he had to deal was a widespread moral relativism. His philosophy is in large measure an attempt to work out the logic of a morality that does not depend upon religion.

Alas, it cannot be done, except in a man's head. As soon as he puts down his pencil and gets up from his desk, he will run into someone who wants to insist on an opposing philosophy. A morality founded in logic rather than faith leads to arguments about how to live rather than creative living. A man who faces nothing but arguments begins to doubt himself. The man who doubts himself learns quickly to distrust his neighbor and soon demands the protection of some powerful and beneficent third party. The third party's power outlives its beneficence, and both the man and his neighbor (who also felt the need for protection and probably complained that "some people" had been "too successful") find themselves reduced to thralldom. That is the story of ancient Greece. It is quickly becoming the story of America.

At around the beginning of the eighteenth century there broke out a religious revival that changed the world. The tinder for it, as we have noted, can be found in the sixteenth and seventeenth centuries and even in the Middle Ages. But it was early in the eighteenth century that it really caught fire. In its light, large numbers of people saw for the first time the reality of their individual importance, power, and potential. They saw for the first time that the way they lived and the way they raised their children had a lasting significance. They saw for the first time that the immediate was less important than the eternal. Bolstered by their newfound confidence, they set out to do great things in the world. The economic transformation I described in this book was but one of the things they achieved.

The light by which they were guided blazed up periodically throughout the nineteenth century. It shines in the background of *McGuffey's Reader*, the stories of Horatio Alger, and even the philosophy of Ralph Waldo Emerson. By the time of Upton Sinclair and John Dewey, it had begun to die out. Unless it flares up again, we are doomed to wander in the darkness.

Notes

Chapter 1: The Achieving Society

1. David C. McClelland, *The Achieving Society* (New York: D. Van Nostrand, 1961), p. 102.

2. John Kenneth Galbraith, *The Great Crash, 1929* (Boston: Houghton Mifflin, 1954), p. 54.

3. Cited in George Gilder, *Wealth and Poverty* (New York: Basic Books, 1981), p. 50

4. For a complete discussion of the issues in this section and the next, the reader is referred to David C. McClelland, J. W. Atkinson, R. A. Clark, and E. L. Lowell, *The Achievement Motive* (New York: Appleton-Century-Crofts, 1953).

5. Reported in Thomas J. Peters and Robert H. Waterman Jr., *In Search of Excellence* (New York: Harper and Row, 1982), pp. 56–57.

6. McClelland, *Achieving Society*, p. 43.

7. Adrian Furnham, *The Protestant Work Ethic* (London: Routledge, 1990), p. 34.

8. McClelland, *Achieving Society*, pp. 211–26.

9. Ibid, p. 44.

10. Ibid., pp. 324–29

11. Ibid, pp. 231–33.

12. Robert Jacobson, "The Austrian School of Strategy," *Academy of Management Review* 17, pp. 782-287.

13. Cited in Peters and Waterman, *In Search of Excellence*, p. 38.

14. McClelland, *Achieving Society*, pp. 340-42.

15. Milton and Rose Friedman, *Free to Choose: A Personal Statement* (New York: Harcourt Brace Jovanovich, 1980), pp. 21–22.

16. McClelland, *Achieving Society*, pp. 189–90.

17. Walter Lippmann, *An Inquiry into the Principles of the Good Society* (Boston: Little, Brown and Company, 1937), p. 358.

18. John Stover, *Transportation in American History* (Washington: The American Historical Association, 1970), pp. 9–10.

19. Mansel G. Blackford and K. Ausin Kerr, *Business Enterprise in American History* (Boston: Houghton Mifflin, 1994), p. 368.

20. John Naisbitt, *Megatrends Asia* (New York: Simon & Schuster, 1996), p. 40.

Chapter 2: The Cycles of History

1. Galbraith, *Great Crash,* quote is from the introduction to the 1988 edition, p. xi.

2. McClelland, *Achieving Society,* p. 109.

3. The material in this section is a summary of ibid., pp. 70–105.

4. Except as noted, the material in this section is a summary of ibid., pp. 107–29.

5. Copleston, *A History of Philosophy* (Garden City: Image Books, 1962) I, ii, 96.

6. Ibid., I, ii, 95.

7. Ibid., I, i, 261–62.

8. McClelland, *Achieving Society*, pp. 310–35.

9. William Durant, *The Life of Greece* (New York: Simon and Schuster, 1939), pp. 98–126, 245–86.

10. The material in this section is a summary of McClelland, *Achieving Society*, pp. 132–45.

11. This paragraph is derived from the argument of Nathan Rosenberg and L. E. Birdwell Jr. in *How the West Grew Rich* (New York: Basic Books, 1987).

Chapter 3: The Appearance of Character

1. John Wesley, *The Journal of the Rev. John Wesley, A. M.*, ed. Nehemiah Curnock, standard ed. (New York: Eaton & Mains, 1876) VII, 343.

2. Gerald R. Cragg, *The Church and the Age of Reason* (Baltimore: Penguin Books, 1960), p. 40.

3. Benjamin Franklin, *The Autobiography of Benjamin Franklin* (New York: Barnes & Noble, 1994), p. 133.

4. Quoted in Leslie F. Church, *The Early Methodist People* (New York: Philosophical Library, 1949), pp. 78–79.

5. Quoted in Max Weber, *The Protestant Ethic and the Spirit of Capitalism,* trans. T. Parsons (New York: Charles Scribner's Sons, 1958), p. 175.

6. Lippmann, *Good Society,* p. 383.

7. Kenneth Scott Latourette, *A History of Christianity* (New York: Harper and Row, 1953), p. 228.

8. Justin McCann, *St. Benedict* (Garden City: Doubleday and Company, 1958), p. 108.

9. Thomas à Kempis, *The Imitation of Christ,* trans. R. Knox and M. Oakley (New York: Sheed and Ward, 1960), p. 41.

10. Maurice B. Line, "Why Isn't Work Fun?" *Library Management* vol 11, no. 4 (1990): pp. 15–17. I should add at this point that in failing to use the politically obligatory "he or she" when referring to unnamed monks, I am not being insensitive. The monks were men, and the use of "he," "his," and "him" in writing about them is perfectly appropriate. As much as possible, in cases where there may be some question about the sex of the persons being talking about, I have tried to use words that grant a priority neither to men nor to women. I have fallen short in this regard only through my refusal to use the ever popular but grammatically challenged "they" when referring to the degendered (neutered?) individual.

11. William G. Dyer and Jeffrey H. Dyer, "The M*A*S*H* Generation: Implications for Future Organizational Values," *Organizational Dynamics* 13, no. 1 (summer 1984): pp. 66–79.

12. Roland H. Bainton, *Here I Stand: A Life of Martin Luther* (Nashville: Abingdon, 1950), pp. 39–64.

13. Weber, *Protestant Ethic,* pp. 79–92.

14. David Zaret, "Calvin, Covenant Theology, and the Weber Thesis," *British Journal of Sociology* 43, no. 3 (September 1992): p. 372.

15. Weber, *Protestant Ethic,* p. 81.

16. Harold B. Jones Jr., "The Protestant Ethic: Weber's Model and the Empirical Literature," *Human Relations* 50, no. 7 (June 1997): p. 760.

17. Otto W. Heick, *A History of Christian Thought* (Philadelphia: Fortress Press, 1966), II, 43.

18. Weber, *Protestant Ethic,* p. 159.

19. Lippmann, *Good Society,* p. 164.

20. William Durant, *The Story of Philosophy: The Lives and Opinions of the Greater Philosophers* (New York: Simon and Schuster, 1926), p. 45.

21. Quoted in Ross A. Webber, *Management: Basic Elements of Managing Organizations* (Homewood, IL: Richard D. Irwin, 1975), pp. 33–34.

22. William Myles, *A Chronological History of the People Called Methodists, of the Connection of the Late Rev. John Wesley; From Their Rise in the Year 1729, to Their Last Conference, In 1812*, 4th ed. (London: Thomas Cordeux, 1812), p. 118.

23. Weber, *Protestant Ethic*, pp. 157–58.

24. Max Weber, *The Sociology of Religion*, trans. E. Fischoff (Boston: Beacon Press, 1963), pp. 237–38.

25. Marvin Olasky, "Sex and the Presidency," *Wall Street Journal*, June 27, 1998, Sec. A, p. 18.

26. Paul Johnson, *A History of the American People* (New York: Harper Collins, 1997), p. 872; see also Larry L. King, "LBJ and Vietnam" in *A Sense of History: The Best Writing from the Pages of American Heritage* (New York: American Heritage Press, 1985), pp. 788–802.

27. Weber, *Sociology of Religion*, pp. 252–53.

28. Weber, *Protestant Ethic*, p. 44.

29. Umphrey Lee, *The Lord's Horseman: John Wesley the Man* (Nashville: Abingdon, 1954), p. 19.

30. William James, *The Varieties of Religious Experience* (New York: Modern Library, 1936 [1902]), p. 291.

31. Weber, *Protestant Ethic*, p. 176.

32. McClelland, *Achieving Society*, pp. 146–48.

33. Ibid., p. 70

34. Latourette, *A History of Christianity*, pp. 813–21.

35. Michael Waltzer, *The Revolution of the Saints: A Study in the Origins of Radical Politics* (New York: Atheneum, 1970), pp. 114–47.

Chapter 4: The Literature of Hope

1. Talcott Parsons, *The Structure of Social Action* (New York: McGraw-Hill, 1937), pp. 129–77.

2. Alfred Marshall, *Principles of Economics*, 3rd ed. (London: MacMillan and Co., 1895), I, ix–xiii, 1–51. Marshall made it a point to stress the importance of values and character. He inveighed against the then-emerging concept of "an 'economic man,' who is under no ethical influences and who pursues pecuniary gain warily and ener-

getically, but mechanically and selfishly" (p. x). Again, he described the essential characterics of an advanced society as "a certain independence and habit of choosing one's own course for oneself, a self-reliance; a deliberation and yet a promptness of choice and judgment, and a habit of forecasting the future and of shaping one's course with reference to distant aims" (p. 5). He may never have heard the term "achievement motivation," but that is very certainly what he was talking about. Economic progress, he said, depended more upon "strong moral character" than upon "great skill and mental ability" (p. 7).

3. Weber, *Protestant Ethic,* pp. 59–60.

4. Adam Smith, *The Wealth of Nations* (New York: Modern Library, 1937), p. 741; see also pp. 746–48, in which Smith describes the influence of small religious sects.

5. Benjamin Franklin, *The Autobiography of Benjamin Franklin* (New York: Barnes and Noble, 1994), p. 6.

6. Ibid., pp. 23–26.

7. Ibid., pp. 104–05.

8. Ibid., p. 4.

9. Quoted in Preserved Smith, *The Enlightenment, 1687–1776* (New York: Holt, Rinehart and Winston, 1934), p. 522.

10. Ibid, p. 347.

11. Franklin, Autobiography, p. 120.

12. Johnson, *History,* p. 235.

13. Smith, *The Enlightenment,* p. 346.

14. Franklin, *Autobiography*, p. 120.

15. Smith, *The Enlightenment,* p. 344.

16. Franklin, *Autobiography,* p. 67.

17. Benjamin Franklin, *A Benjamin Franklin Reader*, ed. Nathan G. Goodman (New York: Thomas Y. Crowell, 1945), pp. 287, 291, 283, and 284.

18. Ibid., pp. 285–87

19. Smith, *The Enlightenment,* p. 114.

20. Franklin, *Autobiography*, p. 100.

21. Ibid., p. 139.

22. Franklin, *Reader*, pp. 283 and 293.

23. Walter Havighurst, "Primer from a Green World" in *A Sense of History,* p. 154.

24. Ibid., p. 155.

25. Ibid., p. 158.

26. Ibid.

27. "The Broken Window," *McGuffey's Second Eclectic Reader* (New York: Van Nostrand Reinhold, 1879), pp. 131–136.

28. "The Good Reader," *McGuffey's Fifth Eclectic Reader*, pp. 39–42.

29. Havighurst, "Primer from a Green World," pp. 155–57.

30. Johnson, *History*, pp. 405–08.

31. Ralph Waldo Emerson, "New England Reformers," *The Essays of Ralph Waldo Emerson* (New York: Random House, 1941), p. 371.

32. Malcom Cowley, "The Hawthornes in Paradise," *A Sense of History*, p. 228.

33. Quoted in F. A. Hayek, *The Road to Serfdom* (Chicago: University of Chicago Press, 1944), p. 20.

34. Emerson, "Wealth," *Essays*, p. 494.

35. Emerson, "Experience," p. 250.

36. Emerson, "New England Reformers," p. 383.

37. Emerson, "Heroism," p. 152.

38. Emerson, "Wealth," p. 498.

39. Emerson, "Wealth," p. 508.

40. Emerson, "Prudence," p. 133.

41. Emerson, "Prudence," p. 137.

42. Emerson, "Character," p. 273.

43. Emerson, "Fate," p. 443.

44. Emerson, "Self Reliance," p. 28.

45. Emerson, "New England Reformers," p. 380.

46. Emerson, "Spiritual Laws," p. 89.

47. Emerson, "New England Reformers," p. 369.

48. John Tebbel, *From Rags to Riches: Horatio Alger and the American Dream* (New York: MacMillan, 1963), pp. 25–26.

49. Harvey Wish, *Society and Thought in Modern America*, 2nd ed. (New York: David McKay, 1962), pp. 352–53.

50. Quoted in Tebbel, *Rags to Riches*, p. 130.

51. Ibid., pp. 67-68.

52. Horatio Alger, *Joe's Luck* (Cleveland: World Syndicate Publishing, 1900); pages are not numbered.

53. Ibid. Again, there are no page numbers, but this is the last sentence in the

book. The date of publication, I should add, is also uncertain. The year 1900, which I have used above, does not appear in print. It was penciled in by a librarian.

54. Tebbel, *Rags to Riches*, p. 71.

55. Marshall, *Principles of Economics*, pp. 33–51, in particular pp. 36 and 38; see also p.1.

Chapter 5: The Age of Achievement

1. Stephen Hess, "Big Bill Taft," *A Sense of History*, p. 578.

2. Roger Butterfield, *The American Past*, 2nd ed., revised (New York: Simon and Schuster, 1966), p. 342.

3. Joseph Frazier Wall, *Andrew Carnegie* (Pittsburgh: University of Pittsburgh Press, 1970), pp. 929–30.

4. Robert L. Heilbroner, "Carnegie & Rockefeller," *A Sense of History*, p. 433.

5. Wall, *Andrew Carnegie*, pp. 88–89.

6. Heilbroner, "Carnegie & Rockefeller," p. 431.

7. John M. Blum, Bruce Catton, Edmund S. Morgan, Arthur M. Schlesinger Jr., Kenneth M. Stamp, and C. Vann Woodward, *The National Experience*, 2nd ed. (New York: Harcourt, Brace, and World, 1968) p. 452.

8. Wall, *Andrew Carnegie*, p. 827.

9. Heilbroner, "Carnegie & Rockefeller," p. 438.

10. Wall, *Andrew Carnegie,* p. 321.

11. Ibid., pp. 315–318.

12. Ibid., p. 301.

13. Ibid., pp. 645–652.

14. Daniel A. Wren, *The Evolution of Management Thought*, 4th ed. (New York: John Wiley & Sons, 1994), p. 87.

15. Wall, *Andrew Carnegie*, p. 237.

16. Ibid., p. 337.

17. Ibid., p. 44.

18. Heilbroner, "Carnegie & Rockefeller," p. 439.

19. Wall, *Andrew Carnegie*, p. 46.

20. Ibid., p. 130.

21. Quoted in John Lukacs, "The Historian as Celebrity," *A Sense of History*, p. 412.

22. Andrew Carnegie, "Wealth," originally published in the *North American Re-*

view in June 1899; here quoted from Thomas Donaldson and Patricia H. Werhane, eds., *Ethical Issues in Business*, 5th ed. (Upper Saddle River, NJ: Prentice Hall, 1996), p. 214.

23. Wall, *Andrew Carnegie*, p. 829.

24. Ibid., pp. 824–25.

25. Heilbroner, "Carnegie & Rockefeller," p. 430.

26. Ibid., p. 446.

27. David Freeman Hawke, *John D.: Founding Father of the Rockefellers* (New York: Harper and Row, 1980), p. 28.

28. Ibid., pp. 47–53.

29. Ibid., pp. 69–73.

30. Ibid., p. 69.

31. Ibid., p. 11.

32. Heilbroner, "Carnegie & Rockefeller," p. 445.

33. Hawke, *John D.*, p. 8.

34. Heilbroner, "Carnegie & Rockefeller," p. 449.

35. Hawke, *John D.*, p. 22.

36. Heilbroner, "Carnegie & Rockefeller," p. 450.

37. Hawke, *John D.*, p. 18.

38. Mansel G. Blackford and K. Austin Kerr, *op. cit.*, p. 161.

39. Hawke, *John D.*, p. 219.

40. Ibid., pp. 181–87.

41. Ibid., p. 122.

42. Heilbroner, "Carnegie & Rockefeller," p. 457.

43. Quoted in Ibid., p. 441.

44. Wall, *Andrew Carnegie*, p. 78.

45. Hamlin Garland, *Main Traveled Roads* (New York: New American Library, 1962), p. ix.

Chapter 6: Director's Law

1. Hawke, *John D.*, p. 2.

2. Ibid., pp. 212–217.

3. Adam Smith, *The Wealth of Nations* (New York: Modern Library, 1937), p. 651. This is a reprint of the fourth edition, which was published in 1789.

4. Richard B. Morris, "Then and There the Child Independence Was Born," *A Sense of History,* p. 75.

5. Ibid., p. 74.

6. Quoted in Milton and Rose Friedman, *Free to Choose: A Personal Statement* (New York: Harcourt Brace Jovanovich, 1979), p. 4.

7. Smith, *The Wealth of Nations*, p. 14.

8. Ibid.

9. Max Weber, *The Sociology of Religion,* trans. Ephraim Fischoff (New York: Beacon Press, 1963 [1922]), pp. 213–21.

10. These are the words of George William Curtis, quoted in Wall, *Andrew Carnegie,* p. 444.

11. Robert Hessen, "The Effects of the Industrial Revolution on Women and Children," in Ayn Rand, *Capitalism: The Unknown Ideal,* (New York: Penguin Books, 1967), p. 111.

12. James, *Varieties of Religious Experience,* p. 360.

13. Wren, *Evolution of Management Thought,* p. 97.

14. John Tipple, "The Anatomy of Prejudice: Origins of the Robber Baron Legend," *Business History Review*, 33 (winter 1959): p. 521.

15. Quoted in Wren, *Evolution of Management Thought,* p. 136.

16. A. J. P. Taylor, *Bismarck: The Man and the Statesman* (New York: Random House, 1955), p. 208.

17. Hayek, *Road to Serfdom,* this is from the introduction to the edition of 1956, p. xxxix.

18. J. P. Mayer, *Max Weber and German Politics*, 2nd ed. (London: Faber and Faber, 1956), p. 21.

19. Quoted in John M. Blum *et al., op. cit.,* p. 549.

20. Quoted in Blackford and Kerr, *Business Enterprise,* p. 202.

21. Ibid., p. 155.

22. Hawke, *John D.,* pp. 145–150

23. Ibid.

24. Alan Greenspan, "Anti-Trust," in Rand, *Capitalism,* p. 65.

25. Reprinted in Roger Butterfield, *op. cit.,* pp. 328–29.

26. Quoted in F. Greenbaum, "The Social Ideas of Samuel Gompers," *Labor History* 7 (1966): p. 39.

27. Quoted in Wren, *Evolution of Management Thought,* p. 174.

28. Wall, *Andrew Carnegie*, pp. 475–528.

29. Ibid., p. 526.

30. Ibid., p. 625.

31. Blackford and Kerr, *Business Enterprise*, p. 191.

32. See for example Rand, *Capitalism*, p. 50.

33. Blackford and Kerr, *Business Enterprise*, pp. 199–200.

34. Ibid.

35. Quoted in Wren, *Evolution of Management Thought*, p. 116.

36. Weber said this in 1909; quoted in Mayer, *Max Weber*, p. 129.

37. Quoted in Wren, *Evolution of Management Thought*, p. 140.

38. Ibid., p. 141.

39. For a more detailed discussion of this issue, the reader is referred to Friedman and Friedman, *Free to Choose*, in particular pp. 128–149.

Chapter 7: The Literature of Despair

1.Felix Shay, *Elbert Hubbard of East Aurora* (New York: Wm. H. Wise, 1926), p. 551.

2. Elbert Hubbard, *Little Journeys to the Homes of the Great* (New York: Wm. H. Wise, 1916) I, xxxiv.

3. Ibid., pp. xxx–xxxi.

4. Shay, *Elbert Hubbard*, pp. 46–47.

5. Hubbard, *Little Journeys*, I, xxxi.

6. Shay, *Elbert Hubbard*, p. 159

7. Hubbard, *Little Journeys*, I, xxx.

8. Ibid., p. xxxvii.

9. McCullough, "The Unexpected Mrs. Stowe," *A Sense of History*, p. 344.

10. Butterfield, *American Past*, p. 331.

11. William A. Bloodworth, *Upton Sinclair* (Boston: Twayne Publishers, 1977), see especially pp. 28–37, 40–41, and 49.

12. Jon A. Yoder, *Upton Sinclair* (New York: Frederick Ungar, 1975), p. 26.

13. Bloodworth, *Upton Sinclair*, p. 47.

14. Hubbard, *Little Journeys*, XI, 179.

15. Upton Sinclair, *The Jungle* (New York: New American Library, 1960 [1905]), p. 63.

16. Hubbard, *Little Journeys,* XI, 178–79.

17. Sinclair, *The Jungle,* p. 63.

18. Sinclair Lewis, *Babbitt* (New York: New American Library, 1961 [1922]), p. 6.

19. Ibid., p. 22.

20. Ibid., p. 26.

21. Mark Schorer, *Sinclair Lewis: An American Life* (New York: McGraw-Hill, 1961), p. 354.

22. Ibid., p. 349.

23. Ibid, p. 602.

24. Ibid., p. 480.

25. Ibid., p.66.

26. Ibid., p. 94.

27. Ibid., p. 486.

28. Ibid., p. 178.

29. Ibid., p. 398.

30. Ibid., pp. 355–56.

31. Ibid., p. 772.

32. William G. Scott, *The Social Ethic in Management Literature* (Atlanta: Bureau of Business and Economic Research, 1958), p. 70.

33. Ibid., pp. 74–75.

34. Wren, *Evolution of Management Thought,* pp. 105–07.

35. *Ibid.,* p. 120.

36. *Ibid.,* p. 118.

37. *Ibid.,* p. 122.

38. *Ibid.,* p. 125.

39. Walter Lippmann, *Drift and Mastery* (New York: Mitchell Kennerly, 1914), p. 10.

40. Scott, *Social Ethic,* p. 66.

41. Frederick Copleston, *A History of Philosophy* (Garden City: Image Books, 1962) VII, i, 45–46, 55, 94–99; see also William L. Shirer, *The Rise and Fall of the Third Reich* (New York: Simon and Schuster, 1960), p. 98.

42. Mary Parker Follett, *The New State: Group Organization, the Solution of Popular Government* (London: Longmans, Green, and Co. 1918), pp. 137 and 172.

43. Wren, *Evolution of Management Thought,* p. 263.

44. Mary Parker Follett, "The Giving of Orders" in J. Steven Ott, ed., *Classic*

Readings in Organizational Behavior, 2nd ed. (Fort Worth: Harcourt Brace, 1996), p. 177.

45. Wren, *Evolution of Management Thought*, pp. 333-34.

46. Ibid.

47. Ibid., pp. 235–253.

48. Ibid., pp. 320–327.

49. William Durant, *The Story of Philosophy* (New York: Simon and Schuster, 1926), pp. 389–95.

50. John Dewey, *A Common Faith* (New Haven: Yale University Press, 1934), p. 31.

51. Follett, *New State*, p. 6.

52. John Dewey, *Individualism Old and New* (New York: Minton, Balch, and Company 1930), p. 34.

53. Shay, *Elbert Hubbard*, p. 161.

Chapter 8: The Great Descent

1. Alan J. Lerner and Federick Lowe, *Camelot*, (New York: Tams-Witmark, 1960).

2. Robert Heilbroner, *The Worldly Philosophers* (New York: Simon and Schuster, 1953), pp. 214–18.

3. Johnson, *American People*, pp. 681–82.

4. Lewis, *Babbitt*, p. 118.

5. Johnson, *American People*, p. 681.

6. Roger Butterfield, *The American Past*, p. 399.

7. Johnson, *American People*, pp. 739–40.

8. For a beautifully written essay on the first of these crises, see Andy Logan, "You'll Have to See Morgan," *A Sense of History*, pp. 480–92.

9. Friedman & Friedman, *Free To Choose*, pp. 79–80.

10. Ibid., p.80.

11. Samuel Eliot Morison, *The Oxford History of the American People* (New York: Oxford University Press, 1965), p. 931.

12. John Kenneth Galbraith, "Why the Money Stopped," *A Sense of History*, p. 676.

13. Richard J. Stilllman, *Dow Jones Industrial Average: History and Role in an Investment Strategy* (Homewood, IL: Dow Jones-Irwin, 1986), pp. 70-71.

14. Henry Pelling, *American Labor* (Chicago: University of Chicago Press, 1960), p. 150.

15. Johnson, *American People,* p. 744.

16. E. Wright Baake, "Why Workers Join Unions," *Personnel* 22 (1945): p. 90.

17. Morison, *Oxford History,* pp. 944–45.

18. James D. Mooney and Alan C. Reiley, *Onward Industry!* (New York: Harper and Row, 1931), p. xv.

19. John Steinbeck, *The Grapes of Wrath* (New York: Modern Library, 1939), p. 42.

20. William G. Scott, *The Social Ethic in Management Literature* (Atlanta: Bureau of Business and Economic Research, 1958), p. 47.

21. Nathaniel West, "A Cool Million," *The Complete Works of Nathaniel West* (New York: Farrar, Straus, and Cudahy, 1957), p. 143 ff.

22. Erich Fromm, *Escape from Freedom* (New York: Holt, Rinehart and Winston, 1941), pp. 7–10.

23. Paul Johnson, *American People,* pp. 741–57.

24. Allan Nevins, "The Place of Franklin D. Roosevelt in History," *A Sense of History,* p. 764.

25. Butterfield, *American Past,* p. 413.

26. Nevins, "The Place of Franklin D. Roosevelt," p. 768.

27. Johnson, *American People,* p. 742.

28. James McGregor Burns, *Leadership* (New York: Harper and Row, 1978); instances are too numerous to cite in detail, but see for example pp. 93–104 and pp. 232–38.

29. Butterfield, *American Past,* p. 416.

30. Ibid.

31. Galbraith, *Great Crash,* p. 153.

32. Johnson, *American People,* pp. 758–59.

33. Harvey Wish, *Society and Thought in Modern America,* 2nd ed. (New York: David McKay Company, 1962), p. 513.

34. Johnson, *American People,* p. 744.

35. Quoted in Hayek, *Road to Serfdom,* pp. 52–53.

36. Johnson, *American People,* p. 789.

37. Herbert Schlossberg, *Idols for Destruction* (Wheaton, IL: Crossway Books, 1990), p. 182.

38. Butterfield, *American Past,* p. 417.

39. Johnson, *American People,* p. 767.

40. James Grant, *Bernard Baruch: A Biography* (New York: Simon and Schuster,

1983), pp. 269–270.

41. Johnson, *American People*, p. 752.

42. Ibid, p. 754.

43. Fred L. Israel, ed., *The State of the Union Messages of the Presidents of the United States* (New York: Chelsea House, 1966), III, 2881.

44. Johnson, *American People*, p. 952.

45. Amity Shlaes, "The Greedy Hand in the Velvet Glove," *Wall Street Journal*, April 15, 1999, Sec. A, p. 22.

Chapter 9: The Literature of Crisis

1. Barry Glassner, *The Culture of Fear: Why Americans Are Afraid of the Wrong Things* (New York: Basic Books, 1999), p. 4.

2. Paul Goodman, *Growing Up Absurd: Problems of Youth in the Organized System* (New York: Random House, 1960), p. 13.

3. Roger Kimball, *The Long March: How the Cultural Revolution of the 1960s Changed America* (San Francisco: Encounter Books, 2000), p. 59.

4. Sloan Wilson, *The Man in the Gray Flannel Suit* (New York: Simon and Schuster, 1955).

5. John P. Marquand, *Point of No Return* (New York: Bantam Books, 1952).

6. Howard Upton, "Had Enough of the Old Rat Race?" *Saturday Evening Post*, December 7, 1957, p. 118.

7. William H. Whyte Jr., *The Organization Man* (New York: Simon and Schuster, 1956), p. 392.

8. Johnson, *American People*, p. 834.

9. Ibid, p. 853.

10. Butterfield, *American Past*, p. 513.

11. Robert Bork, *Slouching Towards Gomorrah: Modern Liberalism and American Decline* (New York: Regan Books, 1996), pp. 21–25.

12. Ibid., p. 19.

13. Kimball, *The Long March*, p. 90.

14. Ibid., p. 30.

15. Fredric Jameson, "Periodizing the 60s," *Ideologies of Theory, II: Syntax of History* (Minneapolis: University of Minnesota Press, 1988), pp. 207–08.

16. Jerry Rubin, *Do It! Scenarios of the Revolution* (New York: Ballantine Books, 1970), p. 89.

17. Kimball, *Long March*, p. 56.

18. Charles Reich, *The Sorcerer of Bolinas Reef* (New York: Random House, 1976), p. 69.

19. Charles Reich, *The Greening of America* (New York: Random House, 1970), p. 5.

20. Ibid., p. 252.

21. R. S. Desowitz, *Malaria Capers* (W. W. Norton & Co., 1992).

22. For thoroughly documented information about the campaign against DDT and other "crises" produced by the advance of science, go to junkscience.com.

23. Robert J. Ringer, *Winning Through Intimidation* (New York: Fawcett Crest Books, 1973), pp. 40–43.

24. Arthur R. Robinson and Zachary W. Robinson, "Science Has Spoken: Global Warming Is a Myth," *Wall Street Journal*, December 4, 1997, Sec. A, p. 22.

25. Philip Scott, "Hot Air + Flawed Science = Dangerous Emissions," *Wall Street Journal*, April 2, 2001, Sec. A, p. 22.

26. Paul Harvey, "A Time to Be Alive," *Imprimis*, 27, no. 10 (October 1998): p. 3.

27. Quoted in Virginia Postrel, *The Future and Its Enemies: The Growing Conflict over Creativity, Enterprise, and Progress* (New York: Free Press, 1998), pp. 25–26.

28. Kimball, *Long March*, p. 121.

29. Ibid., p. 122.

30. Arthur Marwick, *The Sixties: Cultural Revolution in Britain, France, Italy, and the United States, c. 1958 – c. 1974* (Oxford: Oxford University Press, 1998), p. 10.

31. Richard Lowry, "The High Priests of Journalism: Truth, Morality, and the Media," *Imprimis* 28, no. 6 (June 1999): pp. 2-3.

32. Peter H. Gibbon, "The End of Admiration: The Media and the Loss of Heroes," *Imprimis*, 28, no. 5 (May 1999): pp. 2-4.

33. Marianne Jennings, "The Evolution—and Devolution—of Journalistic Ethics," *Imprimis* 28, no. 7 (July 1999): p. 3.

34. Ibid., p. 4.

35. Rubin, *Do It!*, p. 89.

Chapter 10: The Administrative Society

1. Charles Reich, "The New Property," *Yale Law Journal* 3, no. 5 (April 1964): p. 782.

2. Schlossberg, *Idols for Destruction*, 205.

3. Robert A. Caro, "FDR and LBJ," *A Sense of History*, p. 34.

4. Johnson, *American People*, p. 870.

5. Ibid., p. 832

6. Ibid., pp. 875–76.

7. Ibid., pp. 923–25.

8. Kimball, *The Long March,* p. 248.

9. Friedman & Friedman, *Free to Choose,* pp. 91–107.

10. Schlossberg, *Idols,* pp. 109–10.

11. Reich, *The Greening of America,* p. 228.

12. Reich, "The New Property," p. 787.

13. Philip Howard, *The Death of Common Sense: How Law is Suffocating America* (New York: Time Warner, 1994), p. 126.

14. This is from Locke's argument in *The Second Treatise of Civil Government.* For an excerpt, see Thomas Donaldson and Patricia H. Werhane, eds., *Ethical Issues in Business: A Philosophical Approach,* 5th ed. (Upper Saddle River, NJ: Prentice-Hall. 1996), pp. 195–200. For a review of Locke's political economy, see Copleston, *History of Philosophy,* VI, i, 133–52.

15. Reich, "The New Property," pp. 739, 771, and 778.

16. Schlossberg, *Idols,* p. 187.

17. John Stossel, "The Real Cost of Regulation," *Imprimis* 30, no. 5 (May 2001): p. 1.

18. Thomas J. Peters and Robert H. Waterman Jr., *op. cit.,* p. 170.

19. Peter Drucker, *The End of Economic Man* (London: Heinemann, 1939), p. 205.

20. Rand, *Capitalism,* p. 136.

21. Robert L. Heilbroner, *An Inquiry into the Human Prospect* (New York: Norton, 1974), p. 100.

22. Arthur M. Schlesinger Jr., *The Vital Center: The Politics of Freedom* (Cambridge, MA: Riverside, 1949), p. xiv.

23. Schlossberg, *Idols,* p. 194.

24. B. F. Skinner, *Walden Two* (New York: MacMillan, 1948), pp. 206 and 168.

25. Christopher Jencks et al., *Inequality: A Reassessment of the Effects of Family and Schooling in America* (New York: Basic Books, 1972), pp. 8f.

26. Schlossberg, *Idols,* p. 119.

27. Joseph Fletcher, *Moral Responsibility: Situation Ethics at Work* (Philadelphia: Westminster, 1967), pp. 198–202.

28. Schlossberg, *Idols,* p. 181.

29. Hayek, *Road to Serfdom,* p. 231.

30. Howard, *Death of Common Sense,* pp. 57–58 and 12.

31. Ibid., p. 85.

32. Stossel, "The Real Cost," p. 3.

33. Harvey, "A Time to Be Alive," p. 3.

34. Schlossberg, *Idols*, p. 205.

35. Howard, *Death of Common Sense*, p. 33.

36. Ibid., p. 145.

37. Thomas J. Stanley and William D. Danko, *The Millionaire Next Door* (New York: Pocket Books, 1996), p. 141.

38. Yochi J. Dreazen, "Consumer Spending Jumps, but Optimism Eases," *The Wall Street Journal*, April 3, 2000, Sec. A, p. 2

39. Marianne M. Jennings, "The Real Generation Gap," *Imprimis* 27, no. 8, (August 1998): p. 4.

40. Ibid., pp. 4–5.

41. Andrew Peyton Thomas, "A Dangerous Experiment in Child-Raising," *Wall Street Journal*, January 8, 1998, Sec. A, p. 18.

42. Ibid.

43. Chester E. Finn Jr., "Why America Has the World's Dimmest Bright Kids," *Wall Street Journal*, February 25, 1998, Sec. A, p. 22.

44. Jennings, "The Real Generation Gap," p. 2.

45. Ibid.

46. Michael Medved, "Saving Childhood," *Imprimis* 27 no. 9, (September 199): p. 3.

Conclusion: Character and the Future

1. Glassner, *Culture of Fear*, p. xxiv.

2. Peter Farb, *Man's Rise to Civilization as Shown by the Indians of North America from Primeval Times to the Coming of the Industrial State* (New York: E. P. Dutton, 1968), pp. 89–90. For an example of how one "social scientist" continues to hand on the "findings" of another even after they are known to be bogus, see Ross A. Webber, *Management: Basic Elements of Managing Organizations* (Homewood, IL: Richard D. Irwin, Inc., 1975), p. 89.

3. Hayek, *Road to Serfdom*, p. 176.

4. Robert Rector, "America Has the World's Richest Poor People," *Wall Street Journal*, February 24, 1998, Sec. A, p. 18.

5. Shirer, *Rise and Fall of the Third Reich*, pp. 266–67.

6. Howard, *Death of Common Sense*, p. 154.

7. Ibid., p. 174.

8. Adam Smith, *The Theory of Moral Sentiments* (New Rochelle, NY: Arlington House, 1969 [1759]), p. 446.

9. Durant, *Story of Philosophy,* p. 198.

10. Copleston, *History of Philosophy,* VI, ii, 108–09.

11. Wish, *Society and Thought,* p.353.

12. Copleston, *History of Philosophy,* I, i, 154.

13. Durant, *Story of Philosophy,* p. 17.

14. Copleston, *History of Philosophy,* I, i, 261.

15. Ibid., I, i, 262.

16. Quoted in Durant, *Life of Greece,* p. 466.

17. Durant, *Story of Philosophy,* p. 25.

18. Dennis Farney, "Disillusioned, Coburn Plans Exit as HMO Debate Swells," *Wall Street Journal,* September 10, 1999, Sec. A, p. 20.

19. Albert R. Hunt, "The Other Political Scandal in Washington," *Wall Street Journal,* November 12, 1998, Sec. A, p. 31.

20. Ibid.

21. Howard, *The Death of Common Sense,* p. 126.

22. "'Bull's-Eye' Bill," *Wall Street Journal,* March 4, 1998, Sec. A, p. 18.

23. Virginia Postrel, *The Future and Its Enemies: The Growing Conflict Over Creativity, Enterprise, and Progress* (New York: Free Press, 1998), p. 210.

24. Robert L. Heilbroner, "The Missing Link," *Challenge,* March–April 1978, p. 17.

25. Clinton Rossiter, "Our Two Greatest Presidents," *A Sense of History,* pp. 105-06.

26. Jennings, "The Real Generation Gap," p. 2.

27. Ibid., pp. 2-3.

28. Quoted in Postrel, *The Future and Its Enemies,* p. 139.

29. Quoted in Durant, *The Life of Greece,* p. 284.

30. Johnson, *American People,* pp. 108–17.

Index